M000207222

PUBLISHING
L.L.C.

Books by Annalisa Conti:

Nine, a novel (2018)
Africa, a novel (2015)
All The People, a novel (2014)

The W Series, a collection of short stories (from 2016)

NINE

ANNALISA CONTI

Published by AEC Publishing LLC in New York

www.annalisaconti.com

ISBN-13: 978-0-9965174-5-4
ISBN-10: 0-9965174-5-6

NINE, a novel

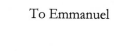
To Emmanuel

CONTENTS

NINE

ANNALISA CONTI

ONE

ANNALISA CONTI

THE WEEK WITH ONE DREAMY START

A soft light.

Blurry space around me, distant walls and ceiling.

My body filled with peace, sunbeams emanating from my skin.

Mike's hand holding mine.

People appeared around me, all sporting wide smiles, their mouths slightly disproportionate to their faces. Their happiness seemed too generous to be contained. They whispered instructions I couldn't understand, as if spoken in another language. I smiled back at them and they caressed my forehead with serene nods.

A person in a golden dress came in, and he started to move his hands in the air. A ball of warm light formed between his palms, small at first but rapidly enlarging and becoming brighter and sunnier. Some other golden gods joined him. They all followed the dance movements and they formed balls of euphoric energy between their hands. The spheres slowly left their creators' fingers and they levitated up in the air; they floated in the room until they reached a stationary position above my body. From there, one by one they started their descent, until they made contact with my skin and they produced instantaneous shivers of pleasure all through my nerves. I closed my eyes, oblivious of Mike and anybody else in the room.

Before I lost consciousness, I could hear everybody singing and cheering in a celebration of life and beatitude. Mike was chuckling, absorbed by the inexplicable marvel.

When I woke up my head buzzed.

There is a certain inertia in life. Some rivers can flow forever: peoples might build bridges above them and cities around them, storms might disturb the fish and birds that populate the riverbanks, but water keeps flowing, carelessly. Some lives are similarly never bothered: they don't face revolutionary events, or they can easily adapt to transformations, as sudden as these may be. Other existences can be challenged with life-altering events. Dams can be built, transforming the river into a lake; glaciers can melt and disappear, letting the river dry out and die. There is always a precise moment when everything changes. What path does life follow from that point onward?

My moment was on a Monday in early August. The fluffy dream that had woken me up earlier that morning had already been forgotten, and I was at work. I was typing on my computer in the Vanity Fair offices in downtown New York, sitting on a couch, too lazy to go back to my desk in between meetings. As I paused for breakfast, I looked outside the windows of the fifteenth floor of the Freedom Tower. I let the tall buildings and the blue sky sink in my eyes, chasing inspiration on the article I had to deliver a few hours later. At the first bite of my Kind Bar, the same chocolate cereal bar I had been eating for years, a rather unusual taste pervaded my mouth. I slowly chewed on it, waiting for the known salty and sweet almond and dark chocolate aroma to hit my tongue. Something was off. I looked at the plastic wrap, to check for its expiry date, before remembering that the bar came from the same box of twelve I had opened several days before. I put my nose on it, and I could smell that same bitter taste I had in my mouth.

Was I working on something so kinky that even my senses were impacted by it? I was finishing an article on American Gods, a TV show based on a fantastic novel by Neil Gaiman. In the latest episode, Spring herself had been the guest star, in a jubilation of flowers and spirituality. And the usual deaths, of course. But not too many.

Was it something I had eaten the previous night? I had to focus really hard to remember the last meal. Mike and I had had a very quiet Sunday dinner at home, where the main dish had been a plain salad with chicken. While cooking the chicken, he hadn't even added any partminger, his favorite Nigerian herb. Mike's mom always put it on every meat she cooked for the family, now like twenty years ago, when he had still been living in London with his parents and siblings. It was even quite unique for Mike not to include any spices in his dishes: his mother's traditional recipes kept him hooked to his origins anywhere in the world he was. Maybe the lack of spices was the issue that morning.

I didn't recognize my moment, so I shrugged it off. I thought I was simply getting older, and I never noticed any other change in the bars. I got back to work without giving the matter a second thought, but I would later realize that my Kind Bars never got back to taste the same again.

THE WEEK WITH ONE FRIEND

"And you say you love your job!"

Rachel had always had the superpower to bring me back on track, especially when I dared to complain about work. She knew there was nothing else I would rather do for a living than spending my days watching movies and TV shows, and then critiquing them on Vanity Fair, eviscerating them on my blog, tweeting about them. And then starting again with attending events about them, going to Comic Cons for them, predicting award results around them. I had painted myself in a corner, as it so frequently happened with her, and now I had to try to get away with it.

"I do, but some movies are real crap!"

As much as I adored my job, summer sometimes brought the worst out of studios, which ended up releasing the most random movies they could find in their closets. As part of my agreement with the magazine, I had to watch all movies that belonged to a certain selection of genres, from science-fiction to black comedy, with anything in between. I didn't have to review them all, at least, but I had to be able to properly contribute to magazine activities that might revolve around them, like the occasional podcast, or a group article, or a press conference that nobody else could attend.

She responded to my text with the poop emoji. Not one of our most mature exchanges, but it was always soothing to pretend we were still in college.

"And I hate to think about crap right before vacations," I replied.

"I always forget: are you doing Spain or Portugal first?"

"Portugal. We land in Lisbon on Saturday morning. We take the rental car and we drive around for a few days. Then we cross the border to go to Spain—"

She responded with the dancer emoji.

"—and we spend a week in Seville and the south of Spain. Then a quick stop in London on the way back."

"Mike's family?"

Exactly.

"Say hi to his brother!"

"Rachel, you know Martin is married, right?"

"I'm not jealous," she texted after about one second, before adding, "What time is your flight on Friday?"

"Some 8:00 pm? Any chance you have time before we leave?"

A crying emoji popped up.

"I have the worst case ever, talking about crap at work. My client is an ass-hole and everybody knows it: the lawyers on the other side, even the judge. Not sure what tricks I can pull out of my hat this time…"

"You always find something," I responded right away, and I really meant it. She was the best attorney and the sharpest person I had ever met. She had always loved her job, even at the beginning of her career, when she used to be just an associate spending days and nights in the office, going home only to shower and change. No wonder she had made senior partner so quickly.

"Thank you darling! I will miss you these two weeks."

"No, you won't. You always find stuff to do."

I added an eggplant emoji, sure she would remember the joke the TV host John Oliver had made in one of his shows, some time ago.

She definitely got it, as she responded with the "guy and girl with heart" emoji.

THE WEEK WITH ONE TRIP TO PORTUGAL

Mike and I were relaxing on a beach not far from Lisbon, the wind from the Ocean kissing our skins. We were holding hands while I was reading the last issue of Vanity Fair, which I had bought at the airport following an old habit of mine, and he was leafing through The Economist. We had always enjoyed our vacations more than anything else in the world: that was our time to be ourselves, free from the constraints of work and the habits of our well-engineered life in New York.

"Did your sister ever get to start Game of Thrones?" I suddenly asked him, prompted by an article discussing when the next season of the show was going to air. An article that, for once, I hadn't written myself.

Mike laughed at my random question, his eyes widening up behind his sunglasses, "I have no idea!"

"I thought you asked her last time on Skype."

"I totally forgot: Alexandra monopolized the conversation!" he apologized, mentioning his sister's daughter, a very bright four-years-old.

"You should tell her that this is the best time of the year to get started: we are widely off season, and next year the show will probably air later, since production becomes more and more complex and expensive every year."

He looked at me as if I was speaking another language, my entertainment fixations so far from the article he was reading about Brexit. He removed his sunglasses to look at me, and he pinched my cheek just like he used to do at the beginning of our relationship, many years ago.

"You're such a nerd," he grinned.

"I know, that's why you married me, right? For the never ending thrill."

Lisbon was a vibrant city, and we took full advantage of it that night. We ate tapas in a fancy covered market, where the best local restaurants had food corners with their specialties; we tasted Portuguese beers and we finally dragged ourselves home much more than tipsy.

I woke up in the middle of the night with the worst of headaches, and with the heavy feeling of someone being in our second floor hotel room. I stood still and I slowed down my breath, to focus on each sound: Mike was peacefully breathing next to me, voices were coming in from afar through the open window, a night bird was scurrying on the railing. Suddenly I heard it, the noise that had woken me up, a sort of metallic grumbling, so close to my ear. I got so scared I almost woke Mike up. Then the sound burst again, this time mixed with a car engine, maybe a truck. A truck couldn't reasonably be in our room. I stood up from the bed, fighting the nausea and the headache, and I peeked outside the window. A trash truck was picking up bins in the street.

How did that noise sound so close? Was I really that drunk? My heart was pounding for no reason, as I scrolled my head in self-disdain and I went back to bed. I promised myself I would try to control my drinking moving forward through that vacation: I didn't want another useless scare.

Before falling asleep, I grabbed my phone to check the time and I found a text from Rachel, just a heart with a "How are you?" as if she knew I needed some comfort right then. My only, irreplaceable Rachel.

THE WEEK WITH ONE TRIP TO SPAIN

"How is Seville?" Rachel texted me a few days later.

"The city is incredible! The hotel is downtown and we get to walk through these old alleys, between multicolored houses. There's a beautiful cathedral, and many monuments."

"Anything juicier?" Rachel asked.

"Well, did you know they filmed some Game of Thrones scenes in the royal palace, the Alcazar? The gardens were used for some Dorne sites, and they are even more beautiful than in the series - but don't tell Mike this is the main reason why I wanted to come here!"

I added a winking face, but she quickly blew it away with the emoji of the facepalm, a woman slapping her forehead. She didn't share my enthusiasm for TV show filming locations.

"You asked for juicy stuff, isn't this at least interesting?"

"I meant interesting for me: are Spanish men sexy hot stallions as they say? I've never been to Spain."

Mike and I had already been to Spain many years ago: we had spent a week in the island of Formentera, about a month after we had first met. Days and nights had gone by in a heartbeat, as we had rolled from bed to beach to bar, and back to bed, at the speed of light. I couldn't say what had been crazier at the time: going on vacation overseas with a guy I had barely known, and who could have turned out to be a weirdo or a murderer, or the fact that I had shown no hesitation when he had asked me to go with him. We had been on just two or three dates before that getaway to Formentera, after we had met at a Vanity Fair event. Mike had already been working as a business consultant for McKinsey & Company for a few years, and Condé Nast had been his client at the time. He had been very excited to participate in the Tribeca Film Festival party, and he had picked his favorite navy tuxedo for the occasion. In some game of destiny, my gown had been the exact same shade of blue, and he had approached me with the lamest move one could think of: "I'm glad you got my message and you picked the right color". "What a jerk," I had thought, just before falling under the spell of his green eyes, gems nestled in the glowing darkness of his face.

"You know me, I don't even see other men, especially when I'm with Mike," I typed back to Rachel.

Then I added, "I got my own black stallion!" and I could see her laugh, proud of her friend.

"I see you are feeling better than the other day," she regained her poise, a few seconds later.

"Definitely, but no more wild drinking, at least for now."

"Any other symptoms?" she added with a smiling face.

"Nope. We've been eating everything and anything in the past three days and I'm perfect. Maybe I should reduce the raw meat and fish: you never know how well they are preserved, and I wouldn't want to get food poisoning. We're not in New York after all."

ANNALISA CONTI

TWO

ANNALISA CONTI

THE WEEK WITH TWO REASONS TO LOVE SEPTEMBER

Coming home had always been a rich feeling for me: a mix of nostalgia for the places and people I had just left behind, especially the times we had gone to Mike's family in London, and the relief of finding again my house, my bed, my life. I was more attached to my normality than I cared to admit, and I loved the comfort of having a routine, knowing what was going to happen the following morning or the following day, planning for my date nights with Mike, receiving the almost-daily "Welcome to another hopefully ok day" text from Rachel. I cherished those recurring moments, the quiet expectation before them and the satisfaction due to them. I wouldn't change my life for anything in the world.

Even going back to work never annoyed me: I always found a kind of safety in having a schedule, even a tight one, especially for things that I was genuinely interested in.

September meant the beginning of Fall TV season, with all the new shows planned by the networks, and the new releases on Netflix and Hulu. The annual critique article was waiting for me to bring it to life, compiling a lush collection of must watch and can avoid shows for my readers and Twitter followers. That was one of my favorite times of the year: the networks sent me screeners for many new shows, that I devoured in a few days and nights, taking furious notes for each episode and making mental comparisons with previous seasons or older shows, to provide the most complete judgments and opinions. This endeavor usually helped me go through Mike's first week back to work: some years he had to travel to the other side of the world right from the first day, the price to pay for being a partner in one of the top management consulting firms. This year he spent that first week in New York, but he came home every night so late that I was already asleep on the sofa, my computer on my lap, an episode of something still rolling.

September also marked the beginning of movie award season. Like every other year, the month was going to be a perfect storm of events and excitement, new movies to watch and critique, waiting for even more new movies to come out and blow journalists and viewers off their seats with emotions and powerful stories. I couldn't ask for more. The stress for all the deadlines and to-dos, and the slight stomach pain that usually accompanied me in the heaviest month of the year, were manageable side effects, compared to the adrenaline that roared through my veins day by day. This year I was less stressed and even more enthusiastic than usual, if at all possible, but also somewhat more bothered by the stomach pain. My stomach had always been my weakness, as all my anxieties had always converged towards the center of my body, giving me a wide range of symptoms through the years. I attributed the increased abdominal annoyance to the pressure, the hot humid air that still oppressed the city, and I forgot about it.

THE WEEK WITH... TWO?

I kept working on my series of articles on the award season, compiling the first reports from the Toronto Film Festival, where the new Damien Chazelle movie had been presented and it had received dazzling standing ovations. I published a nerdish perspective on the Venice Film Festival, titled "How can the normal movie-goer enjoy art-house films?". I chronicled the premiere of the latest Marvel blockbuster, which this time enjoyed the presence of a high caliber actor like Nicole Kidman, and Denzel Washington in a very exceptional role for him. I did all this with a hand on my stomach, as the pain had decided to increase day after day.

The tenth morning in a row that Mike heard me complaining about it while we were still in bed, he insisted with a firmer voice, "You ought to go to the doctor, this is not normal. Or at least take the test."

"Take the test?"

"Yes. Or am I the only one who observed the symptoms?" he widened his eyes. "You completely abstained from raw fish and meat after Portugal. You didn't drink any alcoholic beverage in London with my family, even if Martin kept offering you—"

"Well, I didn't want to drink the night we had dinner at your brother's, that's not my fault!"

"You didn't drink at my parents', either," he smiled back at me, as if he were speaking to a child who couldn't admit her mischief. "Or last weekend while we were dining with Rachel."

This didn't mean anything: I hadn't felt like drinking or eating sushi for some time, so what? Was it a crime?

"And your stomach has been aching for several days now: don't you think perhaps this might be the right time to take the test, and see if that could be the explanation?"

His eyes were becoming brighter with every word, as if speaking out loud was making the possibility more real.

Take the test.

I touched my stomach and I sighed.

We had decided to have children at the beginning of the year. We had both always known we wanted them, but he had been the one pushing to give ourselves a deadline: we were still quite young, but we weren't getting any younger, so why increase the risks of having troubles? Some of our friends had recently had painful stories of miscarriages and hormonal treatments, so right after Christmas we had agreed that the time had come for us to give it a try. Our approach had maybe been more rational than other people's, but we were both way more rational than other people. That was how we worked.

I had spoken to my doctor and I had found out the right week to stop my birth control. Mike had gone the full length, buying the little computer to test for urine hormones in the morning, to identify fertile days, and stocking for pregnancy tests. He had applied the structured diligence of the seasoned business consultant to this other aspect of our lives, and now he was trying to logically convince me to take the test.

"My period is supposed to arrive today, so why don't we give it a couple of days, and we see what happens? I promise I will take the test if nothing happens, and I'll go see the doctor," I tried.

"Amber, let us stop turning around this. It's Saturday, we have all the time we need, so let's do this."

I tried my best puppy eyes to pity him out of it, but it didn't work. He went to the restroom to grab a box of tests, and he came back to bed to read the instructions out loud. He got some sort of comfort from the fact that the test should be repeated after three days to confirm the result: whatever the response, we still had a second chance in just a few days.

Without saying a word, because none came to my mind, I slid out of bed and I locked the bathroom door. I peed on the test stick, my mind still a blank canvas. I left the test on the sink and I went back to bed, where we waited for a couple of minutes, Mike talking about something else while I was staring at the wall.

We both went back to the restroom and we checked.
Pregnant.
"I knew it," I didn't know why I said that.
"I hoped for it!" he whispered as he took me in his arms, his voice shaking. "Let's do it again in three days, and we'll see if it still shows the same result," his struggle to keep calm was evident.

I was way more relaxed than him: that was not real. Nothing would be confirmed until the second test, and even then. There were many false positives, so only a blood test could give final confirmation. I still had time.

We didn't talk about it for three days.

We didn't even mention the test when we had dinner with Rachel on that Saturday night, and I laughed the usual laugh when she asked me if I had any news, yet. I had told her about The Reproduction Plan as soon as I had stopped the pill, and since then she had never missed a beat, asking me every week if the bun was already in the oven.

I didn't even think about it when we were home after dinner, watching a French documentary recommended by Mike's father. Called "Demain", tomorrow, it presented the consequences of climate change not as a remote possibility but as a clear development of today's global habits. According to the documentary, agriculture, energy, economy and governments were currently managed in a way that didn't leave any hope for the future. Twenty years from now all global oil reserves would dry up, and we would not have any form of energy to replace carbon fuels, if we didn't do anything today. Since food today required energy to be produced, people would also starve, in a chain reaction that would cause the collapse of the world as we knew it. The collapse could be avoided, though, if we changed things right now. Food could be produced locally and without the use of fossil energy, as some examples all over the world were already showing. Oil could be fully replaced with renewable energies, from wind to solar to geothermal, in a process that many countries had already undertaken. The economy could become more local, and governments could focus on their people, rather than on the interests of their own components.

The documentary had me thinking about the world my generation would leave to our children: would it be a condemned world, a dark place without energy and food, where people would starve and kill each other? Would it be a happy but prehistoric place, in some ways, where globalization would have been recognized as a failure? Where people would not travel because it would be too expensive, everyone would farm their fruits and vegetables and raise their animals locally, in small communities where the advancements of technology would have been forgotten, because not anymore useful for survival? These questions sounded as interesting as terrifying to me: it looked like future generations might live in a world very different from the place I knew. How would people my age guide our children in this new world? How would we know what they needed and teach them?

THE WEEK WITH TWO COINCIDENCES
MAKING A CLUE

Distant hypothetical questions suddenly became more concrete when my period, usually reliably on time, didn't show up.

Then the day came to take the test for the second time.

"Do you feel like peeing?" Mike asked me once he got home from work on Tuesday night.

I didn't catch it right at the beginning, and I looked at him with wide eyes.

So he continued, "I mean, pee on the stick?"

The verdict appeared on the tester's screen faster than the three minutes advertised on the box, and even faster than the two minutes it had taken the first time I had peed on the stick. The world was sending us a message: do you really doubt it, do you really need a second test? Rational double-check was our motto in the family, so yes.

Pregnant.

"Are you going to make an appointment with the doctor?"

"I'm already on it," I responded while I was turning on my computer to access my doctor's practice website.

"Might I come? Do you think I ought to come?"

I had always loved his spontaneity in taking care of me, the most natural thing he could do in his everyday life.

"I don't know. You can come if you want, but I don't think there will be much going on: she will take a blood sample, and I don't think we'll see anything if she does a scan."

I could almost hear him typing on his phone to look for a more precise answer.

"Wow, the doctor is available only a month from now, according to the website!"

"A month from now?" he kept typing for a new search.

"Yes, she might be out, since she is completely unavailable for the next four weeks. I will call tomorrow morning and see if she has any openings."

"The NHS says you have to see a doctor before the tenth week, so it will be fine. Don't worry."

I had never worried a single day since I had met him. The emotional part of my brain was also still procrastinating and thinking nothing was real, so that helped me keep my poise. But the rational part of me was already starting to plan: we would need to refurbish the second bedroom, we would need to childproof all corners, maybe even buy a new apartment sooner than we expected.

Then I relaxed: we had time, time to get used to the idea.
Time to get fat.

My phone vibrated right then, "I hate my life," Rachel
complained with a shotgun emoji. "How are you?"

I responded with the expressionless face emoji, the one with
one flat line for mouth, and two equally flat lines for eyes. That
pretty much represented my state of mind.

"Do you think it shows?" I asked Mike the following
morning, evaluating my image in the full mirror in our bedroom.

"Would you believe me if I said no, which in this case is the
truth?" he grinned at me, while he was adjusting his suit.

"No."

"Then please don't ask me," he laughed.

In the office, when it was late enough to be sure that
somebody would answer the doctor's practice phone, I tried to
get an appointment. The secretary was very kind, but there was
nothing she could do, besides a polite "you can try to call again,
to check if somebody cancels their appointment". I wanted to
say something to defend the urgency of my need, but I couldn't
say it out loud, I couldn't hear my voice pronounce the words
"I'm pregnant". To me it was like accepting that it was really
happening, with all its consequences. Things were going to
change, the perfect balance Mike and I had acquired after years
of getting used to each other, dealing with each other's

dissatisfactions and savoring common joys, that fine and well-constructed balance was going to collapse. I had never liked changes, because I had always had a very conscious need to keep my life under control, and knowing that I didn't have any type of control on this inevitable change was already making me uncomfortable. Could I still pretend that nothing was going on, that we could keep going to the movies on Friday nights, dining out with friends on Saturday nights, spending tiring vacations visiting cities, exploring wild nature and playing sports?

"Are you happy?" I tested him when he got home that night, late as usual.

"I am happy to build this with you, I am happy to let our happiness grow even further. Are you happy?"

I voiced the equivalent of the expressionless face emoji.

I kept calling my doctor's office every day, just a few minutes after it opened in the morning, until on Friday I was finally able to secure an appointment for the following Monday.

As I was walking back to my desk from the private room I had booked to make my call, I started to feel it: my hands contracting, my back aching, my sight getting blurred. My arms burdensome, my legs restless, my back uncomfortable on the chair - but that was possibly the chair. The document I was working on, a review of one of the movies presented at the Toronto Film Festival, was staring back at me, blank. I rubbed my hands on my face, looking for my lost focus.

Was that the sign? Was that going to be my life for the remaining many months? That was a compromise I couldn't make, I couldn't let go of my job. My job was the thing that defined me, my job and my relationship with Mike. Was I going to lose them both?

I dropped my face in my hands and I spent several seconds completely still, not allowing any single muscle to move. Until my phone vibrated. I dragged my hand towards it to unlock it, and I read the email I had received from Mike: "AVIS Reservation Confirmation | Uptown (West 97th Street & Columbus Ave)".

Crap.

Mike had rented a car to go to my parents the next day, and I had completely forgotten about it.

As we drove through the entrance of my parents' house in Connecticut, I couldn't help myself thinking that already looked like some grandparents' place. I had been born in Connecticut, but we had lived in Manhattan for a few years during high school, since my father had gotten a new job and he hadn't wanted to commute every day. As soon as they had been able to, at some point during my college years, my parents had moved back out and even further away from the City. They were now living in a small sad town about three hours from Manhattan, where I had convinced Mike we would not visit more than once per month. Since they didn't come to Manhattan very often, as they had gotten into a complicated relationship with the City, that was pretty much our visitation right. For years I had barely visited at all, but Mike, with his tight sense of family, had pushed to increase the frequency. Now they seemed happy in that ancient wooden house, with the garden and the porch, community bridge games during the weekend and church services. The life of old people.

"My dear!" my mother hugged and kissed me, and I couldn't stop thinking that she looked older, thinner. In a sort of hallucination I saw her holding a baby in her arms, smiling at me as she hadn't done in years, my grouchy father both proud and moved by the new role in his life. Did they really look different or was it just me?

I held Mike's hand even stronger. He looked at me with a question in his eyes, to which I responded with a subtle nod: yes, everything was fine.

I shook my head. Nothing was real. Not yet.

THE WEEK WITH TWO MORNING SURPRISES

When I saw the voicemail notification on my phone and I recognized my gynecologist's number, I took a deep breath. The news was in. No more doubts, no more hesitations, no more telling myself this could all be a mistake.

The doctor had been very professional the day before in her practice. She had known me for more than fifteen years, since the first time I had walked into her office to get a prescription for an oral contraceptive. I hadn't wanted to go to my mother's gynecologist, somewhere in Connecticut, so I had asked a friend for a referral. What I hadn't known at the time was that she was just a gynecologist, not an obstetric, so if things were getting real she was going to have to refer me to another physician. We had always had a very professional relationship through the years, annual check-up after annual check-up, and again this time she had modeled her behavior on mine. I had been calm, I had gone there just to get my blood and urine tests and to talk about next steps, in a very transactional way.

The voicemail I received on my phone, while I was in a staff meeting and I had left my mobile on my desk, was very serene, too.

Doctor Li's soft voice soothed my ears, "Hello, Amber, this is Doctor Li speaking. I have just received the results of your blood work and your urine test, and I can confirm that you are pregnant. Congratulations. Should you decide to move forward with this pregnancy, you should see an obstetric-gynecologist in the next couple of weeks, as we discussed yesterday. I am estimating a potential due date in early May, next year, but the Ob-Gyn could give you a more precise date after your first exam. Feel free to call me back at my practice if you have any questions or if you need a referral for a specific physician. Best of luck."

I listened to the voice message three times, every time wickedly grinning at the "should you decide to move forward" part. That must be the standard statement the doctor had to use with all women, some guidelines she had to follow to ensure nobody felt forced to have their baby. It still sounded unnecessary in my case, since I had discussed with her our Reproduction Plan at the beginning of the year.

I was focusing on those side thoughts just because I couldn't decipher what was going on in my brain. An unreadable fog occupied my mind. From the mist, a list of things to do started to pop-up before my eyes, as if this new adventure was just another project. Book appointments with doctors, have tests conducted, start to think about how to rearrange the second bedroom, what furniture we needed to buy, what supplies, item after item, line after line. There was also the cousin's wedding next year, not more than one month after the potential due date: would we be able to go? How would parental leave work for our jobs, how many paid weeks would we be able to take, and how many unpaid weeks would I be willing to allow myself?

I shook my head to make all the bullet points disappear and I took a deep breath: one step at the time.

I was waiting for Mike when he came home from work, late that night.

"I got the results today," I greeted him.

His eyes jumped out of his face, "Why didn't you ring me?"

I was not ready to tell you.

"I wanted to speak about it in person," I said instead.

He grabbed me in his arms and he held onto me, then he looked at me straight in the eyes, "So, is it real?"

All I wanted was to say no, to tell him there had been a mistake and we had to keep trying.

"It's real," I said instead.

I could see his eyes shine up, brighten up, "I love you so much, Amber! It is terribly exciting to be making this with you. Are you happy?"

I opened my mouth to say something, but nothing came out. Happiness had always been a very precise feeling for me, that I couldn't identify in my heart at that time. I sealed my lips again for a second, and then I resolved to throw back the question at him, "And you? Are you happy?"

He smiled, a flaming explosion of delight on his face. Then he grinned, "I am not quite sure, though: let's see when shit gets real."

I laughed with him, for the first time that day.

I was in what looked like a hospital room, wearing nothing but a pale gown. I was sweating and screaming, my legs spread open with my feet up in the air, squeezing Mike's hand with mine. Machines were humming, IV lines and catheters were coming out of my body. I was in labor, and it was not going well.

I had been in labor for hours, between painful contractions and ineffective epidural injections. Nurses were yelling at me when to push, and I was doing my best to follow their orders and the rhythm they were imposing to the whole action. My energies were fading away at each push, my brain was getting numb and my will to keep going was losing its grip on me.

After more hours of ordeal, a person who looked like a doctor came into the room, he observed the situation for a few seconds, and he decided I needed an emergency C-section. Right now. Somebody put a gown on the doctor, who started to cut my abdomen open like a butcher, with a long vertical incision. Some other doctors joined him, and they all started to work on my open belly.

When the time came, Mike left my hand hanging outside the bed and he rushed to grab his child from the hands of the nurse. Nobody seemed to notice my torn body, and the blood spilling out of it. Before I passed out, I could hear the baby starting to make noises and everybody cheering around Mike, not paying any attention to my heart monitor as it suddenly went flat. As I was dying on the labor bed, someone kicked it out of the way, to make space for a crib to get installed in the middle of the room. Mike was laughing and chuckling, too absorbed by the marvel of his newborn baby to realize he had just lost his wife.

I woke up from the nightmare and I opened my eyes, recognizing my bedroom and heavily sighing with relief. My phone told me it wasn't even four in the morning, so I did my best to go back to sleep.

I woke up again a few hours later, this time almost unable to breathe, my chest compressed by an overwhelming force. I sat up on the bed, and I clutched on Mike's arm to wake him up to help me. Then it hit me all at once: a brutal sense of nausea shook me so violently that Mike almost screamed. I ran to the bathroom and I threw up everything we had eaten for dinner, that somehow hadn't gone farther than my stomach. I sat on the restroom floor for many minutes, while Mike held my forehead and he refreshed my wrists with a cold wet tissue. He tried to convince me to stay home that day, but I had a staff meeting I couldn't miss; instead he helped me get dressed and he put me on a taxi to go to the office.

What a wonderful way to start the day.

In the taxi I held my phone tight in my hand, staring at the ongoing chat with Rachel, the cursor blinking next to the words "iMessage".

"I feel so bad today", I typed, before repeatedly tapping on the delete button.

I tried again, "I miss you so much", "When can I see you?", "I so need to talk to you", "I so need a glass of wine and I can't even drink".

All deleted. I sighed.

"How was your day yesterday? Did you stay long in the office? I'm so busy right now with all this Twin Peaks revival breaking news!"

Blue arrow, sent.

"Long night, part in the office, part out," she responded with a wink.

I smiled: that was exactly what I wanted to hear.

"Performance rating?" I asked.

"B plus."

I chuckled, "That's it? Did he mess up?"

"The performance was not outstanding. I've had better, but B plus is not bad, don't get me wrong."

"So who's the lucky guy this time?"

"Friend of a colleague, met in a bar yesterday night."

"Hot?"

She replied with a fire emoji, then she added, "Smoking hot! But unfortunately some things express their full potential only if you can handle them to perfection…"

"I love you, Rach," I finished typing as I was sitting at my desk in the office.

The sense of nausea didn't leave me all day, and focusing on my writing was more complicated than ever. I went to the cafeteria to get a hot tea, and while I was pacing back to my desk I tried to compose the article in my head, "David Lynch… Iconic visuals… Laura Palmer… Maybe I'll do a series of dedicated articles on it, I'm sure it will be divisive and obscure. When is it coming out, next year? Will it be done before the baby arrives? Will I still be on maternity leave? How long will I be on leave? I have no idea. Maybe I'll get to start the series, but then who can finish it if I'm out? Todd? He likes we... he could be good for this. I will have to be back for th. season of Game of Thrones, though, that's for sure: that's . biggest hit of the year. I can't miss it. I can't miss the Oscars in Los Angeles, either, or the Golden Globes. And I was supposed to go to Cannes next year, but that is most likely not on the table anymore. And Tribeca? That's local at least..."

My head was heavy and foggy when I woke up the following morning. What happened in my dream, this time? Memories couldn't emerge from the dust, but maybe that was a good thing. The only clear thing was that I had to run to the bathroom again, and throw up.

I was munching on some crackers on the subway when a young woman sat next to me, a kid on her lap. When I focused on the kid, my eyes were captured by the difference in skin tones between the daughter and her mom. As common as that was in Harlem, where we lived, I had never stopped to think about it: our child was going to be mixed race. Was it still unusual today in New York City? Or in London? Probably not. Mike was multiracial too, after all, but his dad's Irish colors didn't get passed to any of his children, who all looked like perfect copies of their mother, a stunning ebony beauty. Would that be the case for us, too? Would I walk around with a child who didn't even look mine? Would people ask me if I had adopted the baby? Would he or she have an identity crisis during primary school, being convinced by some bullying classmates that I couldn't be his or her mother?

What would my parents think? How would they react to the fact that they were about to become grandparents? They had asked for grandchildren many years before: they had crossed a strange period of their lives, filled with the fear of getting old, and they had wanted something new and young. At the time I had been twenty-five years old, with no boyfriend, and their requests had fallen flat. Once their age-related crisis had been over, they had stopped asking, especially after Mike and I had gotten married. They later had started to see our friends popping out kids, but probably they hadn't wanted to jinx it and reduce their chances of eventually seeing a grandchild, so they had stayed put, quiet and smiling, hoping for the best. I couldn't imagine their reaction to the news: would they be excited and simply go crazy like some new grandparents did? Would they be relieved that we finally made it? How would they behave: would my mother remain loyal to her abrasive honesty, and comment on her grandchild's skin color? Would my father impose an even stricter discipline on the baby than what I had experienced during my younger years, regardless of the baby's gender?

I didn't have the answers to any of those questions, and I couldn't stop thinking about them.

THREE

ANNALISA CONTI

THE WEEK WITH THREE WAYS TO
COMPLIMENT YOUR DAUGHTER

It is amazing to see how things disappear if you just stop thinking about them.

Mike had to leave the country on a business trip for about ten days, one of the many times per year he had to hop on business class flights around the world. I had always been sarcastic with him about how he secretly enjoyed those trips and the feeling of extreme coolness that came with them, between champagne and business lounges, but this time he was sorry to leave. I ended up spending all my time either by myself or with people who couldn't yet be made part of our little secret and, as a result, I didn't think about it. Save when I had my head deep in the toilet in the morning, or when Rachel winked and she asked me if I was pregnant yet, pretty much every time I saw her.

The only day I was forced to focus on what was going on in my life was when I resolved to make an appointment with an

Ob-Gyn doctor. I already had a favorite hospital, the same where some of my friends had had their children, so I spent some time on the hospital's website to pick the physician with the best resume and the nicest-looking face, and then I called her practice.

"The doctor is already fully booked for May," the secretary told me with as little empathy as it was humanly possible.

"I'm sorry, what?"

"The doctor is already fully booked for May. She can take only so many new patients with due dates in the same month, and considering what you told me about your last period, it looks like you will be giving birth in May."

"Very well. Is there anybody else available in her practice?" I tried.

She took a few seconds to look at calendars, before she sighed, "No."

"Nobody? So what do I do now?"

"Let me give you the number of another practice in the hospital, maybe you will have more luck there."

The second practice had no availability. So did the third.

"What do you want me to do, have the baby at home by myself?" I yelled at the secretary.

"There is another practice that might have some availability for May, but I'll have to call you back tomorrow to confirm."

Twenty-four long hours, and when the phone rang I had all my last hopes up.

"Doctor Mallory confirmed her availability," the woman announced.

I scrambled through the hospital website to find the doctor's profile, and I read through it as quickly as I could: Julia S.

Mallory, M. D., board certified in Obstetrics and Gynecology, Assistant Professor of Clinical Obstetrics and Gynecology, Assistant Attending Obstetrician and Gynecologist at New York's biggest hospital.

Let's do this, Julia.

"That sounds great!" I responded with a heavy sigh of relief.

"The doctor wants to see you next week for your first appointment."

I accepted, even if Mike was still going to be out of the country: we wanted to get it done sooner rather than later, and he was surely going to be there during all subsequent appointments.

Now I just had to wait.

When my phone rang on Saturday morning and I saw my parents' number on the screen, I almost wanted to say something, to hint at something. I had so many conflicting emotions inside me that I needed to share them with someone. It normally would have been Mike, but he was far away in time and space. I didn't know why exactly I felt that way towards my parents, since we had never had a friends-like relationship, but I couldn't help it.

"Hi, honey," that was my mother on the phone. "How are you?"

"Everything is good, how are you?" the answer came out automatically, the usual facade.

"I'm glad you feel good, I was a tiny bit worried last time we saw you: you didn't look very good."

What?

"What are you talking about?"

"Well," she started, somehow embarrassed by her own words. "Maybe it was just an impression, but it looks like you gained some weight. Your cheeks looked fuller, a bit swollen, so I thought maybe you were sick and you didn't want to tell us."

What the hell?

"Or maybe you just gained weight on vacation?" she kept going, merciless. "See, I didn't think about that, maybe that's just it?"

She paused, as if she was waiting for me to respond. I had nothing to say that I could actually tell her.

"Or maybe you're just ageing. That happens, too. Marjorie's daughter started to get fat when she passed thirty-five, maybe the same thing is about to happen to you?"

What the hell?

"I have to go. Goodbye."

THE WEEK WHERE THREE IS FAMILY

"Good morning, I have an appointment with Doctor Mallory. The name is Gillingham."

When I arrived at the Ob-Gyn doctor's office, conflicting thoughts occupied my mind: did I want the doctor to tell me that everything was fine, that I was going through hell every morning but otherwise I was perfectly healthy, and with an equally healthy baby in my belly? Or was I hoping for a different response, some variations of the "there has been a mistake, there is no baby" scenario? I couldn't say.

Checking in, meeting the nurse, getting undressed. Everything went by in a blur, like falling into somebody else's dream. This had never been my dream. I had many girlfriends who had always wanted babies, since they had been kids themselves, and they had welcomed their sons and daughters like gifts from the skies. I had a few friends who had been more normal growing up, but then they had started to feel the desire to have children once they had met their Mr. Right Guy. I had known Mike was my Right Guy since the first time I had looked into his eyes, and I had never doubted him or our relationship, but the animal instinct for reproduction had never grown in me. As a child I had been terrified by the idea that my parents would at some point have a second kid, who would replace me, use my room, break my toys. I had been used to having my things in their place, and my time to spend by myself. I had been loathing the disturbance. As a teenager I had hated babies, as they had held no interest, not being able to talk or interact. They had been like animals to me: I had been afraid of them, and they had felt it. Every time somebody had given me their children to hold in my arms, we had stared into each other's eyes for about a second, and then the child had started to cry. Hopelessly. Things had improved when my friends had started to have children. Those babies had become the sons and daughters of somebody I loved, and that love had trickled down to my friends' descendants. But still, I didn't have the urgent desire of having one of my own: my life with Mike was perfect. I didn't need anything else, or anything more, and I didn't want it to change. I didn't want the tears of a newborn to interrupt our conversations. I didn't want a baby to force us to travel on vacation to only certain countries and on only certain types of trips, to choose child-friendly hotels, in child-friendly cities. I didn't want to give up the things that made me, me, and those that made us, us. I didn't want to lose myself. Or Mike.

The doctor's room was cold, and I was there by myself, waiting for the physician to arrive. Doctor Mallory, a bright woman in her forties, chatted for a long time to collect my clinical history and my family's information. She performed some routine checks, keeping her smile up and kindly explaining what she was doing, and then she took a sonogram. She was very excited when the first image popped up on the screen.

"That's your baby, that's the head."

She kept smiling while she was taking measurements.

For the first time the truth hit me in the middle of my chest: that was it, there was no mistake. My breath accelerated. I had a thing inside me, a thing that was going to grow inside me, deforming my body, kicking my organs around my belly. That thing was going to change my life, forever. That thing that now I was watching on the scan's screen, while it was moving its arms, making the doctor laugh with tenderness. I had never had a panic attack, but I guessed that was how it might look like: I wanted to cry and scream. I forced myself to keep smiling, while Doctor Mallory kept repeating "everything is great here, you are both very healthy" as she handed me a picture of the sonogram. I quickly hid it in my bag. How could she say that everything was great? Where was the exit from that nightmare?

I rushed out of the examination room, I booked my next appointment with the secretary, I left the building and I was back on 85th street, full sunshine, fresh air, still heavily breathing.

How could I get out of this?

I was trapped, locked in someone else's fantasy, living someone else's life. And Mike wasn't even there to hold my hand.

I couldn't sleep that night, and exchanging silly texts with Rachel didn't help alleviate my struggle. I couldn't shake off my mind the weight of responsibility: we were adding a new human being to this planet. The liability was a shapeless shadow hanging over my head, the duty to educate the child to become a good human being, someone who shared our values of respect, honesty, and kindness. And I wasn't even considering the issue of race, and how being half white and half African-American would influence the life choices of the baby. How could we make sure the baby would inherit our qualities without any of our flaws? What if the opposite were to happen? The baby would grow up to be a complete ass-hole.

The night was foggy and uncomfortable, but at least Mike was coming back that day.

As soon as he opened the door, I flew in his arms and I held on to him. He wanted to know everything about the doctor, in addition to the few details I had told him the previous night over the phone.

His eyes were bright with excitement when I finished my recollection of the appointment, but I reminded him that we still needed to be cautious: we had to wait for the blood test results and I had to schedule a nuchal translucency, a specific scan that would measure some parameters of the fetus's nape to evaluate the risk of Down Syndrome. He complied with my request with a smile. That was my Mike, the man who always honored people for who they were. He knew he couldn't change a person's feelings or mind operations, and the best thing to do was to respect whatever certainty anyone had, whatever emotions they felt. He could criticize and debate, but he always accepted one's ideas, and he was going to curb his enthusiasm until we would both feel comfortable in sharing the news with our families and friends.

In a glorification of the American Way of sharing and cheering, a colleague had a baby shower in the office just a few days later. This was quite a common thing, since Vanity Fair had a considerable number of women among its staff. But it was the first time I was participating in someone's baby shower thinking I might have that very same thing in a few months. The thought struck me, for I had always considered such celebrations very cheesy, and now I was finding myself wanting one for me.

I was wearing a black dress. Mike had bought it for me as a present during our summer trip to Spain, and it was a very beautiful fall dress that fitted me perfectly. At least it had done so when we had bought it, because on that baby shower day it already didn't fit anymore. I had put it up in the morning, defying the mirror to tell me I was getting fat.

Mike had caught the preoccupied look in my eyes, "Are you ok?"

I had looked back at him and I had dared asking, "Do you think it shows?"

This time he hadn't laughed at me. He had examined with great seriousness the outline of my belly, pondering for a few long seconds.

"I think it's fine, but try to stand straight."

I loved his candor.

I stood straight as a stick, especially during the baby shower, where my paranoia had pushed me to think everybody was inspecting everybody else's belly, to guess who was next. I put all my belly-covering tricks into action: holding my breath, pulling my chin up, pushing my shoulders down and out.

I was exhausted at the end, and already looking forward to telling my boss and my colleagues, not to have to play that game anymore. How quickly had I gone from not wanting to tell anyone to counting the days before I could let everybody know.

I had a similar feeling later that night: going out to dinner with friends and not being able to tell them was quite hard to manage. Not only due to limited food options and forbidden alcohol, but also for the constant need to hide my thoughts and my body. I had been excited to see those people, and spend a nice evening with Mike after his work trip, but I couldn't fully enjoy any of it. I was very hungry, but after a few bites I wasn't anymore. I wanted to stay out and have fun, but I also wanted to go home and go to bed.

Everything looked normal, but at the same time it didn't.

History repeated itself on Saturday, when Mike and I had brunch with Rachel. I had spent the morning planning how I would respond to her usual pregnancy question, now that the answer was different. I hated myself for plotting to lie to my best friend. She had always asked me the question with her half smile, that expression that said "I know you, don't try to fool me", the same she used in court when she fought against the opposing lawyers on a case. I never knew how to handle that penetrating gaze of hers, but this time she didn't ask.

"Perhaps she somehow already knows and she is satisfied with it," Mike hypothesized on our way back home. "Perhaps she is just waiting for you to be ready to tell her."

THE WEEK WITH THREE HEARTBEATS

"What are you thinking about?"

I raised my head when I heard Mike's smiley voice.

We were spending a quiet Sunday at home. He needed to rest from his trip and do some work in the afternoon, and I started to think about the announcement to my parents. What should I say? I suddenly stopped: it was too early to think about it, we needed to wait for the Down Syndrome scan. I sighed.

"Are you ok?"

Mike was sitting next to me on the sofa, typing emails on his computer. Those three words, "are you ok", with a question mark at the end, were becoming his mantra.

"You can tell me anything. Strange pregnancy sensations? Incoming hormonal storm? Intestinal gases?"

I laughed, and he smiled back.

"We will need to tell my parents—" I hesitated.

"And you don't want to do it," he finished the sentence for me. That reassured me: if he got it, then it wasn't that crazy of a feeling after all. Or maybe he knew me so well that he could even follow my convoluted logics.

"It's stupid."

"Nonsense," he immediately replied. "I know it is not an easy task to announce such news."

I nodded, and he continued, "I've been thinking about it, and I can certainly announce it when it's time, to both parents."

I loved him so much.

"But not only for you," he kept talking. "Also for me: I want to do my part, I want to prove that I'm taking my own responsibilities in this shared job. After all I am fifty percent responsible of what's going on…"

"And you're one hundred percent responsible of putting this little something in my belly!" I winked.

He laughed back at me, he softly threw his computer and my phone on the coffee table, and he pulled me in his arms.

"Let's see if I still remember how it works," he said, kissing me while I giggled, and holding me even tighter.

The week went by fast, between nights of confused dreams, morning rides on the vomiting roller coaster, and more and more silly text exchanges with Rachel, trying to ditch her questions and avoid making any involuntary reference to the huge elephant in the room. The waiting game was finally over on Friday, the nuchal translucency day. The name sounded very complex, but the test was nothing but an ultrasound, conducted with a more precise machine.

"Are you excited?" I couldn't stop myself from asking Mike, on our Uber to the hospital. He gave me a large bright smile, and that was all he was going to say for now.

My eyes wandered outside the window during the whole ride, recording the images flowing by: Randall's Island and the East River, the Franklin Delano Roosevelt Drive and Astoria, Roosevelt Island and Brooklyn down south. My brain was numbed by the sound of my pounding heart, and a bloody sense of fear in my mouth.

I shadowed Mike through the hospital, as he followed the instructions we had received, to find the test room, check in, and get admitted into the small exam room. A nurse showed me to the bed, Mike to the chair at the end of the bed, and she sat down in front of a portable ultrasound machine.

"You will see on that screen everything I'm seeing here on the machine," she announced, pointing a finger to the big screen hanging on the wall in front of the bed, a few inches from Mike's nose.

She started to explore my abdomen with the machine's probe, and I couldn't help myself from looking more at Mike than at the screen in front of us. His eyes wide open since the first time the baby showed up, he started to convulsively stare at me and at the screen alternatively, as if he wanted to confirm that he was looking inside of me, that the small thing with arms and legs was really in my belly. I knew from the look on his face that seeing the profile of a human being on the screen melted his heart. His eyes became even wider when the ultrasound probe hit the heart and we could see the chambers, contracting and relaxing with timed perfection.

The little alien was thriving and firmly holding on to my interiors, sucking all the energy it needed to develop into a terrifying xenomorph, eager to devour us. I sighed at the violence of my own imagination, a reminder of how unready and probably unfit I was to be a parent. But then, would I ever feel ready or fit?

The nurse took the measurements she needed and she promised us the results in a few days. She kept taking pictures of the baby to check that everything was in the right place: two arms, two very long legs, a beating heart, a round belly, a brain with two hemispheres. Once the scan was over, she walked us to a different room, where a blood sample was taken from the tip of my finger, the last component of the Down Syndrome screening.

When we left the hospital, Mike was still astonished.

"I saw your ovaries," he whispered. "I saw your inside, isn't it insane? A technology that allows us to see inside us, and to see that there's another person inside you, who moves, who has a beating heart, who has its own will. When the baby didn't want to move, it just didn't move. It is not just another piece of your body, it is a person. And we made that person."

He kept looking at me with fascinated eyes, and the more I looked at him the more I tried to form an image of the baby in my mind. Would it look like Mike? Would it have his beautiful and unique mix of Nigerian built and Irish freckles? Would it have Mike's father's blue eyes or his mother's dark magnetic fields? Or would it look like me, pale, blond, boring?

A thought jumped to the front of my mind, from the back drawer it had sat in for some time: Mike's parents were coming from London on Monday, for their annual escape to New York to visit their son and enjoy the city. Every year I looked forward to those ten days, as Mike's parents were two of the people I admired the most. Mike's mom, beautiful and noble, hypnotized me each time she spoke to me, with her penetrating eyes and wit. There was something irresistible about her. Mike's dad had an intrinsic kindness, and the most charming smile Ireland had ever produced, according to his own words. Together they were a symphony, where each instrument had memorized its partition after more than forty years of uninterrupted rehearsal, and the result was exhilarating. This year they had perfectly timed their trip, as we were going to receive the nuchal translucency results in time to share the news in person. We had a family lunch planned on Saturday, for which we had convinced my parents to come all the way to Manhattan: that would be the perfect moment to let everybody know. Four birds with one stone.

So much had already happened around this baby that it seemed impossible that nobody knew about it, yet. All I wanted was to tell Rachel, as soon as I could.

THE WEEK WITH THREE CHEERS

"In-laws arrive today?" my phone buzzed and the message from Rachel flashed on my screen.

"Yes!"

"Have fun with your other lover," she added with a kissing emoji.

"Don't be jealous of Mike's mom: I will always love you more!" I replied with a waterfall of hearts.

"I know, I know. But it still pisses me off to think she will know first, since she's his mom."

"She will know what?" I asked.

"When you are pregnant!"

Ah Rachel, if only...

Going home from work that night, a young man sat in front of me on the subway, holding a small baby in a carrier. I got fascinated by the way he was looking at his child: a sort of glowing aura emanated from his eyes. I found myself smiling.

Was that happiness? I had always thought that Mike and I were already the happiest a person can be, and the addition of a child would just reshuffle our cards, rather than spread them out in the wind. We had promised ourselves we were not going to be less joyful with a baby in our lives; maybe less organized, less focused on ourselves, but equally cheerful. The thought soothed me.

When I entered our apartment, Mike was already there with his parents and their enchanting energy. The cold fingers of reality touched me in the middle of my chest: we would have to tell them very soon.

Mike woke up on Thursday morning with a clear idea in his mind.

"Did you receive the nuchal translucency results?" he asked me as soon as his brain was awake enough to put the words together.

Sitting up in bed and trying to fight the usual nausea, I shook my head, my eyes still shut.

"Why don't you send a message to Doctor Mallory?"

"Right," I yawned back to him, "I will send a message as soon as I get to the office. They're supposed to respond in twenty-four hours."

His satisfied smile showed me his mission was accomplished.

To be sure, he texted me a couple of hours later, "Did you send the message to the doctor?"

He didn't want to be mean or controlling, but that was how we had always worked: reminders and to-do lists were our daily bread, mostly because of our jobs. I had to manage my time very tightly, since I had many overlapping timelines to stick to. Multiple TV shows I was covering were on air on the same day, some at the same time. For some of them I needed to prepare a few drafts beforehand, to tackle different potential developments and be ready to publish my article on the Vanity Fair website as soon as the episode was over. It was a very different type of project management, compared to Mike's job: he had large teams of consultants who worked for him in several weeks' assignments, sometimes with very stretched deadlines, global travel plans, multiple client meetings. I had never been completely sure of what Mike exactly did in those meetings, but I liked to tell myself that he was like a mechanic, for businesses that required their oil pipes to be cleaned up.

Of course I had forgotten.

A physician's assistant messaged me back that same afternoon, informing me that the genetic tests conducted on my blood had given negative results, and the Nuchal Translucency was showing normal measurements. That meant the risk for Down Syndrome was very low. I asked back if there were other tests to be conducted or we were good to go and announce to the families. In a corner of my heart I was hoping that the nurse would respond cautiously, inviting me to talk to the doctor during our next appointment, a few days later, to clarify my doubts and discuss the next steps. But she was very straightforward.

"You're good to go," she typed back. "Everything is normal and everything looks good so far. Great news!"

Great news?

The news was that there were no more excuses now, what was so great about it? There were no more reasons to stay put and keep waiting, no more alibis.

The baby was going to come.

That racially undefined and unfitting baby was going to come and end our freedom. Mike had been dying of excitement, struggling not to tell his parents right away; he needed to let his enthusiasm roam free and embrace everything and everyone. And I owed it to him to accept that new status, and make it official, to ourselves and everybody we loved.

I stared into the void for quite some time, and then I finally resolved to text him the news.

He called me right away, and I could sense his smile on the other side of the phone when I picked up.

"Splendid! Can we announce to my parents tonight?" I could tell he was alone in his private office, since he was yelling.

Panic's tentacles closed in on me. I desperately grasped a life jacket, to enjoy the last few crumbs of normality, whatever that meant.

"Well, my parents are coming for lunch on Saturday anyway, why don't we tell them all together? It would be nice to my parents, too, not to be left behind."

Mike fell silent.

He softly sighed before accepting, "Sure, that's a wonderful idea."

I touched the red button on my phone to end the conversation, and a million images flew through my mind. Short speeches to communicate the news to everyone. More annoying phone calls from my mother, asking how the baby was doing. The "I knew it" from Rachel, and her affectionate smile, contemplating how common I had become with the whole marriage-and-kids gig. Months of getting fat and tired and depressed ahead of me. Years of effort, dedication, and lack of recognition ahead of us. Sleepless nights. Tears. Mike loving someone else but me, maybe even more than me, and always denying it.

I took my head in my hands, my elbows on the table, and I sighed.

In some cases you could just hope for the best.

We met my parents in front of the restaurant Mike had picked for Saturday brunch. I watched as the four parents exchanged awkward hugs, the result of the ocean usually separating us. They had seen each other just a few times before we had gotten married, and in the years since the wedding they had met not more than once a year, when the Londoners had taken their US vacations. It was always interesting for me to analyze the polite greetings they exchanged, the forced interest in one another, the desperate search for points in common and conversation topics. Our parents were very similar on some aspects, that was why both Mike and I had grown up to be equally decent human beings, but completely different on others. My parents had spent their lives between New York City and

Connecticut, never leaving the United States, not for lack of interest but just for lack of habit. They had been blindsided when I had introduced them to that boyfriend of mine, not only a foreigner, but also a clearly strange mix of genes, with his dark skin and piercing green eyes. On the other side, Mike's parents had travelled their whole life: his mother had moved from Nigeria around Africa when she had been younger, to then land in London. There she had met her husband, with whom they had travelled the world countless times; they had explored cultures and countries, and they had transmitted this urge to travel to their children.

We sat at the table and we ordered our food. Mike had it all planned, and he waited for drinks to be served to put his plan into action. I was grateful that he would be making the announcement: I still couldn't picture myself saying the words out loud.

He raised his coffee mug, he glanced at me with an expression that implied how this would have worked better with alcohol, and he started his speech.

"I am so happy to see our family reunited here today, all together. It is such a rare occasion, and I wish this could happen more often. And perhaps it will in the future."

Uncertain looks flew around the table, and Mike's mother mouthed to her husband, "Is he drunk?"

Mike kept braving the audience, raising his cup higher, "I want to make a toast, because we have a little news to share with all of you and to celebrate."

He paused for drama, and I could see my father's eyes open wider, as he was guessing the news. Mike beat him, but it was just a matter of milliseconds.

"We are expecting a child!"

We had long discussed the formula to use: was it going to be a "we are" or an "Amber is"? Or even something quirkier like "you are going to become grandparents"? We had agreed on the "we are", since we had both taken part in the act of producing the little alien that was growing in my belly.

I had a blast following each parent's reactions: my father's eyes went from wide open to fully watery before Mike had even finished his sentence, my father's mouth emitting a silent cry of deep sentiment. I had never seen him making such a scene in my life, and it was deeply entertaining to watch him grab my mother's arm and shake it, in a mix of disbelief and marvel. My mother looked moved, too, but mostly relieved: being an only child, I was her only hope to become a grandmother one day, and she was now visibly thanking some gods that I had finally done something to make her happy. Mike's parents were already used to being grandparents, since both his brother and sister had children; their excitement was more moderate, but profound nonetheless. His mother was thrilled to have a new addition to the family, and she tenderly caressed my cheek from her side of the table. Mike's father was proud of his son, and he started to laugh hysterically, trying to grab a waiter to order a bottle of champagne.

It was a complete success, followed by the usual list of questions on the due date, and how was I feeling, and how were the first test results. Mike had even brought the picture from the Nuchal Translucency. My mother held her breath, she covered her mouth with her hand and she let her breath go only after several seconds, with a loud "wow". My father then caught the picture and a "this is so impressive, it looks real!" came out of his excited lungs. Mike's parents politely waited for mine to finish consuming the photo with their eyes and hearts, and they took a good look at it as soon as they could hold it in their hands.

"These things get more and more modern: next scan you'll be able to see who the baby looks like!" Mike's dad couldn't curb his enthusiasm.

The more I looked at my parents, the more their features changed, as if they had instantly transformed into grandparents. My mother, never eager to make compliments, held my hand tight and she told me I was beautiful, and the baby would be the most marvelous in the world. My father, the authoritarian and severe businessman, was the happiest I had ever seen him, more than at my wedding, more than at my college graduation. I was part jealous, for the first time having to share my parents with someone else, however superficial our relationship had grown out to be through the years, and part relieved, ready to finally dump on someone else the pressure they had never ceased to exercise upon me.

Telling Mike's brother, Martin, and sister, Meredith, during a skyping session later that weekend, was much less stressful than telling our parents.

Our conversations with Meredith were always accompanied by the laughs and screams of her two young children, who were as free of spirit as their mother, a fashion designer who had recently moved with her family to Cape Town, South Africa. This time Meredith added her own shrieks to the chorus: once she had heard the news, she started to cry and grin at the same time, mumbling how her little brother was going to have a baby and give more beautiful cousins to her children. It was a celebration of family and passionate love.

Martin was quite the opposite. A professor of Economics in London, he kept his severe mask on even with the family. Mike and his brother would mostly skype on their own, talking about politics and finance, and other things I could barely follow. Martin's wife, Elizabeth, their two daughters, and I would join the sessions towards the end, once all the serious items on the agenda had been processed, and we would share our lighter news, compliment the kids for their latest achievements, enjoy some broader family time. When Mike and I both showed up on the screen at the beginning of the video call, Martin couldn't hide his surprise: what was that unexpected change in the procedure? What was going on in our lives, big enough for Mike to disrupt their routine? With a very British "I see", Martin called Elizabeth. After the announcement was properly communicated, a wave of excitement burst out from Elizabeth and their older daughter, who started to scream "Baby! Baby!". Martin couldn't contain his joy, and he was even heard saying "This is fantastic!".

We also started to plan for the following weekend: we wanted to meet with our closest friends in New York to share the news with them, and we set up video conferences with Mike's friends in the United Kingdom. We trusted our parents to spread the news to the remaining members of our families faster than the speed of light, and we were not deceived by Mike's parents, who didn't lose a second to tell their own siblings and relatives, even from this side of the Ocean. Family is a beautiful thing.

As the news of our incoming heir crossed the Ocean and it got disseminated like a drop of color in a glass of water, a sense of suffocation started to crawl up in my throat.

"Can I tell you something?" I asked Mike one night, after his parents had gone to sleep in our second bedroom. My voice was shaking.

"I know you wanted to tell everyone as soon as possible," I took a breath and I kept going after his nod. "But now that our whole families know, it would be terrible if something happened... Not for us, we are strong and we can handle anything, but for them: they would suffer, and they would pity us, and I don't want them to do either."

He had a way of looking at me, when I said something that he somehow expected from me, and that further confirmed to him the kind of person I was, "I knew you would think something like this: you always think about everybody else."

"Right. You and I know this could happen, because things happen, and that's life. And it's ok, but they would be so sad, they would be devastated by it. And they would be even more sorry for us than we would be for ourselves, causing them even more sadness, in a vicious circle that—"

"Don't worry," he stopped me and he sighed, putting his arms around me, "If anything happens, we'll handle it, we can do it. Don't worry."

Don't worry: that was easy to say. But I wasn't worrying, I was just hoping for the best, and preparing for the worst.

FOUR

ANNALISA CONTI

THE WEEK WITH FOUR WORDS: HOW IS THE BABY?

My plan to prepare for the worst unfortunately didn't include an emergency procedure to contain the newest phenomenon brought to life by Mrs. and Mr. Gillingham senior: the How Is The Baby feast. After the announcement they suddenly forgot I even existed, and they started to just ask how the belly and the baby were doing. I had completely disappeared, and I couldn't understand how or why: the baby was not there yet, and the belly was my belly, it was not an extension of the baby itself. Was I suddenly not important anymore? Was I just a biological incubator for a new grandchild for Mr. and Mrs. Gillingham senior? I was still there, blood and flesh and pissed off darts coming from my eyes. Mike tried to calm me down one night, when I finally told his mother to please ask about my own wellbeing, not the one of a baby who was inside my body, not going anywhere without me and therefore fully depending on my own health.

He didn't succeed, but I blamed the hormones, and I hissed to him, "Remember, you promised you wouldn't love this baby more than you love me."

My disappearance wasn't part of any of our deals.

The nightmare that woke me up on Friday morning, after what looked like a B-movie rape scene in an alley, wasn't part of the deal, either. Or the unstoppable nausea that still marked the first several minutes of my day, every day. Or the tiredness, the weakness, the thirst. At least I was going to see Rachel that night, to celebrate Mike's parents' departure and finally share my news with her. One thing I was sure of when I rang Rachel's doorbell: she would love me even more, caring about the baby as an extension of me, and not vice versa.

She was in a cheerful mood when she opened the door, a glass of wine in her hand, half full or half empty, depending on when she had refilled it for the last time.

"My dear," she squeezed me in a tipsy hug, "how are you?"

It was early, but she was already celebrating the end of the week.

"I have so many things to tell you, this week was so crazy! That's why I'm already half drunk."

She poured some wine in a glass and she handed it to me. I had spent my twenty-five-minute subway ride, from West Harlem down to Rachel's loft in the West Village, thinking about how I wanted to tell her: what words, what jokes, what tone I wanted to use. I wanted her to understand that I needed her more than ever. I wanted to be sure she would be there for me all the way through. I needed her strength. But at that point I didn't find anything to say, so I just stared at her and at the wine in her hand.

"Fuck," was all she said.

Had I ever refused a glass from her collection of French reds? Probably not.

"Fuck, are you...?" she added after a couple of seconds of complete silence.

The funny thing was that she had asked me that same question a hundred times already, without any stress or hesitation, as if she had always known that the answer would be negative. But now she knew I was going to say yes, and she was as scared as I was.

"Are you...?"

"Yes."

I couldn't say the word either.

She sobered up in a second and, with a small tear in her eye, she put the glasses back on the dining table and she hugged me with her whole body, wrapping me up with her warmth.

She let go after a few long breaths, to look at me straight in the eyes, her hands grasping my shoulders, "I love you, and you and Mike will be amazing parents."

That was her way to tell me not to worry, and that everything was going to be fine.

"How far along are you?" she then gently pulled me towards the sofa, getting started on the usual list of questions about the hows and whens of the situation. I had to stop her quite early in the process, though.

"Can we order food? I'm starving."

She smiled back at me, "Are you going to be a fat mama?"

"Jeez, Rach, it's dinner time and I'm hungry! And I haven't gained an ounce!"

"Yet," she finished the sentence for me. But then she burst out laughing, and I could put my concerns back in a drawer in a far corner of my mind.

We ordered from a nearby Asian restaurant, where she got some sushi rolls and I picked a chicken pad thai. By the time the food arrived we had exhausted my news.

"So," she began while mixing soy sauce and wasabi in a corner of the plastic cover of one of her trays, "I have a sort of news too."

That was going to be interesting.

"Sex, drugs and rock & roll?" I yelled.

She laughed hard, her best laugh, "Of course! You know me babe: not so much the drugs, unless you consider alcohol one of them, but a lot of sex and rock & roll!"

"Who's the guy?"

My pad thai tasted so good that I just wanted to eat and listen to her.

"A new guy at the gym. Not that new," she rushed, as soon as my left eyebrow jumped up, since I knew how she liked younger guys. "He's well above the legal age, if that's what you're thinking about, and fully consenting."

"I hope so," I mumbled, my mouth full of noodles.

"I promise, one hundred percent consenting. And he's so young and athletic that, oh my God, I swear nobody has ever done the things he does—"

"Rach!"

"What? Now that you're an old pregnant lady you are also prude?"

"I'm eating: I don't want to think about your sex performances while I'm eating. And given my state I could

74

throw up at any moment. Do you want me to throw up on your sofa?"

"No, you should be fine, we just had sex on the carpet, but not here on the sofa," she grinned at me, putting a large piece of Rainbow Roll in her mouth.

I looked at her and then at the carpet, and I burst out laughing as hard as I could. Ah!, the weekend activities her carpet could reveal.

THE WEEK WITH FOUR NEW ITEMS FOR THE CLOSET

The weekend was a whirlpool of morning calls with Europe, brunches and dinners, all carefully planned to share our news with our friends on both sides of the Ocean. Everybody exploded in congratulations and good wishes, in a crescendo of excitement. Infected by their euphoria, on Saturday night I had a vision in my sleep, of Mike and me, and a little copy of Mike. We were all walking on a beach, hands in hands, bright eyes all around. The three of us.

On Sunday morning I had the first breakfast in months: the vomiting roller coaster seemed to have left me alone for one day.

By the time I finalized my weekly piece on the HBO Sunday prime time show, quite late on Sunday night, I had almost forgotten that the second doctor's appointment was coming up the following morning.

Mike was going to be there this time, and he was very excited about the idea of meeting Doctor Mallory and taking another peek inside my belly.

The doctor didn't show any sign of surprise when she entered the room and she saw Mike sitting on a chair beside the bed. Either her deeply rooted professional code of conduct was preventing her from having any reaction to the fact that Mike was African American, or she was a true New Yorker, used to everything and anything in life. I wished we had that same absence of reaction any time one of us introduced the other to a new circle of friends or colleagues: even in the very progressive New York City or London, some people could be embarrassed or even bothered by a mixed race couple. In less cosmopolitan parts of both the US and the UK, and in many other countries we had visited during our trips around the world, we had encountered a vast range of attitudes, from pride to complete disapproval. We had been stared at, pointed to, laughed at, insulted, threatened, harassed, often all during the same trip.

This time the doctor's visit was rather underwhelming: no scan, no images, no pictures. A strange microphone was pointed towards my belly button, and the baby's heartbeat sound came suddenly out of it. Mike's grin came out, too.

"Everything looks great," the doctor said, with her usual friendly but efficiently confident tone. Mike was enthusiastic about her: he was always at ease with professional people, and she had good answers to all his questions.

"Is there any other test we ought to conduct?" he asked.

"Well, we did the Nuchal Translucency, and the results are telling me that your risk is about one in ten thousands, which is the minimum the machine can detect. That's as good as it gets.

We could do an amniocentesis, but it is an invasive test and there is a risk associated to it, since we need to insert a needle in Amber's belly and collect some amniotic fluid, to examine the genetic material—"

"Would you recommend it?" I couldn't stop myself from asking.

The doctor smiled and she seemed to be looking for a precise formula in her head.

"We have a hospital policy not to explicitly recommend any test or treatment," she continued. "We give our patients all the options, and we let them decide."

Mike and I exchanged an unsure look, Doctor Mallory read the hesitation on our faces and she sighed, "I can't tell you what to do, but in your case, considering that you are below the age of thirty-five and that all the tests so far have given good results, if you told me you decided not to do it I wouldn't be too concerned, and I wouldn't suggest you reconsider your choice."

Sometimes physicians were driven more by liability constraints than actual treatment decisions.

"There is also another non-invasive genetic test we could run. I usually don't offer it to my patients because it is not covered by insurance and most people decide not to take it, but it could provide us with some additional information on potential chromosomal defects."

Mike and I exchanged another look, which he accompanied with his typical raising of the left brow.

I spoke for both of us, "Why don't we do this additional non-invasive test? What is it?"

"We just need a blood draw. The test looks for the fetus's cells in your blood, and we run detailed analysis on a few chromosomes, which are connected to fetal anomalies.

Combined with the Nuchal Translucency results and the other blood tests we already conducted, this builds a very good picture of the situation. And it also tells you the gender of the baby. Do you want to know it?"

"Sure we do!" I responded quickly.

"You mentioned this test is usually not covered by insurances," Mike's brain was processing the cost model. "How much do you think it would cost?"

"We have a very good agreement with the lab that runs the test", she nodded. "They usually charge the patient around two hundred dollars."

We were happy to pay a few hundred dollars to have a better chance of having a healthy baby, there was no doubt about it. We left the clinic shortly after, once the nurse had made a new hole in my arm to suck some blood for the genetic testing.

Mike hopped on a taxi to go to the office, not far from the hospital, and I took a good walk to reach the R subway stop, where I sat on a train all the way to the World Trade Center. The doctor's words were still clear in my head: we were going to know the baby's gender soon. I hadn't thought about it, yet: was it going to be a boy or a girl? Did I have a preference? That was the first time I was asking myself that question, but the answer was surprisingly clear for me: I hoped it was a boy. Not for me, not for Mike or our families: nobody had ever openly told us they would have preferred a boy, and we had never really touched upon that point in any conversation. I wanted the baby to be a boy for the baby himself. Life could be so much harder for girls. The United States were a very modern country under many aspects, and many people understood the value of gender equality, but not everyone. Being a woman was still a disadvantage, because of diffused sexism in many contexts. As a journalist who focused on nerdy topics like fantastic movies and TV shows, I had received my abnormal share of insults and threats on the internet; Rachel often had to fight twice as hard as her male colleagues in court, and in the end she had developed a warrior attitude towards her job; a few of my friends from high school had gone on and studied engineering, to later find themselves underpaid when compared to their male peers; many women still suffered from discrimination and harassment all over the world, and sometimes the situation seemed even more bitter here in America.

This clarity surprised me. Those thoughts must have seethed on the backburner of my mind for a long time, and now they were popping out, unstoppable. I didn't want my baby to suffer for the simple reason of being born of a certain gender. Our child was going to be of mixed race, a condition already delicate even here in Manhattan, and I didn't want to add a second burden on its shoulders.

But then who knew: maybe in twenty years all discriminations would just be a distant memory. Maybe.

"We will soon know the baby's gender!" I texted Rachel a few hours after the physician's visit.

Her quick reply, "Shit is about to get real," shook me: things had already started to go down fast after that second doctor's appointment.

I had decided to tell my boss, because I didn't want to hide anything from Lauren, and I didn't want her to think I was keeping anything from her. Our relationship had been built on mutual trust over the many years we had worked together, since I had joined the Condé Nast family. She had pushed me farther towards deciphering my core passions, investing my time in the movies and shows I believed in the most, and ultimately building my brand as a journalist, not only within the magazine but also in the outside world. I wanted to tell her myself, before either I started to show, and she would guess, or she would randomly find out from someone else.

"Do you have a minute?" I was walking in the corridor towards her office, when I saw her turning a corner and coming towards me.

"Sure, let's go to my office."

We sat and she lightly smiled at me, "What's your question?"

I hesitated for just a second, "It's not a question, more a news: I'm pregnant."

That was the first time I ever said the word, and the sound of it was like an earthquake. I could see the walls crumbling down, the window shattering, the two of us being ripped apart by the explosion. Mike would say that I had watched too many disaster movies lately, for a piece I was writing on how the era of the disaster movie had ended just when things had started to go bonkers in the worldwide political landscape. Maybe he would be right, but hearing the words pronounced by my own voice made the whole thing real for the very first time. I was more than three months pregnant and I still couldn't believe it.

"This is such a good news!" she chirped, while standing up from behind her desk and coming to my side, to lock me up in a maternal embrace. "For a second I thought you were resigning and I got scared!"

She fired all the questions that came to her mind, from the due date to my emotional status. Somehow she looked more excited than I did.

"Do you think you will take longer than the regular leave? Maybe you guys plan to go to London for a time?"

I had affirmative answers to both questions, and she was very understanding about it, vigorously shrugging when I started to talk about replacement plans and dismissing my concerns. I wanted to take advantage of the company's parental leave, as much as I could: I had always worked very hard in my life, in school and in my job, and I believed this was my chance to take a break - a very busy break, but still a physical cut from the usual life. I wanted Mike and me to build a relationship with the baby in its first few weeks. Luckily, Mike had a very generous paternity leave. Then I wanted my parents to come and help me for a while, when the baby was maybe four or six weeks old, so that they would feel comfortable enough to take care of it, at least for a few hours each day, and I could take a break. They would be so ecstatic to spend some time with their grandchild: my mother had already started to text me and call me more often than she had ever done in my adult life, in an effort to get me used to her presence.

Maybe I was being unrealistic, maybe I would be one of those mothers who are not able to leave their children even for a split second. Maybe I was going to become attached to it even more than I was attached to Mike, and maybe the same thing was going to happen to him. This was the scariest scenario: the two of us losing our perfectly balanced relationship to focus on the new arrival, the external element. I promised myself that I wouldn't let this happen to us.

I couldn't have picked a better day to speak to Lauren: the following morning I was getting dressed and my usual work pants, the skinny chinos I had about twenty pairs of, didn't fit anymore. I looked at my profile in the tall mirror of our bedroom, and I could see that little belly roll trying to escape the jail of the pants' button. I could barely breathe. I had never really realized how skinny my pants were, and this sounded like a punishment for never having wanted to give a try to the more modern, more loosely fitting soft pants that many of my fashion-focused colleagues had been wearing for years.

Mike was leaning behind the closet door, looking at my desperate face reflected in the mirror.

"Shopping this weekend?" his best consolatory smile flashed on his face.

"I'll buy online: I don't want to feel fat while I try maternity clothes in a maternity shop, where everybody has huge bellies bumping around."

At least I made him laugh.

I had saved an article on my phone browser, a few months before, on the best online shopping spots for fashionable moms-to-be. Not that I would call myself fashionable, but at least I wanted to be able to wear something that still reflected my style, while hosting a growing alien inside my belly. Later that night, back at home after work, eating a non-raw-fish sushi selection and waiting for Mike on one of his long days at work, I extensively surfed the web to find something that would suit me.

The article had some great suggestion at hundreds of dollars each, some fairly good ones around the one hundred mark, and then there was asos maternity, with its wide range of affordable-to-fancy clothing options for all pockets. I also had some precious remote help from Rachel: I sent her the links to my potential picks via text, and she efficiently responded with emojis, from poop to dancing woman. By the end of the night I was able to find skinny tailored pants, with an elastic maternity band; fluffy blouses to go with the pants; leggings for the weekends. I was completely satisfied with myself.

"Did you also find a winter coat?" was the first thing Mike asked me once he came home, when I quite proudly showed him the results of my shopping challenge. He had the unique capability to find the little missing element in anything anyone would do. The detail was not even little this time, since we were already in November, and New York City would soon become the freezing hell we all hated and we complained about as loudly as we could.

"Do you think I should?" the rhetorical question came out of my mouth before I could stop it.

"Yes dear, I think you ought to. You won't fit in your sexy winter coat by the time we leave for London for Christmas."

Right.

We were taking the usual two weeks off for the end year Holidays, ready to board for a family Christmas at Mike's parents' house in London. Mike was right: my cute flattering coat would not make it to mid-December.

"Can I wait for another couple of weeks for that? It's still too early to think about winter."

"You can do anything that pleases you, just buy the snow boots before they go out of stock."

The winter boots were Mike's ultimate obsession: I had survived for many winters with my rain boots and thick wool socks, but this time he wanted me to get proper ugly Canadian snow boots, the chubby ones with special grip soles.

"Because you know you could fall in the snow, with an unbalanced center of gravity. And being yourself—"

"I know I'm goofy, you don't have to remind me," I told him with my best hurt puppy face, the one that never failed to make him laugh.

"Perhaps you would like me to remind you how you fell on the sidewalk during summer, arse on the ground, bruise-covered butt for at least a week," he laughed and he tried to hug me.

I escaped the hugging, but he was faster than me, and I was happy to lie in his embrace on the sofa for a little while longer.

"Do you want to hear about the changes I'm thinking about for the apartment?" he offered later that night.

Changes? What changes?

"Well, it would be a good opportunity to change the heaters, since it's always so hot in here during winter. And we need to move the table out of the second bedroom, and rearrange our room to make space for a smaller table, so that you don't lose your writing space."

"We can just put a small table at the end of our bed, it will fit," I replied, bothered.

He couldn't or didn't want to sense the annoyance growing inside of me, "I don't think it would fit. I think we need to remove the bedhead, buy some small side tables to replace it, perhaps buy a new bed."

"No."

"No?" he repeated, as if he needed confirmation.

"We don't need to change our bedroom: a small table will fit," I didn't want to look at him.

"That's it? You don't want to talk about it?"

No, I didn't want to talk about it. If there was one thing I didn't want to touch was our bedroom, our intimacy as a couple, the privacy of our nights. The idea of modifying our inner space as a direct consequence of the baby's arrival looked like a betrayal to me, a betrayal of our promise to remain the same. To always come first.

"No."

I grabbed my hurt feelings and I went straight to bed. Mike joined me a few minutes later and he tried to hug me as soon as he slid under the sheets. I pretended I was already asleep.

THE WEEK WITH FOUR RERUNS

I couldn't see anything. I had been blindfolded, and my wrists were tied, too. I knew it was a dream, yet I couldn't stop sweating and asking myself what would come next. I couldn't speak, some tissue filling up my mouth. I sighed, waiting for the nightmare to get worse and trying to wake up. Cold claws swiftly grabbed my feet and they spread my legs. I used all my strength to wiggle out of my monster's grasp, only to have its tentacles wrapped even tighter around my ankles, my calves, my thighs, my hips. I couldn't move anymore. A dead slime penetrated me, and the same frozen death filled my mouth as I tried to scream, bloody tears rolling down my cheeks.

When I finally woke up, Mike was gently shaking me. "You're crying," he said.

I wiped my face and I hugged him, thankful, only to have to jump out of bed after a few seconds, the morning vomiting roller coaster waiting for me at the bottom of the toilet.

"Everything sucks," I texted Rachel as soon as I sat on the subway.

"Wait, you just discovered that pregnancy is not all bliss and glowing skin?"

"It's all nightmares and puke," I added with a nauseated emoji.

"Don't worry, it will be over before you know it! And then you will have a charming mini-Mike who will keep you awake at night and barf all over you. Isn't that adorable?"

I responded with the "face screaming in fear" emoji.

Rachel was quick, "But you will be able to drink again, so everything will be awesome!"

Not sure, Rachel, not sure.

"Hello, Amber, this is Doctor Mallory speaking. I have the results of your MaterniT21 test: we checked chromosomes number thirteen, eighteen, and twenty-one, and all tests are negative. This is great news, as it means we didn't find any chromosomal anomalies. I am also able to tell you the gender of your baby, if you want to know. Give me a call back to my office number."

I found the doctor's voicemail when I got back to my desk after a staff meeting, and I listened to it at least four times. She knew if the baby was a boy or a girl, and I would know soon. The baby was about to become fully real: it would suddenly stop being just a thing in my belly, and it would become a he or a she.

It was the last step of my journey to reality: I had to give up the last veil that was still hiding me from the truth, the truth that a new life was expecting Mike and myself around the corner. It was time.

The assistant at the doctor's office could only tell me that a nurse would contact me back. These phone games never ended up working for me. I waited for a few minutes, fixating the phone in my hand, expecting it to ring again soon and to know what it was going to be. I found myself hoping for a boy even more strongly than before, to spare it from pregnancy and all the issues the female body brings with it - periods, aesthetics, hair removal.

After a while I realized the nurse wasn't going to return my call right away, so I texted Mike. He called me after about half a second.

"Did the nurse ring you?" his voice sounded over excited.

"Not yet, can I call you when she does?"

"I have a meeting from 12 to 3 pm, so text me if it's during the meeting, and I'll try to get out and ring you back, otherwise ring me straight!"

I could see him and his bright smile on the other side of the phone, as if he were there in front of me. He didn't care about the gender of the baby, because he was convinced we would be able to give the best education, and the strongest bases for self-determination, confidence, and personal success, to any boy or girl.

I started to play the conversation with the nurse in my head, with the two options. What if she said it was a boy? I would be relieved. What if it was a girl? I wouldn't be disappointed for myself, and there would be no differences in my feelings towards a girl. But she would be in disadvantage against a male competitor at work, she would be passed over for promotions, she would suffer because of that second X chromosome, and I would love to spare all these defeats to the baby.

I had to eventually stop staring at the phone and go back to work. Wednesday was American Horror Story night, and I was preparing different versions of the article I was going to post that night on the Vanity Fair website: was Character A going to die in this episode? Was the Big Plot Twist everybody expected going to air tonight? Mike hated how I could watch violent television shows or movies and not be influenced by them. Sometimes I would be grossed out, but most of the times I was left untouched by even the most gruesome events on screen. He was bothered by the social side of it: gratuitous violence seen on TV or on a movie screen could have a huge impact on susceptible youngsters. We clearly had no need for cinematographic violence, when we could find so much authentic brutality any day on a newspaper's front page. Paradoxically, the never ending drama, tears, and heartbreaking deaths of shows like Grey's Anatomy had always a longer grip on me. He had never liked those shows, either, because of their impact on my mood. He called it "Amber's Strange Crying Factor": a terrified scream had a way lower impact on me than a mourning one. I had always been a nerd in my emotions, too.

I was following my thoughts as they appeared on my computer's screen, black virtual ink on a white page, when the phone rang. I had the doctor's office number saved in my contacts, so I knew who that was.

"Hello, may I speak to Miss Amber Gillingham?"

"That's me."

Was my voice shaking?

"Hello, I'm calling you back from Doctor Mallory's office, did you call us?"

I could quickly find a quiet room where my words would not be heard from the outside, but I still felt I had to whisper, "Yes, the doctor told me you received my MaterniT21 test results, and that you can tell me the gender of the baby."

"Very well, Miss Gillingham. Yes, we received the test results, and it looks like you are having a boy."

Something grabbed my throat, and an unexpected cork plugged my airways.

"Oh a boy", I squawked, tears filling my eyes.

"Yes, congratulations!"

Somehow the nurse sounded way more excited than I did.

I gave myself a couple of minutes to gain my poise back, before I called Mike.

"Hey, can you talk?"

"Sure, I'm driving, but I can talk."

"The nurse just called me," the throat-grabbing monster hit back at me, but I sniffled and I tried to be stronger this time. "Do you want to know?"

"Sure I want to know!" he screamed from the other side of the phone.

"It's a boy!"

"It's a boy! Oh!" I could see his eyes open wide and bright, "I am so happy! You wanted it so much!"

"Thank you," I whispered.

Thank you for accepting me for who I was.

He took a big breath, "I'm almost there. I have to run, but I will ring you as soon as I'm done with the meeting."

As I was hanging up with him, the thought kept rolling inside me, waves on the seaside: we were having a boy.

I slowly spread my news to the larger circles of friends, colleagues, and family. At the end, Chloe's turn came. Chloe and I used to be close friends in primary school, inseparable at an age when all we had needed to call each other best friend had been to love the same cartoons, enjoy our bike rides together, and secretly laugh about Fatty Betty, Chloe's neighbor. Growing up, we had developed different personalities, which had worn our bond thinner and thinner, especially from my side. She had become the kind of girly man-seeking woman that I couldn't suffer. We had ended up living opposite lives, making choices that kept separating us from each other. We had reached a precarious balance in the past years, exchanging emails every few months and speaking over the phone a couple of times per year, both struggling to keep alive something that had gone in a coma years ago.

"Amber! My God, how are you? It's been so long! You are always too busy to call me!" my phone conversation with Chloe started with a bang.

"I know I have been somewhat out of touch lately, I am so sorry."

"Don't worry, dear, how are you? How is Mike? I saw on Facebook that you went on vacation in Southern Europe this summer, how was it?"

Wasn't it weird to talk about summer vacation when winter was already approaching? It was almost Thanksgiving, and Europe was far behind me, a faded memory of things before the whole baby situation had exploded in my face. I had always had the feeling that Chloe was living in the past, with her husband met twenty years before, her stories, her friends, always the same.

"Summer vacation was great, we really loved Spain."

I didn't want to get lost in her weeds, so I decided to keep going straight to the point, "I actually have some news that I really want to share with you: Mike and I are expecting a baby!"

"Oh my God!" she started to sob quite loudly on the other side of the phone. "Oh my God, I can't believe it! I felt it when I saw you were calling me, I knew something was going to happen. And you are having a baby! I am so happy for you."

She didn't seem to be able to speak further, choked by her tears.

"Thank you," I mumbled, overpowered by her emotional reaction, "Mike and I are very happy too."

"I can imagine, Mike must be so excited! Are you going to breastfeed?"

What?

"What?"

"Are you going to breastfeed? It is such a unique experience, you must breastfeed."

Why did that have to be the first question? Chloe had her own parental views, that included a moral obligation to breastfeeding, an almost vegan baby menu, a very reluctant adoption of only the most highly recommended vaccines, and the refusal of all contact with chemicals, especially medications.

She sensed my hesitation, since I hadn't really thought about that, and she kept chasing me, "Breastfeeding is the best for the baby: don't think twice about it, just do it."

I tried to shut her up and change topic, "We're having a boy, we're very happy about it."

"That's great, just like my Jasper! When is the due date?"

"Early May."

"Oh my God! That would be so great if he could be born on Jasper's birthday! We could have birthday parties together, they could become best friends, we could spend a lot of time together. That would be so amazing!"

I hadn't thought about that.

"What are you going to call him?" she didn't even need to pause to catch her breath at this point.

"I have no idea, Mike and I are just starting to think about—"

"Oh, you need to have a name as soon as you can. Devon and I had a name right away."

"Oh."

"Do you have a stroller?"

"No, we thought we could get one in a few months, and—"

"No no no, you need a stroller right away, you need to get used to it."

"Oh."

"Do you have a baby crib and bed?"

She was clearly showing off how prepared she was to the whole parenting thing, but at that point I decided not to be intimidated by her.

"Listen, Chloe, I still have six months to go. We have plenty of time before we actually need all the baby stuff, and a nice order on Amazon will bring everything to our place in one day. There's no need to worry!"

She mumbled something that sounded like, "You have no idea what you're talking about," that I deliberately decided to ignore, and I used her first and only hesitation to spit out a work-related excuse to rush to something else.

I was physically exhausted when I hit the red button on my cell phone, relieved to get rid of her yappy voice.

I had never liked unsolicited advice, especially from people who had a totally opposite approach to the topic under discussion. Chloe was not the first one to try to choke me with her truth, but she had the immense power to get on my nerves in a heartbeat, with her inappropriate comments and weird ideas. I had already received unexpected reactions from some colleagues and friends, my feminist self-control being deeply challenged when people I considered modern and reasonable responded to my pregnancy with some bluntly sexist comments.

"Well, you reached the age when everybody gets pregnant..."

"Now you will have to give up something here at work, maybe you can make room for some of the younger guys?"

"Now you have to focus on your baby: nothing else matters, especially not your job!"

I didn't know how to answer to those people. My job still mattered, my identity still mattered, and I was still the same person, with the same abilities and career ambitions.

My absolute favorite nonsense comment had come from a woman I didn't know very well, a friend of a friend who had been at one of the news-sharing group dinners Mike and I had organized. She had a boy herself, and when we had told her we were going to have a boy, too, a sad cloud had flown through her face.

"Is anything wrong?" I had asked her.

I hadn't noticed the desperate look on her husband's face when she had responded.

"I had always hoped I could have a girl, so I can understand what you must be feeling now," she had reached for my hand while speaking softly.

"Well, I always thought being a woman was more complex: you have sexism, lower salaries, glass ceilings preventing you from obtaining some of the highest positions…"

"Oh, I have never experienced any of those things," she had replied with her eyes wide open.

"You must have been lucky in your life!" I had tried to remember what she did for a living. "I have collected many examples of discrimination, on my skin and on many of my girlfriends'. I actually wanted a boy," I had concluded.

"Oh no, why would you want a boy? Life is so much easier if you are a girl, mine has always been. You can get free passes for clubs, you can wear nice dresses and makeup, you can obtain anything you want. You just need to smile and wear a short dress, or something that makes your boobs stand out, depending on your assets. And if you flirt just a little, men do anything for you!"

As her husband had rubbed his forehead with his hand and Mike had repressed a grin, I had found myself unable to counter her impeccable logic.

THE WEEK WITH FOUR DAYCARES AND TWO THANKSGIVINGS

"This is the craziest thing I've ever heard in my life!" I should have said, but I was too baffled to even respond.

"I know what you're thinking," Mike raised his eyebrows and he brushed my arm to keep me calm, "but that's how things work. We have no choice."

"You're telling me they will put us on a waitlist, if we're lucky, for a spot in a children's daycare? To start in ten months?"

Mike sighed.

We had always loved Manhattan, the heart of the world, the city where everything was possible. But being the place that it was, crowded with people ready to fight with their teeth and nails to get the best out of it, Manhattan came with precise rules, sometimes nonsensical. If we wanted to put the baby in a daycare, we had to follow the rules. Probably a routine to-do for couples anywhere else in the US, the daycare selection was a proper task in Manhattan. The offer of good centers was limited, compared to the number of people who inhabited the city, and it was essential to put one's name on the waiting list as soon as possible. The experts recommended right after conception, but any time between nine and twelve months before the desired start date could give a couple a fair chance to get access to their favorite daycare. With a due date in early May and a desired start day in early August, based on my general understanding of Vanity Fair's maternity leave policies, we had to make a decision as soon as possible. Which, in the first half of November, sounded completely nuts.

Mike had taken the process very seriously, investigating and finally selecting four centers to visit, in a Monday morning dedicated to the endeavor. On the subway on our way to the first meeting, he was explaining me the process, advance payment and waitlist and all.

The daycare tour was mind blowing. All locations offered special classes from the age of twelve months, including Spanish, Chinese, ballet, music, and science; they all served organic meals; they were all clean and shiny, more than our own apartment; they all had highly qualified and certified personnel who claimed they would prepare one's child to perfection for the admission tests to the top schools in Manhattan. They all cost like our mortgage, but hey, the baby was surely going to become a genius!

Mike had saved the last spot of the tour for what he had already identified as his favorite option: the closest to a subway stop, and also half a block from Central Park, where the educators told us they brought the children for a stroll twice a day, weather permitting. That sealed the deal for us, and a few minutes after the visit was over Mike was happily filling in the application form, and signing the few hundred dollar check that had to go with it.

"Mission accomplished!" he grinned as we were walking out the door.

"You already knew we would choose this: you're so smart..." I teased him with gasping eyes.

He pretended not to notice my mockery, and he went on to list the pros and cons of the four daycares we had just visited, in a very sweet attempt to convince me again that he was right. When we reached the subway platform on 59th street I closed his mouth with a kiss, and he finally relaxed and he smiled back at me.

Mission accomplished. And ready to enjoy our Thanksgiving break.

Routines were my lifesavers, and holidays provided me with the best annual cycles. Thanksgiving Tuesday Dinner had been my special moment with Rachel for years, since we had shared a room during our first year at Columbia University. Tuesday was the perfect night, as we both had to reach our families for Thanksgiving dinner on Thursday, braving the weather for a drive to Connecticut or a flight to Naples, Florida, where Rachel's parents had moved after retiring.

I checked my phone as I was leaving the office that night, to remind myself where Rachel had booked our dinner. "Flowers, upscale organic vegan gluten free restaurant", twenty-something minutes away with the A C E subway lines.

"Why in hell did you pick a vegan gluten free restaurant for our Thanksgiving dinner?"

"LOL!" Rachel texted back after a few seconds. "Just to piss you off."

That was love.

"I love you too," I responded with a middle finger emoji.

She replied with the grinning face, and she added, "The menu is actually good, with pasta, salads and tofu."

"I am not going to eat a soy-based steak, FYI."

"They have a great vegan crepe with tofu and tapioca cheese. And you will eat enough animal fats on Thursday at your parents' place, anyway."

Fair point.

"Do they serve wine, at least?"

"Of course they do," she texted back. "But you're pregnant, remember? That thing on your stomach is not fat, at least not only fat…"

I responded with the poop emoji, and I got off at the following stop.

"Please let's never give up our Thanksgiving dinners," I told her after our shared mushroom-based starter, which I had to admit tasted pretty good.

"Why should we?" she offered me her tipsy smile. She was enjoying the wine for both of us.

I smiled back. She was right, why should I stop enjoying my life? Why should I give up the things that best defined me and that filled me with joy? I squeezed her hand and she caressed my face.

"I love you, fat mama."

"I love you, drunk sex-addict."

The drive to my parents' house was the thing I enjoyed the most about spending four full days with them. The highway 95 ran between towns and forests, marvelous greens and browns, not close enough to the coast to see the ocean, but sufficiently to smell the salt if you were paying attention to it. I savored each step of the trip: collecting the car at the rental office, leaving Manhattan late on Wednesday night to avoid traffic, and reaching our destination after midnight, greeted by my mother's sleepy and thankfully almost silent hugs. This time the routine was challenged by my bladder: for the first time since I could remember, I had to ask Mike to stop somewhere halfway to use the restroom. I felt pregnant. Not yet fully used to it, but more and more faced with the evidence of it.

Thanksgiving used to be a weekly endeavor for my mother and me in my childhood. We would spend the previous weekend and few weekdays planning together for the menu, which would end up always being the same; I would toddle after her while grocery shopping, eager to run around the shop to grab something for her; I would silently observe her as she would pick the perfect turkey. The day before Thanksgiving would be dedicated to getting the turkey ready: she would let me mix the stuffing ingredients in the gigantic bowl, all my strength focused on pushing and rotating the wooden spoon, desperately trying to obtain a blend good enough for her. In the meantime she would bake the bread, because she had always had this idea that bread tasted better when reheated for a few seconds on the following day. On the T-Day we would wake up early to finalize the turkey setup, put the beast in the big oven, and dedicate the smaller oven to pie baking. It had never mattered that it would be only the three of us, my parents and me: my mother would always want Thanksgiving dinner to be as big as possible, as rich as possible, decorated with all the foods and table items she could think of.

The idyllic Thanksgiving routine had broken when I had reached puberty and I had become a horrible teenager, as my mother would put it if asked. I had refused to help her any longer, and she had never lost an occasion to show me how much better she had been dealing with everything without me, how more perfectly cooked the turkey and more fabulous the dinner table.

Moving out to go to college and, a couple of years later, my parents relocating to Connecticut, had put a dignified end to our feud: I had been now allowed to show up on Thursday at lunch time, ready to eat.

Mike had dedicated considerable effort through the years to the mission of establishing a more decent rapport between my mother and me. Now the latest tradition would dictate Mike and me arriving to my parents' place decently late on Wednesday night, and sleeping in on Thursday morning. By the time I would be ready to help my mother, only the apple pie would be left to make, the apples, cinnamon, sugar and flour ready on the kitchen counter, butter and eggs at arm's distance in the fridge. She would follow my every movement with her eyes, ready to clear her throat at any minor hesitation and speak up at any major issue, like picking the wrong knife to cut the butter. Mike had greatly trained me to grin at every reproach, like the mature adult I was supposed to be.

This year I woke up on Thanksgiving Day after a surprisingly serene night, and I jumped from the shower to my clothes even before Mike was fully awake. While I was peeling and cutting the apples, the back of my head tickled, and as I turned around I caught my mother spying on my belly from behind my shoulders.

"Are you trying to X-Ray me to see the baby?"

She lifted her eyes from my stomach to my face for a few seconds, "Oh no, I was just looking at the belly: it's showing now."

"I know," I responded, already missing my usual flat line, "I almost can't hide it anymore."

"Why would you want to hide it? It's such a normal thing."

I sighed.

"But it still is my body that's getting deformed out of my control."

"That's the deal with it," she lightly patted my ego and my arm. "The excitement and the hormones are there to cover up the fat and the bloating."

My mother always knew how to make me feel better.

"Are you looking forward?" she added after a few seconds.

"It's still hard to imagine. Are you looking forward to having a grandchild?"

She exploded with pure enthusiasm, "I am so looking forward! I will spoil him so much, I will allow him to eat all the things he won't be able to eat at home, and to do all the forbidden things. He will have his toys here and we will invent secret games that you will never know of. I will be his friend!"

You will be his friend?

"Wait a second, you never spoiled me, you were never my friend. Did I pick the short straw and the baby gets the long one?"

What was this story? My mother had always been very strict with me, reinforcing my father's obsession for severe discipline on anything: food, rules, going out by myself. She had also added her nice touch of merciless honesty during my worst teenage years, when I used to wear glasses and braces, boobs hadn't yet showed up and I had been a lonely nerd. And now she wanted to be my child's permissive superhero?

"That's a mother's role, that's going to be you: you will teach him discipline and rigor, you will have him eat vegetables and stinky fish, you will punish him if he does something stupid. But I get to be the fun one now: I'm his grandma! I will follow your basic rules, I won't give him fried chicken or boxes of cookies, I'm not completely crazy yet, but I will let him have a piece of chocolate, a little more ice-cream than what he gets at home, a burger when he's holder, homemade and organic, of course. He won't see me all the time, so I want him to love me."

I couldn't believe my ears: my mother had suddenly become cool. Years and years of being the uncool kid who couldn't go out at night, and now my mother was in such a desperate need for love that she was ready to do anything for a baby who wasn't even born. It sounded so unlike her. But also so grandma-like: after all, the role of the grandparents was to love and spoil their grandchildren. It was the reason why parents kept asking their children to reproduce: to have a second chance at being cool parents, when discipline and education were not their responsibility.

I sighed, and I promised myself that I would be different: I had no idea how, but somehow I would mix empathy and discipline, love and rules, to give the baby a better experience.

I didn't even have time to reply to my mother's declaration of love for the still unborn grandchild, when my father's joyous yaps completely destabilized me for good, "Good morning baby boy! Did you sleep well?"

"Dad, who the hell are you talking to, there's no baby boy!"

"I know, I know," he dismissed me with a shrug, keeping up a smile addressed only to my belly. "But you are here too, in a way, right?"

"It is not!" I yelled at my father, and my shrieks brought Mike running into the kitchen.

"Oh come on, Amber," my mother obviously needed to add something to the conversation. "Your father is just excited."

I threw a desperate peek at Mike, but nothing came out of his mouth.

I cleared my throat to fight angry tears, "That would be nice if I could still exist for you guys, at least for a few months. Then I know that even Mike will become less important after the grandchild arrives, and I will be relegated to a far third place in your lives."

I eyed Mike to bring my father away from my sight as soon as he could, and I went back to cutting the apples for my pie, enraged as ever. My mother kept speaking words I didn't hear. I had expected my parents to go completely crazy about the long awaited heir, but not that soon.

It was going to be a long Thanksgiving Day.

The morning after, my most vivid memory was how I had thrown up everything shortly after we had left the table, in what had immediately reached the top of my Worst Vomiting Roller Coaster rank. Now I was looking at myself in the mirror of the guestroom Mike and I always used at my parents': had my belly just completely exploded? How could my breasts suddenly be that big? And most scarily of all: how much more was I going to expand? I couldn't stop myself from being myself, and thinking about the worst possible outcomes, certainly inspired by how disastrous the holiday weekend had been that far. What if something were to go wrong now? Anything could still happen: development defects, viruses, miscarriage, death. How would our families take such news, now that everyone was getting attached to that yet unborn baby? How would Mike take it? How much would he suffer? And how much pain would hit me, as a consequence of everyone's desperation? I was not ready for the baby to come, but I was even less ready for a tragedy to occur, instead. Only one word came to mind: inadequate.

What is life
You ask me, my son
Life is the infinite flow of things
People you leave behind
Clothes forgotten in hotel drawers
Questions not asked
Answers already vanished

ANNALISA CONTI

NINE

FIVE

ANNALISA CONTI

THE WEEK WITH FIVE INCHES ADDED TO THE WAISTLINE

I left my apartment building early on Friday morning and I looked up at the sky, gray with clouds, uncertain between snowing and clearing up. My breaths were short and fast as I walked to the subway, I could feel my weight.

"I am so fat!" my fingers typed fast on my phone.

"You're not fat," Rachel's reply popped up almost immediately, surprising me. "You are expecting a baby. The beauty of pregnancy. You will lose all your weight so quickly after he's born, trust me! You're not like me: if I ever get pregnant I will gain sixty pounds and never let them go!"

She was right, but I couldn't forget the image I had seen in the mirror that morning: my belly was out, front and center. And new wrinkles seemed to appear on my face every day. I hadn't even had a terrible night, with just a glimpse at the vomiting roller coaster, but my eyes were opaque.

In a clear improvement of the situation, my mother's text came in.

"Hello, Amber, dad and I hope everything is fine with Baby Boy. I think you might be getting bloated, so I asked Sheila for a slimming herbal tea against water retention. She suggested something called Ultra Slim. It's a caffeine-free herbal tea from Vegan Conscious Teas, the brand I love. Let me know when you buy it. Also, I can ask her for some laxatives if you need them. Don't be ashamed to talk about these little female issues with me. How is Mike? Loves, mom."

With sniper precision she had hit all targets: asking about the baby, then about Mike, completely forgetting about me, mentioning embarrassing bodily functions, implying I was fat. Strike. She had been mastering the art of diminishing me for years, even if she had never again matched the perfect score she had achieved for my Prom. She had managed to buy me the dress she wanted, a puffy pink explosion, instead of the dark blue gown I had chosen; she had demanded that my date showed up at our place in advance, to evaluate the poor kid; she had hated him, a rather normal, slightly emo geeky guy; she had told him he wasn't dressed properly for Prom; he had dumped me right outside my building's entrance, forcing me to go to the ball by myself, taking the subway with my pink gown and hideous shoes. She had called me every ten minutes to know how things were going, and since I had never picked up she had resolved to jump in a taxi and come see for herself. I had never wished for instant death any harder than the moment she had grabbed my arm and she had dragged me outside to yell at me. In front of the whole school. The following day I had moved out of my parents' apartment, squatting at a friend's place until I would find a solution. I had ended up spending that summer working at a children's camp upstate, the perfect way to stay out of reach until the last week of August, when I had gotten access to the room I had secured in one of Columbia's dorms.

In all this, mornings were not even the worst part of my days: my stomach was especially swollen in the evening, after many hours spent sitting on my butt in the office, focused on my computer and never enough stretching. But at least I had Mike by my side at night. Every time he saw me with a hand on my belly, soothing my straining skin, he smiled at me, "You have such a cute belly!"

"It's not cute," I would always scold him, "It's horrible. I'm disgusting."

"Nonsense! You haven't gained a pound. It is just the belly, and all the water you drink."

"Right."

"It's a very sweet baby belly," he would then add, and he would hug me each time.

That wasn't the only evolution, though, as I was slowly getting used to saying the words out loud: I'm pregnant. Eventually it stopped sounding like a curse, as I was repeating the words more and more frequently every day, to colleagues, to friends, to the cleaning lady.

Everybody was very excited about it, and each person was showing their affection and attentions to me. It was a constant celebration, which caught me by complete surprise. It all sounded very ancestral, the miracle of a pregnancy in the community, a new life that would soon come and make the world a better place. Beautiful dreams.

At work, my childless female colleagues invited me more and more often to lunch. Maybe they wanted to take advantage of the last few months of Amber as they knew her, before the baby came and it transformed me into some new animal. Or maybe they were trying to get a sneak peek of how it really was, the whole pregnancy situation, to get ready for it when their time would come.

The most heartwarming reactions came from my male colleagues, though, who all revealed themselves for the teddy bears they were. Some of them asked me how I was feeling on a regular basis, sincerely interested in my health; someone suggested me to take it easy when they saw me at my desk later than usual, busy with a movie review of the latest Christmas blockbuster. It didn't matter their age or role, they all now saw me like a special entity, who deserved a smile every time they crossed me in a corridor. They had all become a father or a brother, wanting nothing but my wellbeing.

THE WEEK WITH FIVE SENTENCES TO KILL SOCIAL CONVENTIONS

"I feel good," I was telling Rachel at dinner on a cold Sunday. Mike was home, working.

She nodded while she was chewing on her salad, to encourage me to tell her more.

"I reached a good balance."

I bit on my burger, while warming up at Rachel's smile, and I kept going.

"I am getting used to all this, my body that changes day after day. I mean, I am not excited about being pregnant: I still feel horrible every morning. It's improving, but the vomiting roller coaster is still up and running. I still have nightmares from time to time, but I think it's normal. I have no idea of what I will do with a baby in my arms, but I think it will come. I'm definitely not enjoying my pregnancy as some women do, drowned in hormones and feeling finally complete as a human being."

I ingurgitated half the burger in one bite, and I waited for Rachel to say something. She kept smiling and chewing, so I kept going.

"I am happy to recognize the original Amber: still rational, nerdy, not more emotional than needed," I concluded with pride.

Rachel stared at me for one long second, as if she were trying to read beyond my eyes, looking for something. Then she shook her head and she squeezed my hand, "Let's make a toast to our good ol' Amber!"

Too bad nobody else wanted to cheer for the real Amber, as I understood during a work trip to Los Angeles.

The weather was soft in the City of Angels, a nice break from the first drafts of winter that had started to blow over New York. I got to the hotel on a late Tuesday afternoon, the memory of sunset almost lost in the air. As I was getting ready for dinner, I glimpsed at the mirror, and I realized I would have to acknowledge my now evident truth to everyone I would meet that night. When I walked in the dining hall, I saw Vibin rushing towards me: he was one of the editors of Vanity Fair's tech section, a fellow nerd I always enjoyed a good conversation with.

"How's Chicago, Vibin?" I greeted him, curious to know about his recent move from Connecticut to Illinois.

"It's been great! The kids love the new school and they are looking forward to the first snow, but Shumaya is concerned about winter. They're saying this year will be brutal, but we will see. How are you?"

The segue was too perfect to miss it, "Well, I'm happy your kids are enjoying the new life. And I have some news: I have a little one on the way, too."

His eyes opened wide, in the largest smile I had ever seen on his face, "This is such great news, Amber! Children are such a life-changing earth-shattering blessing! How are you feeling? When are you due? Do you already know what it is? Are you excited?"

His pressing questions submerged me, but they were not hard to answer. Apart from the last one: was I excited? Since I knew him quite well and I thought we had a good relationship, albeit mostly professional, I went for the truth.

"I wouldn't call myself enthusiastic: my relationship with Mike has always been perfect and fulfilling, and we didn't need to add a baby to call ourselves happy. We decided to have children now, just because now it's the right time for us to do so. Some things might need to be adjusted, but we are sure we won't give up our strength and connection as a couple. We're pretty confident in our organizational skills. I definitely wouldn't say I'm thrilled, but I am very satisfied that everything is going as planned, and the baby has been healthy so far."

While I was speaking, I could see the corners of his mouth sliding down on his face, as if the invisible strings that had pulled them up at the news were getting strained by the energy of my unexpected words. When I was done with my explanation, he puffed an "Oh", uncertain of what to say. My answer was too different from what he was expecting, and not an answer he cared to hear: his two children were the love of his life, a love that had completely replaced whatever relationship he used to have with his wife, without him being able or willing to do anything about it. He had muted his regrets long ago. He was now longing for my understanding, and he was expecting me to deliver a joyous answer that would make him feel comfortable about his own feelings for his kids. Or his wife. He couldn't process my words because they were something he had never considered, and that was now clogging his system.

Looking for a way to unblock him, I quickly sputtered, "But we are also very excited! It will be great! The kid will change our lives and we will love it!"

The relief was immediately evident on his face: my forced smile, confirming I was on his side of the fence, was enough for him to feel good about himself. He could now express his deepest joy by lightly patting me on the shoulder.

I left Vibin with my eyes wide open in horror, and I went to talk to another close colleague, a witty woman who wrote in the politics section. It turned out Vibin's was not an isolated case, as I tried to be honest with her, too, and she had the exact same reaction. I then bent the knee to social conventions.

Like Bill Murray in Groundhog Day, my two days in Los Angeles forced me to live the same conversations over and over again. Meet someone I hadn't seen in many months, announce my pregnancy, smile at the congratulations and pressing questions, confirm my incredible excitement for the situation, rejoice together. Move to the next person and repeat. Again and again. I became an expert in fake smiles, simulated cries of joy, and assorted versions of "Oh my God".

By the time I boarded my plane back to New York I was exhausted, frustrated by how people would do anything to hide their insecurities and regrets about their lives, even to themselves. Especially to themselves.

NINE

My phone vibrated, and I deleted an email from my mother without even reading it. I didn't need her to diagnose me with some other pregnancy symptoms. Not now.

THE WEEK WITH FIVE FINGERS IN A HAND

"Here are some symptoms you might be experiencing in your fifth month: achiness in the lower abdomen, backache, headaches, constipation, heartburn, indigestion, flatulence, bloating, leg cramps, swelling of ankles and feet, occasional swelling of hands and face, varicose veins of legs and vulva, hemorrhoids, forgetfulness, absent mindedness, fetal movements."

The more I read, the more my heartbeat accelerated and my breaths became shorter and quicker. I listened to my body: was that the onset of backache? Were my legs cramping, or swelling, or were varicose veins popping up? Was my constant stomach pain the result of the combination of heartburn, bloating, and flatulence? Did I forget to turn off the gas?

The book Mike had bought a few months before, What To Expect When You Are Expecting, hadn't provided much help that far. If anything, it had kicked off my hypochondria for some of the horrific symptoms it was mentioning. It had also led me to worry about the few discomforts I was experiencing, the vomiting roller coaster and the on-and-off nightmares, which weren't discussed at all in that fifth month chapter. At least the morning encounters with the toilet were becoming less physically challenging.

One manifestation was completely missing: where were the baby movements?

Lying in bed one night, Mike was reading a pamphlet on Russian politics, snorting and snickering at each page turned. My complete focus was on the latest review of the annual Star Wars movie. I was diligently comparing the New York Times piece to my own words, published a few days before on the online edition of Vanity Fair; the Times' critic had a different perspective on the movie, and he called "a fraudulent mashup of themes and characters from all previous entries of the franchise" what I had praised as "a modern reinterpretation of the classic Star Wars topics of self-discovery, feminism, and interracial cooperation". I was so immersed in my study that I almost missed the bubbles in my stomach. I had been experiencing those bubbles for a couple of days, and I had thought my intestines were getting more and more upset at how the baby had been pushing them around to make room for himself. After a few seconds, a new set of bubbles forced me to detract my attention from my precious tablet, to stop and listen to them. I even put a hand on my belly, to understand what was going on: was I sick? Was I going to throw up, on a special roller coaster ride?

When the bubbles came back in a different area of my belly, closer to my groin, I figured it wasn't my intestines showing their dissatisfaction, rather the baby struggling to find its space among my organs, and I was feeling its movements. Inside me. I shook my head to throw away the image that had suddenly popped in my brain: a baby Alien bloodily emerging from the lacerated abdomen of an unfortunate host, in any entry of Ridley Scott's movie saga.

"Are you ok?"

Mike must have peeked into my internal turmoil with the corner of his eye, as I had my right hand on my groin and a scared look on my face. I shook my head again to remove Alien's Ellen Ripley's screaming face from my sick imagination, and I tried to put up a smile.

"I think the baby is moving. Do you want to give me your hand?"

Mike couldn't have asked for more, as his ear-to-ear smile confirmed when I grabbed his hand to put it on my belly.

"Did you feel that?" I asked him at the following bubble show.

He remained silent for a few seconds, trying to capture any movement with his fingertips.

At the end he shook his head, softly deceived.

"Maybe it's still too early to perceive the movements from the outside," I ventured at the end.

He looked at me with the sweetest smile on his face, and he kissed me, "I love you".

Christmas was all around you in New York City, in the best Love Actually tradition, only two weeks away. The Rockefeller Center tree was lit and crowded with tourists; boutiques on Fifth Avenue and across town had been decorated with their shiniest lights and most festive gimmicks. It was the best time of the year, especially for Mike: Thanksgiving had always been my American celebration, while Christmas meant going to London, spending at least a week at his parents', with his brother and sister and their kids. This year it was going to be an even bigger celebration, with our new addition soon coming to the family. His parents were going to be certainly not as crazy as mine, since this was going to be grandchild number five for them, so I was hoping for some much needed rest, and milder enthusiasm.

In this Christmas atmosphere and with the trip to London coming up in just a week, we went to the hospital for the detailed scan, the fifth month's close encounter with the baby. As for the nuchal translucency, Mike was way more looking forward to it than I was. Those tests were the only way for him to feel what was going on in my belly, what was growing inside me, while at that point I could perceive the baby's movements and imagine him stretching and jumping on my stomach.

The nurse explained us that the test might take a long time, and that we might even be required to come back for a second try, if the baby was not cooperating and showing her the many body parts she had to check and measure. It turned out the baby was more than happy to dance along, putting up a perfect show for us and the nurse. The most moving component of that forty-minute scan for me was to watch Mike's face: the smiles he couldn't hold back any time the baby displayed something new for us, the awe he couldn't hide when the nurse pointed to the beating heart, made of moving chambers and contracting walls. The nurse counted five long fingers and she took pictures of each hand and foot, the spine and the skull, the belly and the legs. She spent several minutes on the face, to inspect the bones and give us a good image of the profile, a tiny nose and lips somehow showing up in transparency. We had told the nurse that we knew it was a boy, so she did her best to give us sound evidence to prove the information. And there it was: Mike's pride was unmissable as he admired the baby's penis, disproportionately long and almost passing the middle of his thigh. The baby had surely gotten something from Mike's Nigerian origins.

When we left the hospital, pictures in our hands, the idea of a child going to pop up in our lives in just a few months didn't sound that unbelievable anymore. In some short weeks I had gone from refusing to believe it was happening, to getting quietly comfortable with the idea. That had to be how things worked for any revolutionary change in one's life: we first refused to see it was happening, then we might get angry at the idea of it, then we finally started to make room for it in our minds and in our lives. I found amazing how the human brain worked, how it could process any change and make it part of the usual flow of things. I just hoped my brain would keep working in the fine way it had done for years, even during the last months of my pregnancy and especially once the baby was born. I didn't want to become one of those women who only focused on and who only talked about their children. I still had interesting things to do in my life.

"Look who smiled for Auntie Rachel today?" Mike gloated, while handing the scan pictures to Rachel across the table, later that night at dinner. It was our last chance to see her before leaving for the UK on the following Friday.

"Oh my God!" she uttered, leafing through the photos. "Look at his nose, so cute. And... wow, this is rated R: look at this penis."

She frowned, "This is a class A tool. Does it run in the family? I knew I should have tried harder with your brother, Mike. I guess there's always time."

"You do know my brother is married, don't you?"

"Nobody is perfect."

"Didn't they teach you about harassment at Harvard Law?" I joked.

"You know, my dear, being an attorney is a matter of giving the interpretation of the law that best fits with your client's needs, and that a judge can accept with clean conscience. It's a delicate balance, which only the best can achieve," she concluded with a toast to herself.

"Anyway," she added after a long sip from her glass. "Talking about Auntie Rachel: when are you guys moving closer to me? They are about to put on the market an apartment in my building: three bedrooms, rooftop, fairly priced."

Mike laughed and he raised his glass to Rachel again, "To our friend who never gives up! You have been living on Morton for four years?"

"Five."

"Five years, and you have been restlessly trying to convince us to follow you downtown ever since. We are absolutely fine where we are. Our flat is perfect for us and we have a bedroom for the baby. Not everybody needs a duplex, my dear."

"I'm just saying, Mike, in case you want to put your big-shot consulting partner money on a good investment. You know I would do anything to keep you guys as close as possible to me," she grinned.

"We love you, too. We even got you a Christmas present" I announced, placing a small packet on the table.

I watched as Rachel ripped the paper and she opened the Chanel makeup box: mascara and two lipsticks for "the busy elegant woman", as the leaflet said.

She smiled and she came around the table to kiss me on the cheek, tell me she loved me, and quickly hug Mike, before she placed her own gift box on the table.

She sneered. That was never a good sign.

"This is for both of you, guys, but Amber should open it," she pushed the box in front of me.

I untied the red ribbon and I opened the black box, to reveal a sumptuous creation of tissue paper that was hiding the kinkiest lingerie I had ever seen in my life. Red and gold, the corset had complicated straps to make it adaptable to any belly size, and holes in the nipple area, but "not for breastfeeding", as Rachel kindly pointed out. The panties were completely transparent and they had a whip hanger "for any occasion". The package also included a whip, obviously, and a very useful handcuffs and silk ribbons set, "to express your wildest desires".

Mike was laughing his ass off as I looked at Rachel straight in the eyes, "I've always known you have the sluttiest taste in lingerie, that's why I never go shopping with you. Let me just ask you one question: where in hell did you find slutty pregnancy lingerie?"

She looked up, proud and straight in her best impression of Game of Thrones' Daenerys Targaryen, "You know my house motto: Fire and Sex."

"I'm telling you: it doesn't fit!"

Mike was trying to be helpful and zip up my dress, but he got himself drowned in a shower of yells when I had to stop him from cutting my breath. The dress didn't fit anymore, or better, my new body was not the right size for that dress.

Panic ensued, "What do I wear now? This was the one dress I was planning to wear also for New Year's, and it already doesn't fit!"

We were getting ready for Mike's office Christmas party on Saturday night. I had tried on that same dress the previous weekend, and it had zipped at that time. It also had squeezed my boobs in a slightly more pronounced way than what I was hoping for, but that was fine one week ago. Now it was not fine anymore: the dress almost exploded.

After a second set of yells, that led Mike to unzip my dress all the way down, I threw the dress on the bed, and I looked at myself in the mirror. The front view was almost normal, but the profile betrayed the truth: my breasts were enormous. My belly was still small, and it would have easily gone under the radar, but my boobs were huge. Deformed. That was the word that jumped to my lips right away: deformed. My face, arms and legs were still the same, my stomach was mostly under control, too, but my breasts had gone up at least a couple of sizes. Which was not much in itself, but all the dresses I owned were exactly my size, and quite fitting on the chest.

Mike's attempt to cheer me up with a half-joke on my boobs, "I certainly love them!" didn't have any visible effect, as I ignored him and I kept throwing angry looks at them in the mirror.

"Amber, we ought to go soon. Is there another dress you could wear?"

I was still hypnotized by my distorted reflection in the mirror, and I didn't even answer him. It took me several more seconds to come out of my catatonic state and reconnect my brain.

"Let me try the green one."

"I had to wear the green dress, but it makes my boobs look even bigger," I texted Rachel on the taxi.

A sad emoji, followed by the Munch's scream emoji, came back after a few seconds.

"Who are you texting?" Mike's whisper suddenly interrupted my search for the perfectly sad and horrified emoji to add to my last text.

"Rachel."

"Complaining about the dress and the boobs?" he then asked with a large grimace, squeezing my hand not to make me go mad at him.

Damn, he knew me way too well.

Mike had been working at McKinsey for several years now, so I had already met many of his colleagues, and the Christmas party was the annual occasion to chat with his closer friends and their significant others, people our age. This year the recurring gossip on who was aging with less dignity and whose wife had clearly exaggerated with her Botox had been clouded by baby-related congratulations. Everybody already knew we were expecting our first child, and Mike's smile kept broadening as the night went on, one eighth of an inch for each person who told me how beautiful I was, how lucky he should feel, how the baby was going to be absolutely fabulous. He showed me and my belly off like the best prize he could ever win, the Academy Award of life. It was the cutest.

The evening was livened up by embarrassing performances of younger drunk colleagues, and incredibly boring celebration speeches for people who had been promoted to partners or who had reached relevant anniversaries in the company. Some things never changed.

In a quiet moment, I found myself looking outside one of the windows of the downtown Manhattan's hotel where the party was held. The sky above the bay was clear, Lady Liberty was shining on her island, green and beautiful, and boats were floating on the Hudson, full of drunken parties. It was such a nice night.

"Just stop whining," I told myself as I reached Mike, his buddy Ryan and his wife on the dance floor. Jumping at the rhythm of the latest Calvin Harris and pretending to sing lyrics with my squeaky voice was the perfect way to forget my complexes, the only one which didn't involve alcohol. What was the name of that non-alcoholic but somehow inebriating cocktail, anyone?

THE WEEK WITH FIVE STEPS TO CHOOSE A NAME. OR JUST GO WITH BARACK

What's in a name, really?

Mike and I hadn't started to think about a name for the baby, and for a very simple reason: we had no idea. Some people picked their children's names when they themselves were not even adults, either based on family practice, favorite actors, names or people they just happened to like, but we had none of those. The middle name was going to be either my father's or Mike's dad's name, following Mike's family tradition, but we were still out hunting for that first key component of the baby's identity. We didn't have a favorite letter we wanted it to start with, or any favorite sound we wanted it to include, so we went the other way around. Mike purchased the Big Book of Names, and we got ready to dedicate to it part of our Christmas break.

A couple of days before Christmas, on a late Friday night, we had just boarded our plane to Heathrow, when Mike took the book out of his computer bag and he placed it on my lap.

"Do you want to go first?" he asked me.

Following my perplexed expression, he went on and he showed off his highly renowned and paid consultative skills, "I created a process in five steps, for which I have prepared a series of notes on my phone," he started while tapping on his mobile, either not noticing or just ignoring the amused look on my face.

He pointed his right pinky at me, "First, each one of us goes independently through all the names in the book, noting down the ones we like; second, we exchange lists and we are allowed up to five vetoes each; third, I create a consolidated list, in which we rate the names, on a one-to-ten scale; fourth, we take the top five. As a fifth step, we will use the next few months to reflect on those five names, remove some of them if they are not suitable anymore, and add some wild cards if something new stimulates our creativity. When baby boy arrives, we look at him in the face and we choose his name."

His face could now relax into a large grimace, the one that had his teeth somehow become whiter and brighter, and which could suddenly hypnotize anyone who had the bad luck to be addressed with it. He called it the Mike It Rain face, for its legendary power to capture any client. I called it the Crazy Clown face. When he needed to convince me about something, he added a smidgen of Puppy Green Eyes to it, to obtain a Crazy Sexy Clown face that I was, indeed, never able to resist.

Following his instructions, I opened the book at the letter A.

It was much more entertaining than I had expected, since the book offered a selection of juicy information about the names, like origins, famous nice people and famous bad people, including dictators or serial killers. It contained any name for any kind of parents, from the extremely religious ones who might want to pick Christ, to the contemporary democrats who would love Barack, to the frankly suspect couple who would want to name their offspring Adolf. I had my dose of fun in tapping some sure to be vetoed names on my notes, like Rollo or Guido, together with some more palatable ones: Andrew, Henry, Thomas. Nothing too creative, but I was hoping for Mike to add a touch of exotically European flavor to the selection.

I was happy to kiss Mike goodnight after I completed my assigned job.

An extreme turbulence woke me up, and I noticed with horror that oxygen masks were dropping from the ceiling, and flight attendants were running around terrified. Everyone on the plane was screaming. Mike was nowhere around me. My belly was huge, a nine months heavyweight. I wore a mask on my mouth and I did my best to adopt a brace position, like the first officer was yelling on speaker in a never ending loop, while the captain was trying to tame the plane. I admired the perfect setting of this live disaster movie. The aircraft kept going down, oblivious of the strenuous efforts the commander and the rest of the crew were putting on it to try to save us all. After terrifying minutes of falling, the plane hit the ground with a thunderous noise. Then silence. I passed out.

When I regained consciousness, I saw my belly had cracked open like an egg. A perfectly formed boy had come out of it and he was now scouting the surroundings to plan for his survival. He looked at me with an evil expression, and as he started to walk back towards me I knew he was going to eat me: what best food could he find than the one who had kept him alive for nine months?

I woke up laughing at the absurdity of my dream, which had epically failed to scare me. Only Tom Six's movie The Human Centipede had reached comparable levels of gross disgust mixed with a missed opportunity for a great comedic achievement.

I opened my eyes and I crossed Mike's gaze, amazed by my chuckles, "Can you share the amusement?"

What a hard thing to describe... Instead I noticed how, for the first time in months, I didn't feel any nausea. Maybe the insanity of my nightmare had fixed my stomach?

"The vomiting roller coaster left without me this morning," I grinned. "What's for breakfast?"

In reply, he swiftly handed me his phone, asking me to exercise my veto rights on the fifteen names that had survived to his own veto, and then to rate what remained. A short list of pretty decent, but rather unexciting names were left after he had combined our rates. How would we go from there to finding the perfect name for our heir? We still had a few months to complete the final step in Mike's process, and hopefully end up with a choice that would convince us both.

"Cabin crew: prepare for landing," the pilot announced, as I watched London approaching in the distance, in a surprisingly clear dawn.

Meredith, Mike's sister, was already at work in the kitchen when we entered Mike's parents' house. Her husband Paul was busy in the living room with their four-year-old Alexandra, who was lying on the floor with a coloring book, and their two-year-old, George.

"You're here!" Meredith yelled when Mike's father let us in, and she captured us in one of her hugs. She looked at me with her big brown eyes, identical to her mother's, and then she hugged me again, whispering in my ears, "You will be wonderful parents".

A shiver ran down my spine, a mix of pleasure and estrangement. Mike's mom came rushing down the stairs to kiss us, and we were all there together, standing right at the entrance, savoring each smile.

There was a lot of talking and showing off of my belly, that morning, but Mike and I were allowed a nap to recover from the flight and the time difference. That mere thirty minute pause regenerated me. As I was walking downstairs to offer my limited cooking knowledge, Meredith came towards me with a conspiratorial look.

"Would you have a moment to come upstairs to our bedroom?"

I loved their British accent, and I cursed my total lack of musical ear that prevented me from picking up some of those noble-sounding t's and o's.

"You see, I brought you something from home," she explained, once she had closed the door behind our backs. "You don't have to take them, but I figured I would bring them, just in case."

She opened a luggage to show a rich collection of baby clothes.

"Oh," was everything I could say.

"This is not a gift," she answered to my clear discomfort. "No gifts before the baby is born. This is just an assortment of George's clothes that I don't need anymore, and that you can borrow if you like them."

She smiled and she took my hand, "I don't want you to feel uncomfortable. What do you think?"

I thanked her and I accepted with a nod. She then helped me stuff the clothes at the bottom of my luggage, "So that you can just shovel them in a drawer when you're back home, and completely forget about them until you need them", and she left the room.

I stared at those clothes: they were so small, and the baby was going to be small enough to fit into them, a tiny fragile thing that could break at any step. It was even more fragile right now, still in my belly, an undeveloped human being, unable to breathe and survive on its own. Anything could still happen, I couldn't stop myself from thinking, and having all those clothes was contributing to make real something that wasn't yet real at all. I was trying to keep things as they were, to preserve my own sanity and to protect the people I loved from a greater later deception, but nobody else was on my side on this. The baby was already so concrete for everyone, that I could see its ghost floating above my head, a little pale cloud shaped like a human.

I sat on the floor, eyes wide open and fixated on nothing. I lowered my head and the colors of the room got covered by the yellow of my hair, so I closed my eyes. Tears ran down my nose and they dripped on my lap. Where was Rachel when I needed her? I would have given everything I had for a minute with her.

"I already miss you, how long are ten days?" I tapped on my phone.

"Not that long," she responded immediately with a heart.

THE WEEK WITH FIVE UNMISSABLE BOXING DAY SALES ITEMS

The ghost was still hanging in my bedroom when I woke up on Christmas day. It was compressing my chest so strongly that I barely noticed that I hadn't had any nightmare, for the first time in a long time. Or that the vomiting roller coaster had skipped my stop, now for the second morning in a row. I spent several minutes in bed, motionless and with my eyes closed, silently cursing anything I could think of: the inevitability of things, my hormones, myself. As I started to cry I remembered that Mike was still sleeping next to me, and I hoped I hadn't woken him up. Christmas was Mike's favorite day of the year, and I would never forgive myself for ruining it for him with my stupid tears. Moving very slowly, I reached out to my phone on the nightstand: 8:32 am, not bad; a few Google and Twitter notifications, very well; a text from Rachel.

"Merry Christmas my best friend, my Sister. Enjoy these days with the best side of the family, and remember that things will be good. I will always be there for you. I love you, as always. And please do not forget to use my Christmas present! And please also tell Martin that I'm not jealous if he's married with kids: I'm a very modern and open person. Remember that, if this works, you and I would be sisters-in-law. How cool would that be?!"

I tried not to laugh out loud, and I silently thanked her for somehow always knowing what to say and when to say it. And she was right: I had plenty to enjoy.

Christmas Eve's dinner had always been a Nigerian feast at the Gillinghams': roasted chicken, turmeric rice, with Meredith's special blend of curry and peppers that made it tastier and just a little spicier than usual, coconut rice, catfish pepper soup, all accompanied by a wide selection of beers and wines, and followed by a long recovery night, sitting on the sofas munching on Nigerian coconut candy. But the real Holiday was always on Christmas day: Meredith's kids, of whom at least Alexandra was now old enough to understand the whole Santa Claus magic, woke up early and they started screaming, in full-blown excitement about their presents. They ran down the stairs to be inevitably amazed by the multitude of packets filling their stockings, trickling down the floor and under the Christmas tree. The view was moving for us adults, too, even if we had been the ones up late at night to create that same magic.

"Next year one more sock will be up there," Mike whispered in my ear. I gave a hint of a smile.

Martin and his family joined us for lunch, well after all presents had been opened at their home and all toys had been tested and evaluated by Stephanie, who was almost three now, and quietly chewed on by Caroline, who had just turned eight months old. Mike's dad immediately grabbed Elizabeth, Martin's wife, to get her help with the last details of the meal; Mike and Meredith set the table while everybody else was somehow managing the four kids, in between greetings, hugs and various celebrations of joy.

I had loved that family for many years now, since I had first met them. Mike and I had been dating for a couple of months, when he had gone the European way and he had simply told me, "My parents will be here for a few days, and we ought to all have lunch together on Saturday."

To my surprise, as somehow we had already been on the Formentera vacation together but we hadn't yet seriously discussed our relationship, he had just introduced me as his girlfriend.

Through the years, children had come to enlarge the crew, and I was relieved to know that the baby was going to have a bunch of cousins who were being raised all around the world, with whom to build strong relationships and an even more open mindset. After all the years spent with Mike, discovering how different and astounding every corner of the planet was, with its peoples and cultures, I would have been disappointed to raise a solely American child, someone who might think the United States were not only the best place but also the only possible place. I loved how that mix of Africa, Europe, and America was going to make the baby a citizen of the world. I didn't expect him to free mankind from its worst plagues, but the baby surely would be willing to approach anything with open mind and heart.

Christmas lunch distracted me from my dreams of the future, with the British side of tradition: roasted turkey with stuffing and gravy, masterfully cooked by Mike's dad; Elizabeth's famous multi-potatoes, a choice of mashed, roasted, and fried potatoes with various sauces; roasted and boiled vegetables; and the unmissable Christmas pudding, this year also presented in a pregnancy-safe alcohol-free version that had been prepared just for me.

It was one of the best Christmases I could recall.

The top spot in my ranking was still my twelve-year-old Christmas, the last one with my maternal grandfather. Grandpa Cliff was a World War II veteran, who had been a teenager at the time he had enrolled, shortly after Pearl Harbor, and who had collected a bottomless stockpile of stories from the war. During my twelve-year-old Christmas he had recounted his most heart stopping adventure: how he had escaped from a prisoner-of-war camp in Germany with the help of an Italian soldier. The story was still vivid in my mind, after many years, and I could remember each passage. I held my breath with grandpa, fleeing the camp with this Italian prisoner who could speak a few words of German; I got cramps in my legs while they were walking all the way from central Germany to the border with Switzerland; I froze with them crossing the Alps; I startled every time they struggled through northern Italy, relentlessly moving south; I sighed with relief when they finally reached Rome in June 1944, just a few days after American forces had liberated the city. In my mind, that Christmas had been the last time I had seen my mother truly happy, the last time she and I had enjoyed a normal relationship. Grandpa Cliff had died the following summer, I had entered my rebellious teen during fall, and my thirteen-year-old Christmas had sucked.

Waking up the following day was one of the hardest tasks I ever performed: the mix of jet lag, overfeeding, adrenaline low due to the end of the Christmas festivities was pushing me back down every time I tried to open my eyes and stand up. At least I had had a great night's sleep, and the vomiting roller coaster was not in sight. Mike was equally tired but more resilient, so around ten in the morning he dragged me out of bed with the promise of a light breakfast and a shopping run for Boxing Day.

"Shopping?" I asked him with just one eye open, while looking for a lost slipper.

"Let's go to Oxford Circus: it will be incredibly crowded, but that's the best Christmas spirit we can find!"

After having fought an ocean of Londoners who were desperately trying to find the best deals across the many downtown's boutiques, we somehow found ourselves in front of a baby shop.

"Wait a second, this is the shopping you wanted to do?" I stopped before the entrance to ask Mike.

"Well, I believe they have special sales for Boxing Day."

"You tricked me."

I looked at him with my best frown, to which he put up his most charming grin and he gently pushed me in by the elbow.

Obviously he was right: we would have been stupid not to take advantage of Boxing Day sales, so I tried to stop my brain from feeling rushed and conned into that. In the end, we were all behaving as if the baby was already there, so buying a stroller wasn't going to add much awkwardness. We were going to need one at some point, anyway.

"Also," Mike was adding as we entered the shop, "I can get us an upgrade with my miles on our way back, so that we can check in more stuff, and make anything fit."

"Ok buddy, let's do it!"

We left the store one hour later, with a stroller, equipped with newborn, baby, and toddler seats, a car seat, a baby carrier, a high-tech blanket, and a stuffed animal, because why not. We threw everything in a taxi, and we were greeted by excited laughing faces when we came back home. So much for wanting to keep a low key pregnancy. When a fairly large family was involved, at least larger than my own family of myself and my parents, nothing could really be low key.

At least a to-do was crossed from the list, and that was always a great feeling.

NINE

SIX

ANNALISA CONTI

THE WEEK WITH A SIX PACK, SORT OF

The days after Christmas flew by in a blur of dinners with friends, time spent with the family eating even more food, and watching my belly literally explode in front of me.

"It's just Christmas", I told the mirror when Mike and I came home after the holidays.

"Right, Mike?" I then gazed directly at him. "It's just Christmas: we gained the annual five pounds, and we will lose them in a couple of weeks, as usual."

Mike was standing right next to me, looking skeptical, but keeping his smile as bright as he could. Was he trying to be indulgent with me, some "let's not displease the pregnant lady" situation?

Maybe.

Coming home also meant getting back to our comforting morning routine: waking up early, placing my mat in the second bedroom for some soft yoga moves, accompanied by Mike's weight lifting snorts. While I was showering and Mike was shaving, I realized our morning habits would need to change.

"We will lose our workout space."

"I know," he answered, his voice distorted by the noise of the electric shaver. "We'll just have to subscribe to an actual gym."

Right. We hadn't been in a gym for years, since we had moved to West Harlem and we had decided to work out at home in the early mornings.

Another change.

I shrugged: going to the gym was not such a big deal, after all.

I turned the water off and I took a minute to breathe and cool down before moving to the makeup and dress-up stages. I was glad I had already bought maternity clothes, as my belly was now big enough to require a proper attire. The mirror, always honest, was showing me what looked like somebody else's image, this new person who had my face, my arms and legs, but the torso and stomach of a pregnant woman. The Pregnant Woman, that was me now. People would say "my pregnant colleague", "my pregnant friend", "my pregnant neighbor", "the annoying pregnant lady I had to leave my seat to on the subway today", and that would be me. I would suddenly stop being "my entertainment colleague", "my friend who's a journalist at Vanity Fair", "my white neighbor who's married to the handsome black guy", "the annoying lady on the subway who was texting stupid things to her girlfriend and laughing out loud". I would just be identified by my body shape, my current state. The mirror threw back the image of the corners of my mouth facing down, my shoulders flaccid and my back relaxed: The Pregnant Woman, Depressed Edition. And what would happen next, after the baby would arrive? I would probably just become somebody's mother, as if giving birth to another human being was going to remain in the world's memory as not only my biggest, but also my only relevant achievement.

"What are you doing now?" Mike found me making grimaces at my reflection.

"Face gymnastics."

He gave me his best perplexed look, and he blew me a kiss while he was tying his necktie. A couple more minutes and we were walking towards the subway in a cold January morning. We rode together until Columbus Circle, where he left me with a tender embrace as my train kept going towards Chamber Street and my office in the Freedom Tower.

The day started slow and quiet, with New Year's greetings, holiday stories, and some buddy jokes on the size of my belly, "Did you have too much food for Christmas?"

Until it happened.

Meredith had warned me this would happen soon, much sooner than I expected. She had told me it would creep me out, and to be especially aware of older women.

I should have been careful.

I was filling up my bottle at the water fountain when one of the floor admins, a middle aged lady I didn't know very well, suddenly attacked me.

"Oh my God you are pregnant!" she cried in the middle of the corridor, from a few feet away, and she threw her hands on my belly. Without asking, without giving me the time for a strategic retreat. Her hands were on me before I could do anything to avoid it.

What the fuck? Was I going around touching your own belly, old lady?

"Yes, I am, I'm at six months," I had to say something to divert her claws from my vulnerable entrails.

I took advantage of her short distraction to arch my spine backwards, grab the sides of my blazer to close them, and cross my arms in front of my belly. What a swift move. I was very proud and I must have let a faint smile appear on my face, because she took it as an encouragement to keep talking and asking questions.

Why did people believe they were entitled to touch a pregnant woman's belly? Especially in the United States, where the definition of one's personal space was very precise. Even more so in New York City, a place where people would do anything not to touch you, unless it was to push you out of their way in the street or while running to a subway train.

How was a pregnant body different, then? How could it escape these social rules? Did a pregnancy become a community good, something to be discussed and celebrated, even by people who didn't know the woman herself?

"People just suck," was Rachel's comment a few days later at dinner. "Some things make people forget all social survival skills, and for some reasons pregnancy is one of the topics that drive the highest number of people the craziest."

Mike laughed and he tried to balance out Rachel's bluntness, "People are always excited by babies, it is not intrinsically a bad thing. Some people just can't restrain themselves."

"I'm so looking forward to this baby to arrive!" he rolled me up in his hug as soon as we entered our apartment that night.

"We still have four months to go!" I tried to keep calm as I untied myself from his arms. "Where's all this rush coming from now? Are you already tired of being just the two of us?"

He pondered for a second before he took a deep breath and he answered, "Everyone in the office has been wishing me a happy new year in the past three days, and everybody has been patting my shoulder, explaining me how excited I must feel, and how looking forward I must be to meeting our baby in a few months. Their enthusiasm is highly contagious."

He looked sorry when he opened his mouth again, "I apologize, my dear. I would never get tired of being with you, just with you."

"That's why you wanted to have a baby? To be just with me?"

"Yes," he smiled while dodging my bullet. "You know I wanted to have a baby to have even more of you, a smaller version of you running around."

His excitement was a second layer perspiring from his skin, a physical emission of his body.

I sighed.

To be honest, nobody really seemed to share my calm and rational approach to my pregnancy. Soon friends, colleagues, people became unable to restrain themselves in any socially acceptable way from obsessively asking us if we were ready, or excited, or worried, or scared, or happy, or looking forward, or… pretty much anything we could and even couldn't think about. At first I responded digging deep in my best self-control, nourished during years of yoga practice, with a constructed smile and a happy-sounding noise. But after I lost count of how many times I had listened to the same patronizing questions, I let it go.

"Listen: yes, we are ready. We are reading books and we have our ideas on education and care, and if anything goes wrong we will listen to whatever the doctors have to say. Also, yes, we are as happy as we've always been so far, since the day we met. This will not change our happiness. Lastly, no, I'm not worried about delivery: I will soon take birthing classes, where a professional will tell me what I need to know about it and how to prepare for it. I will hope for the best and I will be ready for anything. And if shit happens, it happens. There's nothing you can do to avoid it and you just have to manage it as well as you can. Starting to worry four months in advance is not useful, and it's even stupid. Why clogging your body with stress and adrenaline, when you can relax and keep working on the endorphins? You will need them when the time comes, when you won't sleep for three days in a row and you will just want to die."

That was so liberating.

Soon, the time came for the monthly visit. Doctor Mallory greeted us with a decisive, "We need to discuss a few things," before granting us the usual peek into the baby's heartbeat that made Mike freak out.

"First, Blood Cord Banking," she pointed her pinkie towards us.

Mike and I had never thought about it, but we exchanged a quick look and we agreed: it would be a great investment. Anything that could potentially save the baby from a fatal disease would be a great investment. Doctor Mallory nodded in satisfied approval, and she gave us the names of the top three companies, instructing us to make a decision soon.

"Next thing, you should register for one of our birthing classes," she continued, handing us a brochure. "One of our nurses teaches them, and they are highly recommended by the hospital."

I grabbed the brochure, yes ma'am.

"And finally, the hospital visit," she scribbled a website on a piece of paper. "It will familiarize you with the delivery department, explaining you what to do and where to go when the time comes."

I took the paper in my hands, yes ma'am.

"It is great to have so many resources to help us learn all we need to know," Mike approved as we were leaving Doctor Mallory's office.

"It lowers the chances of a catastrophic break down," I agreed.

Mike laughed and he hugged me, "We still have all the time in the world to get ready. We won't lose our minds, I promise."

I nodded, somewhat reassured.

Then my belly button popped out.

I had been closely monitoring it, day and night, and I knew it was going to happen soon: its bottom skin was getting closer and closer to the surface. And then one night I saw it, shyly peeking its head out of my belly. The ultimate sign of pregnancy, the point of no return, the protruded belly button. I accepted that additional evolution of my body with a quiet resignation: another piece of me I was not in control of anymore, another sign of time. I didn't even feel nostalgic about my current but already old life anymore, why bother? Why spending time regretting something that would never come back? The baby would grow up and have his own adult life, but we would always remain his parents, an irreversible condition. We would eventually go back to our life as a couple, with our activities and hobbies, but then grandchildren would come, and even different social conventions would define us. This life we had been sharing for a few years now, the feeling that we were the only two people that mattered in the world, and the pure happiness and satisfaction this brought, this moment was already gone. Lost, to be replaced by different moments, different lives.

Now I saw why my mother had been so upset at me during my dark adolescence years. Not only had I changed her life forever, ruining her balance and killing her dreams, whatever they were, but also in exchange I had given her an angry teenager who at best hated her.

I looked at myself in the bathroom's mirror, the pajama top rolled up to uncover my belly, the swollen stomach becoming the most evident part of me. I saw a shadow of the Amber I used to be, now just a halo.

"Are you ok?" Mike's new favorite three words came floating in the restroom from the door, as he stood at the entrance.

I saw the same shadow upon him, and the ghost of the Mike he used to be was holding hands with the older version of myself. I hoped the two current versions of ourselves would keep holding hands as tightly.

"I have a big belly," was all I could say.

He smiled at me and he came closer, to kiss me on a cheek. He gently placed a hand on my belly, to comfort me and to tell me that I was still the same to him. The baby moved exactly at that time, as if he was trying to touch Mike's hand. And for the first time, Mike could feel that movement.

"What was that?"

I laughed, "That's the baby, not my stomach, I promise!"

He couldn't believe how intense the sensation had been on his own skin, and he immediately pulled his hand back.

"Did I upset him?" he worried.

"I don't think so: he's been doing the same thing for a few days now. He moves all the time."

Mike slowly placed his hand back in the same spot, waiting for something to happen. When the baby moved around again, Mike almost let go of a cry, a grown-up man stunned by the strangeness and beauty of life, and by the touch of his son. The sense of Family.

THE WEEK WITH SIX HOURS AT IKEA

What the hell is the Family and Medical Leave Act?

Ah, the unique joys of navigating through Condé Nast's maternity leave policy, trying to understand what the Family and Medical Leave Act, FMLA to its friends, gave to people. Fascinating.

I had to read through many pages of company policies, asking for help to the one colleague who had children while working at Vanity Fair, and in the end I gave up and I dialed the Human Resources Call Center. After twenty minutes of taking notes and asking very stupid questions, I received an email that confirmed HR had opened a ticket for me and my parental leave: six weeks of paid solace, followed by all my remaining vacation days, and six more weeks of unpaid happiness. Such a blessing to have children in the United States, especially with Mike's friends all over Europe enjoying several months of paid maternity leave, in some cases even starting before the baby was born. That was such a dream: having some time for myself, on my own, before the baby came.

"Don't be so tragic!"

Rachel was making fun of me, later that night at dinner. Mike was away on one of the last business trips he had planned for the first half of the year, before my March-to-June travel ban would become active. Maybe I was being too cautious, but what if the baby decided to pop out while Mike was somewhere in Europe? Between finding a flight, going to the airport, flying home and getting to the hospital, several hours would pass, and he would never forgive himself for losing the birth of his first child. Well, I would never forgive him, either, for not being there with me. Surely Rachel would be willing to replace him, holding my hand, telling me when to push, wiping away my tears, and snapping the most inappropriate pictures of me. Lifelong blackmailing power. But in a very friendly way.

"I'm not being tragic, just realistic: twelve weeks is nothing. You barely have time to recover, get used to having a child, accept that you will never find balance in your new life—"

"Start to have sex again," she interrupted me, raising her glass to an imaginary toast.

"Well, they say you can after a minimum of six weeks."

"Wow, six weeks without having sex? That's probably the worst side of having a baby," she laughed.

"When you are depressed and sleep-deprived, I don't think sex is the first thing you think about."

Rachel gazed at me with high eyebrows, disapproving of how I was not laughing at her jokes.

She gave it a last try, "Dear, don't forget who you're talking to."

She kept looking at me straight in the eyes, investigating what was going on in my mind. From the expression on her face, she couldn't find what she was looking for. Or maybe what she found was not what she expected.

I tried to smile, and I squeezed her hand to thank her, "What would I do without you?"

"Your life would be so boring: the married lady with the good husband and the perfect baby on the way. You need me to stay young. And to drink the alcohol you can't touch during your pregnancy. How great is that? Perfect symbiosis!"

"Alright then, make me feel young: tell me about this guy you're dating."

She could make any of her stories sound like a movie, romance or horror depending on how much of a good performer the leading actor was. She would slightly change her voice to play Him and Her, enjoying every second of her narration probably even more than I was savoring the listening. She was born for the stage and she knew it, and she used all her charm and expertise every day in court and with her clients: nobody could resist Counselor Rachel Chambers.

"So in the end you didn't have sex with him, right?" I asked at the end of a very satisfactory performance.

"Nope, he didn't do enough to deserve my little flower."

I almost spit water in her face, at the sound of those words in that mouth.

"I know, many people have already had the pleasure to pick my rose from its garden, and the care of putting it back where it was, but this is not a good reason to let everyone in. No woodcutters allowed in here."

"So?" I pressed her. There had to be something more than a making out session in the back of a yellow cab, for the story to be worth being told.

"So I called my personal trainer for an evening session!"

The words "personal trainer" were not a code for anything, as she precisely meant what she said: her personal trainer. The guy she worked out with almost every morning had been taking full care of her and her wellness for a few years now. What we called a fruitful professional relationship.

We were crossing the George Washington Bridge, the upper Manhattan connection between New York City and New Jersey, when the evidence of the situation became finally undeniable.

Mike and I had decided that specific weekend in mid-January, that cold Saturday morning covered in a white sky, preparing for snow, was the perfect day to rent a car, go to IKEA, and buy some baby furniture. We were going to be busy with friends and family for the remaining weekends of the month, then Mike would have to travel to Europe and the West Coast in February, and soon I would be too big and tired to face the physical challenge of IKEA. The drive, the Saturday crowd, the additional stop at Walmart to stock up on cleaning supplies and shower gel, they were already a lot at that stage of my pregnancy.

I had exorcised my last hesitations and what remained of my resistance to change by compiling a very detailed list of what we needed. Taking inspiration from many different sources, from the internet to friends and colleagues, I had prepared a very efficient excel document to track all the pieces of furniture, the accessories, the kitchen and bathroom tools, with their prices and brands. Making lists always helped me rationalize my problems.

In the car I was reading my list to Mike, "Stuva changing table with 3 drawers, white and birch; Slakting box, gray and orange, for changing table, pack of three. Maybe you don't need these details…"

"Oh no, I love details!" he responded right away, the smile he was nowadays constantly wearing corrupted into a mocking grimace. "Do you also have the dimensions of the box? God forbid we get the wrong pack of three."

"Seven by ten and three quarters, by six and three quarters. Six and three quarters is the height," I whispered, my face purple with embarrassment.

He saw my dismay and he tried to mitigate it, but it was hard for him not to laugh, "I'm not making fun of you, I think you did a wonderful job. You channeled all my excitement and you made it nerdily real."

He kissed my hand as I turned my head towards the window, with the Hudson River and its Valley. My first ever trip to IKEA had been shortly before the end of my senior year in high school, to buy furniture for my college dorm with my father, exceptionally without my mother. She hated IKEA. We had rarely had father-to-daughter conversations before, but that time he had asked me questions about myself: was I scared of going to college, and did I have a plan to make friends, those were the words he had used. Remembering that conversation now was like reading a book from one's childhood, and finding it much less childish than one had thought.

"What else do you have on the list?"

"Skotsam changing pad, white," I restarted with a sigh, "Skotsam changing pad cover, white and orange; Stuva crib with drawers, white; Vyssa Vinka mattress for crib, blue; a bunch of sheets…"

"No no, at this point I want to know the models and sizes!"

He grabbed my hand and he kissed it again, "Come on, give me a laugh!" he then added.

I just gave him a grin and I stuck out my tongue, which made him laugh again, his white teeth shining in the grayness of the air outside the window. I finally cracked, too, and that's when the baby decided to participate in the moment with a deep movement that startled me.

"Are you ok?" Mike immediately asked, following an unconditioned reflex.

"Yep, somebody just decided it's party time in my belly!"

Mike's eyes were sparkling emeralds as he looked at me and he held onto my hand even stronger. I had seen that look many times through the years, but this time he was gazing through me, trying to reach his unborn son to communicate with him, to share his feelings with the little thing that was growing inside of me, the little thing we were making together. His sweetness made me smile.

By the following night, our apartment had started a new life: the second bedroom had lost its desk and office chair, keeping only the sofa bed as a reminder of its previous use. A quick round of Craigslist had found new loving parents for the old furniture, freeing us from the embarrassment of throwing away some beautiful and almost new items. Mike had spent his Sunday building the baby's crib and changing table, while I laundered the new sheets to have them clean and ready when the time would come. I had also taken out from the suitcase all the clothes that Mike's sister had given us during Christmas break, to go through them one by one and place them in the drawers. We had countless onesies and pajamas, little shirts and tiny pants, socks and hats. There was everything we needed. At least for a couple of weeks, according to how fast babies seemed to grow.

I paused to observe how normal those changes now seemed, as if a switch had been turned off in me. At some point the irrational brain had taken control of the rational parts of my mind, and I had accepted what was going to happen in a few more months. I was still ready to fight people who asked me how the baby was doing, instead of asking me how I was feeling, but I was also ready to forgive them. My belly had become the most visible feature of my body, especially since I hadn't gained much other weight; people would somehow be just surprised at how fast my stomach was expanding, and they couldn't stop themselves from asking me how the tenant of that newly created space was behaving.

THE WEEK WITH SIX HUNDRED QUESTIONS FROM CHLOE, OR SO

Once they were done with their comments on my belly, people couldn't resist their urge to tell me how happy they were for me. Friends, colleagues, acquaintances, neighbors: they would all fill up with pure joy as soon as they would see me. Large smiles and hugs would be generously bestowed at any occasion, words of commotion and affection would be pronounced, hands would be put on chests and hearts to certify the authenticity of the feeling.

"Isn't it a strange thing to say, why would they all be so happy for me? Children are an enormous responsibility: two adults make the decision to introduce a new human being on the planet, and the full understanding of rights and duties has to come with the choice. The child has to be taken care of during every living second for several months, then a proper education has to be kicked off: walking, speaking, eating are easy things, compared to building a social conscience, becoming a fair human being, understanding modern issues like gender, class, race. Especially for the baby, who will be born at the corner of Nigeria and Connecticut, a black-and-white person in a world that still will find it hard to classify him as either. Or neither. Or both.

"I can see a life of hard work in front of us, with constant effort and rewards, with failures and comebacks, worries and satisfactions. I can see happiness for the child and his own successes and achievements, but I don't see how that happiness will translate into some additional joy for myself or Mike. You know we have been happy each minute of our life. Mike's excitement for the incoming baby is a mere expression of that same bliss, as cute as it is. Maybe we are just a lucky exception, two people who were able to find and maintain their balance as a couple, to gain fulfillment in each other. We are planning to keep that balance, including our children in that circle of support and mutual growth, to maintain a constant level of joy throughout the years and the challenges of life.

"Some people decide to have children to fill in their contentment gap, to replace something they aren't able to build in two with something they hope to achieve in three, or four. Sometimes it works and sometimes it doesn't.

"Maybe it's all part of the natural instinct: being a parent is such a merciless job that your brain has to trick you into believing it's going to be the greatest delight of your life. Maybe that's going to happen to us, too: the first look at our offspring might bring immediate peace and a sort of heavenly contentedness."

Rachel looked at me after my long tirade, her chin resting on one hand, a sensible expression on her face. I smiled, waiting for her joke.

"You know, Amber," she spoke softly after a little while. "I think everyone is so happy for you because they love you, and they are eager to see you satisfied, and living a full life. Not that life isn't full without children, but since you are now expecting one, they all assume that you and Mike wanted one, and they're cheering the fact that you guys got what you wanted."

Oh.

"They all know how hard it is to raise a decent human being," she kept going. "And sharing their excitement is just a way to encourage and support you and Mike."

Where was my joke?

"Don't be afraid," she finished. "It will all work out for you guys."

"What do you mean? I'm not afraid, that's what I just told you: we are rationally planning our post-baby life exactly to preserve our balance. I'm not going to ruin everything I've built."

"I know," she squeezed my hand.

"I mean, I'm not crazy, I know some things will have to evolve, but not the core things, not what defines us as individuals and as a couple. We will not change."

"I am sure you won't: you owe it to me, at least, to remain the New York bitch you've always been!"

On Thursday night, many weeks after we had spoken for the last time and I had announced her the news of the incoming baby, Chloe called me. When I saw her name popping up on my phone, my first reaction was to put the phone down again, and just let it go. I didn't have anything specific against her, I just needed some mental preparation before talking to her; I needed to force my face to smile, to prepare for the impact with her and her voice.

"Hello?" I finally decided to tap on the green button on my phone's screen.

"Happy New Year, my dear! Oh my God, it will be such an amazing year, the best of your life so far! You must be so excited! How are you? How wonderful was your Christmas vacation? I'm sure your family took incredible care of you and the little bun in the oven. How are you?"

She drowned me in her words, and I could just emerge to grumble, "I'm great, how are you?"

"Oh! I'm so happy you are feeling good! Is the nausea gone?"

There was a full second of silence, while I was waiting for the flow to resume and she was expecting an actual answer.

"Yeah, I was just a little bit sick at the very beginning," I replied in the end, playing it down to contain her empathy. "But it went away really quickly and I've been feeling amazing ever since."

"You are so lucky, I was throwing up every single day when I was pregnant with Jasper. But it didn't matter because I had my sweet bundle of joy in my arms at the end."

I could see her eyes getting wet from my side of the phone, her emotions trying to extend their fingers and slide out from my phone's speaker. I had never been very emotional and I still had no idea of how to handle people who cried as often as Chloe.

I assumed a happy laughing tone, trying to close the faucets, "I know, I have been so lucky so far! I'm really enjoying these months, living every day at the fullest! It's such an amazing time for me!"

Each exclamation point cost me physical energy. At least it seemed to work.

"That's such a good news!" she cried out, "Do you feel ready? Is the bedroom ready? Did you get the stroller and all the things you need?"

That was my time to show off, so I stuck my chest out, "We are completely ready: crib, changing table, stroller, everything has been bought, assembled, and it is ready to use!"

In your face!

She cheered even louder.

"Did you buy clothes?" she suddenly threw in the mix.

"Clothes for the baby? We have some, and we still have time to get more!"

"Oh no, after you pass week twenty-six, never say you have time: the baby could come anytime now."

"Well, that's still early, I still have three months to go!"

There and then I learned a lesson: people always think you don't know anything at all until you've been through it.

"Oh no, don't even say so, do you want something bad to happen to your baby?"

Fuck.

"No, of course not—"

"Did you find a name, at least?" her voiced rose by a tone.

"No, not yet, but—"

"Not yet?" her voice climbed at least one other tone. "Not yet? What are you waiting for? For the nurse to put him in your arms after forty hours of labor? For the birth certificate to be in front of you? For him to start talking and ask you "Why don't I have a name, mommy"? What are you waiting for?"

She didn't even give me the time to answer.

"Your baby needs a name. I'm sure your belly is already big, which means he could come out at any time. Show me your belly."

What?

"What?"

"Show me your belly!" she yelled again, trying to switch to a video call.

I almost panicked, "I can't do a video call, I'm… I'm not home!"

"Then send me a picture of your belly," she barked her order.

"I don't have a picture of my belly…"

"What does it mean you don't have a picture of your belly? How do you keep the memory? I don't understand you, Amber. Well, take a picture now."

"I can't, I'm in my coat now, you wouldn't see anything."

"I just want to see a picture of my old friend with her belly, what's wrong with that?" she whined, and I feared she would get back to her sobbing mood.

There was nothing wrong with that, per se, I just couldn't understand why she wanted to see a picture of my belly: what was so exciting about it? There was nothing remarkable or unique about it, it was just the belly of a six-months-pregnant woman. She used to have one of those not long ago, so why was she interested in mine? It was not a wonder, like a third arm or a giant penis, something you would definitely want to see; it was just a hopefully temporary body situation. A deformity destined to disappear. Or maybe to stay, depending on how lucky I would be after delivery. Maybe she wanted to see it for the same reason strangers wanted to touch my belly: the baby was like some common good to them, something they felt compelled to care for, some inheritance of a past where the whole community would provide support to mothers-to-be. Too bad I was still my opinionated self, rather than just a pregnant person, an uterus with arms and legs, who would soon be just a mother.

"There's nothing wrong with it," I tried to calm her down. "I just don't take many pictures, so I don't have one to show you. But I promise I will send you the first one I take, so that you can look at my belly."

She sniffed, somehow comforted.

"I just want to make sure you're fine," she commented, "I never see you."

Now she was sounding like my mother, but at least I knew how to handle that. I reassured her that everything was perfectly fine and that she would get her photo shoot very soon.

Chloe really reminded me of my mother, with whom she shared a certain vainness and an incredible ability to drive me crazy. I certainly didn't need two mothers: one was already too much.

"Any plans for the weekend?"

Rachel's text popped up on my phone, as I was still staring at it after I had hung up with Chloe.

"Got any Prozac?" I tapped back.

"Did you just talk to Chloe?"

"How did you know?"

Rachel scared me sometimes.

"Well, your mom never calls on Thursdays."

THE WEEK WITH SIX ALIEN MOVIES TO CHOOSE FROM

As soon as the alarm went off, one thought came to my mind, "Why am I here?"

A second later, for some reason my mother's voice resounded in my brain, "Suck it up, Amber. Wake up!"

That was enough to kick me out of bed. That and the reminder of how paramount to my job that event was, and how much excitement I had gotten out of it in the past few years.

It wasn't even four in the morning on that Monday in late January, and I had to be out of my hotel room in less than thirty minutes. The Press shuttle to the Academy's Samuel Goldwyn Theater in Beverly Hills wasn't going to wait for me. I was in Los Angeles to cover the announcement of the Oscars nominations, which I had always seen as a privilege and an honor that the magazine renewed every year for me. The announcement had always taken place in LA around five in the morning, for the Academy's ceremony to receive full coverage across the United States and Europe. Journalists and publicists would crowd the theater, furiously taking notes and producing live feeds and tweets after each category was announced. It was a beautiful auto-celebration of Hollywood and what remained of its star power.

I had been quite happy at the idea to leave New York the previous afternoon, to reach the sunny West Coast. Too bad a frozen rain had held the plane on the ground for three hours, the baby had kept me awake dancing in my belly during the whole flight, and it had been almost midnight when I had collapsed on my hotel bed, begging the gods of sleep to take me into their arms. I had waited for a friendly torpor to come, but nothing had seemed to happen.

I must have eventually fallen asleep, since the alarm startled me at 3:55 in the morning.

Through thick fogs I got ready, I obtained my one daily coffee from the hotel's bar, and I waited for the Press shuttle. Once I reached my seat in the theater, I stretched my fingers to prepare to live-tweet through the announcements, and then I steadily gripped my phone. When the President of the Academy came out on stage accompanied by Chris Hemsworth, I took advantage of the handful of seconds I still had left to snap a few pictures of the handsome Australian, and shoot them to Rachel.

"Oh my God, he's so hot!" I could see her responses with the corner of my eyes, in between nominations and tweets.

"Can I have one of those?"

"Is he still married?"

"Can you give him my phone number?"

I tried not to laugh.

"Why are you even awake so early in the morning? You must be so tired!" she concluded with a rapid fire of heart emojis.

The coffee worked, and I was able to stay awake and productive for a few hours, just the time I needed to type and send my article to Jeremy, the magazine's editor, with clever comments on nominees and snubs, and witty predictions of winners.

The program of the day included a press breakfast at the hotel at nine, followed by a first waterfall of press conferences in the theater, lunch at the hotel, a second round of press conferences at the hotel, a dinner gala and an after dinner party at a separate location. As I was scrolling through my calendar, an overwhelming sense of failure grabbed my throat: how was I going to survive that day? How was I supposed to report back to the magazine on all those events, in the shortest of times and keeping the high standards of insights and juiciness the entertainment articles always demanded?

The questions hanged before my eyes for a long time.

"Suck it up, Amber," I told myself as I was sitting in a lonely corner of the theater, accompanying my silent words with a couple of slaps on my cheeks. "You will have to do it. You can rest tomorrow."

In the confused rush of the rest of the day, I decided to skip breakfast in favor of a thirty-minute power nap, which provided me with enough energy to make it through the morning press conference sessions. I picked up a sandwich for lunch and I used the rest of my time for a second nap, which proved extremely successful and which kept me alive until dinner time. I faced the evening schedule with enthusiasm, and taking many smart notes on my mobile, that I would compile in a series of two or three articles the following morning on the plane. I shamelessly used my pregnancy, and the consequent inability to drink, to cut the after-dinner party as short as I could. I reached my bed with my eyes already closed, brain in full hibernation mode and makeup still on. I woke up the following morning just in time to shower and rush to the airport to catch my flight back to New York. Hollywood lifestyle at its best.

Mike was already home when I opened the door and I crumpled in his arms.

"I'm so dead!" I whined as he watched me go straight to the bedroom to get changed.

"I worked non-stop on the plane and I sent everything to Jeremy as I landed," I kept going, as if I had to justify my weariness to Mike, who was more used than me to business travels and impossible work schedules.

Mike smiled at me, "You deserve a good night's sleep now. Did you have a good time, at least?"

The question made me wonder: had I had a good time? Usually the most enjoyable aspects of those events were the social experiences, the lunches and dinners and parties. Which I had completely missed. I had also always loved to gain insights during press conferences before many other journalists and experts in the field, but this time I had been so exhausted that I hadn't even appreciated that. I sat on the bed and I didn't move for a few seconds. A first tear ran down my nose.

"It was horrible," I finally spat out in between sobs. "I hated every minute of it. I was so tired! Everything sucked, and I sucked too: those articles are crap and Jeremy will have to rewrite them all."

There was something else in the back of my mind, something that had been lingering since I had left home on Sunday afternoon, "I don't want to travel anymore, I can't make it. I can't do it and be pregnant at the same time."

Mike softly caressed my face: he knew what that meant.

"They will have to send someone else to the Academy Awards," I whispered.

"If that's what you want, just tell your boss. She will understand."

She would surely be understanding and kind, as she always was, but what would that mean for me? The baby was not even there yet, and I already had to give up something to make room for him. And not just some random thing: the Oscars were the most important event of the year, the one the whole entertainment staff looked forward to, as a considerable portion of the months leading up to it was dedicated to that one night. I was going to miss the biggest night of my year, for the first time in so many years, just because my body couldn't take it.

I kept crying, silently, with frustration. This time not even Mike's embrace could do anything to stop it.

I was reading on the sofa on Sunday afternoon, accompanied by the sound of Mike's fingers typing on his computer, when the baby decided it was time to give a new sign of his presence. My eye caught some movement on my belly surface, like a shadow quickly flying by. I slid off month seven of What To Expect When You Are Expecting to focus on my stomach. And then I saw it: my skin was moving with the baby. There were bumps and valleys appearing and disappearing, and it seemed like I could peek inside my own belly and see what was going on. It looked more and more like one of those scenes from the Alien movies, where the monster was preparing to make its way outside of a poor host's body. Hopefully the baby's way out was going to be less of a killer one.

I mouthed a "crap" and I kept reading about month seven of my pregnancy. The core of the chapter was the birth plan, a list of questions for the expecting mother, to be discussed with the partner or the doctor. I decided to take a very rational approach to that, and I filled in a spreadsheet with questions, potential answers, and open points. I did some internet research on the elements I had minimal knowledge about, like the pros and cons of eating or drinking during labor; I searched the book for more information where further chapters were referenced, for example to evaluate the benefits of different labor positions. I left on hold some questions for which I would trust Doctor Mallory and her team more than anyone else, since I didn't have any aversion to most medical practices. Did I want to induce or augment contractions? Did I want fetal monitoring? Did I agree with the use of a vacuum extractor? Would I accept a C-section?

I barely repressed my astonishment for some topics that looked too strange or too gross for me to even consider them, and I couldn't stop myself from sharing them with Rachel, "Would you want a mirror to be placed in front of you, so that you can see what happens during delivery?"

"You mean: would you want to see your Lady V being deformed by a head? No, thank you. Next?"

I smiled, "Would you want to touch the baby's head when it starts to peek out?"

She responded with the vomiting emoji. The message was loud and clear. And I agreed with her sentiment: as natural as it was all supposed to be, the physical aspect of giving birth was undoubtedly the least entertaining. I would rather read complex education manuals, like the one Mike had recently purchased on the development of brain cells and neuronal connections in babies.

I left at the end a few items that I needed to discuss with Mike.

"Darling, do you have a second?" I asked him at one point, taking advantage of a yawn and a stretching movement of his arms.

"I am putting together the birth plan," I continued when he nodded, "And I have a few things to ask you."

"A birth plan?" he stopped in the middle of a second yawn, startled.

I read through the progresses I had made that far, until I got to the few points that involved him.

"The first question is: who do you want taking pictures and videos? My answer is: only my husband, only after delivery, only after I've allowed it—"

"And with your universal rejection right," he added with a laugh. "Especially before sending any picture out to anyone. Right?"

I looked at him with a large grin on my face, "I can see we are on the same page, buddy."

"Next question," I kept going. "Would you want to cut the umbilical cord?"

He thought about it for one long second, with a very serious expression on his face.

"Yes, I would love to do it."

"That's what I thought," I smiled back at him with the same somber loving expression he was showing me.

"Now the last question: do you want to catch the baby?" I spit it out as clear as I could.

"Catch the baby?"

"Yes," I tried to explain, "When the baby comes out, usually the nurses catch him and you can stay next to me, so that you don't have to see what's going on down there. And I'd rather you not seeing anything of what happens down there, to keep some mystery in our marriage... But if you really want, you could go and catch the baby."

He seemed perplexed, and he played for time to think it through.

He finally took a deep breath, "I mean, do I really need to be ready to catch him? Are you going to shoot him out of your vagina?"

SEVEN

ANNALISA CONTI

THE WEEK WITH SEVEN HORROR STORIES AND ONE LESSON

Why do we love our children?

A colleague, who had just come back to the office after her maternity leave, told me with spirited eyes, "Be prepared to meet the greatest love of your life, the greatest joy! I had always promised my husband he would remain the person I loved the most, but since the first time I saw my son I realized that couldn't be true anymore!"

I didn't fully understand the meaning of her words, so I just smiled and I nodded at her.

I could clearly enumerate the reasons why I loved Mike, so love itself was not the focus of my puzzlement. I loved my husband for some rational reasons, like trust, loyalty, our common view of life, and obviously how handsome and sexy he was. There were also some irrational arguments, like the way he made me feel when I was with him, and when I was not with him, and the indissoluble attachment that we had mutually developed during the years; there was also the physical side of love, even harder to explain but clearer to the eye. None of these reasons seemed to apply to babies, though, as a small child would hardly respond to any rational need a grown up might have, and a baby could certainly not provide emotional or physical satisfaction to an adult.

What was it, then?

There could be an ancestral component of love. When babies are born, they are completely helpless if left on their own. Nature needed to ensure that parents and other older members of the community would take care of newborns, to guarantee their survival and, with it, the preservation of the species. What better way than installing an invisible switch inside people, which would turn on the Light of Love at the arrival of a new baby? This kind of love would protect babies from the outside world, using their own parents and families as human shields.

There could also be a rewarding component of love. Babies spend nine months in their mother's wombs, growing day after day, moving and manifesting their being alive during most of those months. Pregnancy can be very challenging for women: morning sickness, back pain, gastrointestinal troubles of pretty much any sort, cardiovascular complications, gestational diabetes, and more severe albeit rare problems. Men can suffer during pregnancy, as well, as they see their partners endure painful efforts. Labor and delivery are a whole other story, as they can leave evident scars on a woman's body and soul and, in many countries in the world, they can even cause her death much more frequently than we might think. After all these endeavors and dangers, the baby has to be the compensation at the end of the quest. Parental love could simply be the brain injecting joy and happiness in the bloodstream, to try and balance out all the challenges of the previous nine months.

There might also be a third component: self-love. In the end what's a baby, if not half of a person's genetic baggage? A footprint through eternity? People might look for themselves in their own children's eyes, and love them simply because of the image they see as a reflection. They say a child is the fruit of a couple's love, and it might simply be a concrete expression of a love that already exists, rather than something new and motivated by the existence of the child itself.

Was I being too rational? Was I missing the point, the spontaneous and beautiful nature of maternal love? The permanent bond that connects a parent to their child, and that forces mothers and fathers to support him through his whole life?

I didn't feel that love, yet. I felt the will and responsibility to give everything Mike and I could to the baby, but more for moral duty than maternal love.

Would I feel that love, eventually?

I didn't know how to answer that question, either: I didn't want to lose myself, but at the same time I didn't want to be superficial and irresponsible with such a fragile human being. I wanted to be myself, but I also wanted to succeed in that new assignment, I wanted to do a good job.

Maybe the Light of Love would turn on inside me, too, at the given time.

Weekend brunches with Rachel were a long standing tradition. It was usually only the two of us, sometimes joined by Mike after we had moved in together, many years ago. Rachel and I had always loved the familiarity of that weekly appointment on the calendar, the safe harbor it still represented for both of us, through good and bad times. On that Sunday morning, I walked up the stairs of the West 4 subway stop, enjoying the pale sun and the brisk air on my cheeks, and I smiled as I saw Rachel strolling towards me.

"Were you coming to pick me up at the subway?" I hugged her. "I didn't know this was a date! I should have worn a shorter skirt."

She released herself from my hug to put her hands on my shoulders and look at me straight in the eyes, "It's always a date when it's you and me."

She kissed me on a cheek and she patted me on the head. "Let's go," she added.

We strode arm in arm to the restaurant, accompanied by the rhythm of our heeled steps, and for a moment I was convinced we were still in college: two girls without a care in the world. I grinned and I held her arm even stronger.

"Mike let you come on your own today, that's nice," Rachel noticed with a sip of her first Mimosa. "I'm surprised he didn't ask you to leave your belly at home, to make sure baby boy is not corrupted by Auntie Rachel's bad influence."

"Trust me: if there was a way to do it, he would have wanted to carry the baby himself. His excitement is getting so completely out of control that it seems he's the one with the hormones and stuff. He had tears in his eyes the other night, while he was touching my belly."

"That's sad when your man cries while touching you. It's usually the opposite for me", Rachel noticed with a wink.

I laughed at her sex-addict joke.

"I know," I then sighed, while munching on my toast. "And it's not even the craziest thing that's happened to me this week. People are losing their minds around me."

She threw her inquisitive look to encourage me to tell her more: she loved gossip.

"Well, all the women I know are reliving their pregnancies with me. Somehow seeing me with this big belly triggers their own delivery memories, and it automatically entitles them to share their horror stories with me. So we have the colleague who at first couldn't breastfeed, then she had multiple breast infections, then she followed a special diet to try and produce more milk, which almost onset diabetes in her. Or the colleague's wife who had to give birth on the hospital kitchen's table, because there were no rooms available. I also have the office manager who went through a forty-eight hour labor, before the nurses realized the baby had turned around and he was not facing down anymore, so they had to practice an emergency C-section. If you want I can give you the friend of a friend who had about one hundred stitches, which suddenly broke as soon as she got home from the hospital, then the wound got infected, and then it almost gave her a deadly anaphylactic shock."

Rachel's eyes were wide open now.

"And that's not even all! There's the neighbor who lost so much blood during delivery that she almost died, and then she had to spend one week in the hospital, which was not covered by her insurance, and she almost went bankrupt. Or would you prefer the story of a friend of a friend, whose baby spent several minutes without oxygen towards the end of labor, without apparently anybody noticing, resulting in a severely mentally and physically handicapped—"

The vibrating noise coming from my bag interrupted my storytelling pathos. I fished for my phone and I snorted when I saw the caller's name.

"We were talking about annoying people, and look who shows up," I grinned at Rachel, turning the screen towards her.

"Chloe? Didn't you just talk to her a few days ago?"

"I did. I don't know what she wants," I pressed the volume-down button to stop the vibration and let the call go to voicemail.

A mildly disappointed look dimmed Rachel's eyes.

"What?" I asked her.

"Maybe she needs something. Isn't it strange for her to call you again so soon?"

I sighed. I didn't want to talk, let alone think, about Chloe.

"I will call her back," I conceded.

Rachel gave me a half smile and a brief shake of her head, "You know you won't."

She's always known me better than my own self.

"Where were we, anyway? Right, I wanted to tell you my favorite story among all the insanity I've been exposed to: do you remember Margot, Mike's French friend from college?"

Rachel nodded briefly.

"On skype last week she told us all the details of her episiotomy, for Mike's deepest dismay."

"What the hell is an episiotomy?"

"Right, I had to Google it after the call. It's a practice still used in some European countries, that consists in completely cutting the perineal muscles, the muscles that basically surround your vagina, to create more room for the baby."

Rachel's suffering face was priceless.

"The problem is that sometimes people simply don't recover from the cut, as it happened to Margot: for her, having sex is still a pain after almost three years - and not just because of her now ex-husband."

"Oh my God, people should really keep some details to themselves!" Rachel hissed, crossing her legs tighter before gulping half of her glass to recover her poise.

I took advantage of her hesitation, "I couldn't agree more: why do people need to share such intimate stories? And what do I care? At least I'm not easily shocked, not after six seasons of American Horror Story, but it still boggles me. Everybody seems desperate to give me instructions, so why does no one share their life lessons when, say, you are starting a new job? No one grabs your arm and tells you "ah, when I started my last job the first day I did this and that, my boss told me this and that, my colleagues were like this and that", even if it's something a vast majority of people go through in their lifetime."

"Why are you so angry?"

Rachel's frankness destabilized me, "I'm not angry!"

"Then what is it that really bothers you?"

"Well, I told you: I don't care about those stories. I don't want to hear them."

"Where's your empathy, Amber?"

"What do you mean?"

"Imagine you had an accident," she explained, "or a life-changing experience, something that affected your most intimate being, and you wanted to vocalize your emotions with your friends, to free yourself from a portion of the weight. And also to help them in case something similar happened to them. Now imagine your friends not giving a damn about your experience, not caring, and even being visibly upset by your narration. How would you feel?"

Oh.

My gaze went from her face to my hands on the table.

"All these women want is to help you prepare for the worst, and exorcise the most unknown and yet common experience in a woman's life."

I looked up again, "I'm such a jerk."

She smiled, her eyes bright again, and she caressed my cheek, "You're not a jerk, you're just pregnant."

"That I know very well by now."

"And getting used to it and accepting it is a process: it takes time, and you should just grab all the support you can."

I squeezed her hand.

"And I will be here with you all the way through," she promised.

"It's always so good to see you!" I hugged her as firmly as I could.

THE WEEK WHERE SEVEN NAMES SHRINK INTO ONE

"It was so good to see you, for once just the two of us!"

Cheryl hugged me at the subway stop, where our ways were going to part, as she was headed back home in the Upper East Side. She was married to Mike's work buddy Ryan, and the four of us had had a couple relationship for quite some time now: dinners in four, lunches in four, sometimes a movie, typical situations that happen once you're old enough to be living a two-people's existence. On a rare Sunday afternoon when Ryan had had to work and he hadn't been able to make it to our monthly appointment, Mike had decided to let us ladies enjoy an afternoon tea by ourselves.

Eating cookies and small sandwiches, and drinking jasmine green tea, I had had the most boring afternoon of my life. I couldn't believe how the usually pleasant outings we had the four of us had given birth to that disappointing two-some. Cheryl was a very sweet girl who made a balanced and entertaining couple with Ryan, but she lost any interest when taken on her own. I wasn't sure if my bad mood was driven by some hormonal peak I wasn't even able to detect. The only thing I knew was that I hadn't cared at all about her Saturday afternoon of shopping with her sister, or the full report of her week of meetings at work, or the next baby shower she was going to attend. And when she had asked questions, I had been even bothered by how she had wanted to know "Everything about how you are living your wonderful pregnancy", as she had put it.

Finally alone on the uptown D train, I sighed as I sat down, and I let my head lean backwards and touch the wall. I closed my eyes, and some images replaced the afternoon subway crowd: a deep annoyance a couple of days before, after a lunch with a colleague I usually enjoyed spending time with; the impatience to go home, during a dinner with many friends the previous weekend. As more examples came to my mind, all fairly recent, I told myself that Cheryl could not be the problem. There were far higher chances that everybody was still perfectly fine, and I was the one who had developed some sort of resistance to people. Was Mother Nature playing not only with my hormones but also with my senses, to seal my bond with Mike to the detriment of my relationships with anybody else?

The only other person I still wanted in my life was Rachel. Mother Nature knew what she was doing: Rachel was more a sister than a friend, the main component of the community of women that, in ancient times, would be required to stick around me to help me raise the baby while my mate would hunt for food.

"I already miss you," I texted Rachel right away.

"Are you ok? Do you feel fine?" she typed back in a second.

"I am, I just miss you."

"Come on, you saw me for lunch. Am I that awesome?" she responded with a dancing woman emoji. "Don't you have enough of me already?"

"Never!" I replied with a beating heart emoji.

"Did Chloe call you again and you need support..?"

Well, actually.

"She called yesterday, but that's not why I'm thinking about you."

"Did you pick up?"

How could she know everything?

I started to type, "No, I couldn't. I was—" but Rachel was faster than me:

"Did you call her back?"

"I texted her that I would."

"Did you call her back?"

Damn, Rachel.

"Perhaps your subconscious knows we will have less time to spend just the two of us, in the future, and it's pushing you to get closer to me," Mike was trying to psychoanalyze me when I arrived home and I immediately threw myself in his arms.

"Or maybe just everybody suddenly sucks," I spat, sickened by the idea of Mike not being fully mine anymore.

"Right," he smiled back at me, holding my face in his hands and kissing me, "Everybody sucks but me, that's the best compliment you've ever given me. I love your hormones!"

"Great, let's decide on the name."

My next sentence, so clearly unconnected to anything we had said in the previous minutes, left Mike speechless. I took advantage of it.

"Let's decide on the name: take out the shortlist, let's kick some names out, and let's just agree on one. With the clause that, if the baby really doesn't look like that name when we see him for the first time, we might reconsider."

I didn't know if that sudden determination was coming from the consideration that, well into the seventh month, it was now time to decide on a name. Or maybe Chloe's apocalyptic words, her reminders that anything could happen now and the baby could come out any day, were still resounding in my skull. She had a much deeper influence on me than what I was willing to admit. She was my nail, like in one of those scenes from old cartoons, where Donald Duck was hammering a nail in the wall, and suddenly a crack appeared, small at first, then spreading large and fast, shattering the wall and ultimately making Donald's house collapse on itself. I pretty much collapsed under Chloe's maternal ire.

Mike walked me to the dining table, where his computer and work papers were spread, and he grabbed his phone to show me the shortlist. The smile on his face was more than I could handle, so I responded to it with a perfect poker face.

"You never liked Nolan, we can remove that," I started from the bottom of the list, the easy discards first.

"It's too American," he confirmed, tapping on the Delete button. "How about Edward: can we agree this sounds too old?"

"I kind of liked Edward, good old Ed, but sure, let's take it out."

We went through the five survivors on the list, until there was just one.

"I guess that's it."

Mike's enigmatic expression gave away his perplexity, "This is important, Amber," he frowned. "This impacts our baby's entire life."

I shrugged.

"That's the name you wanted since the beginning," I justified myself. "And I've never had anything against it. So that's our best name."

"That's our best name," he raised his brows.

"Unless we look at him when he's born and he looks like a Barack: in that case we'll call him Barack."

Mike couldn't hold a laugh, "That would be epic!"

With the baby name firmly in our pocket, now everything was ready. From the top of the mountain of my self-confidence, I figured the following appointment with Doctor Mallory was going to be the best opportunity to discuss my birth plan.

Right.

What the book didn't explain was that completing a birth plan was not something normal people would actually do, since normal people would just listen to whatever their doctors would tell them to do, and physicians didn't need some Upper West Side bitch to yell at them because they were not literally following her birthing choices. Maybe I didn't put it in the right way, but the conversation with Doctor Mallory didn't exactly start with the best premises.

After the routine exam and discussion of next steps, she asked me if I had any additional questions. I got right at it, gesturing to Mike to pass me my bag, and grabbing my printed birth plan. I might have just overkilled it.

"I'm reading the book What To Expect When You Are Expecting…"

Doctor Mallory stopped typing on her working station and she made a strange sound, something in between a laugh and a snort, "And what are you expecting?"

What?

"Well, in the book they tell you to put together a birth plan," her discomfort visibly increased with every word, and I tried to capture Mike's eyes for some support. "So I did. And I have a few questions."

"Go ahead."

Now I was legitimately scared of her, and the way she was squeezing her eyes thinner and thinner.

"Well, I'm not sure I even understand some of the questions. For example, they ask you if you would consent to the use of a catheter, and—"

"What does it even mean? What kind of catheter? A urine catheter?" she squeezed her eyes even more.

"I guess so. It's not very clear."

"See? That's the problem: these books, they put so many stupid ideas in your mind, and you end up not even being able to listen to your doctor! My goal is to deliver your baby in the healthiest possible way, for both you and the baby. This should be your goal too, right?"

She waited for me to nod before she resumed her invective, "Very well. So while we will be delivering your baby, we will do everything we need: we need a catheter? We use it. We need pain medications? We give them to you. We need a C-section because there are complications? We do it. We are one of the biggest hospitals in the Country, and we have perfect guidelines that we follow for each procedure. I've seen so many people coming in with their birth plans and then using them as toilet paper at the first painful contraction, screaming for those medications they had sworn they were never going to allow me to give them."

She stopped to catch her breath, and I tried to calm her down with a whisper, "I am very much aligned to you, and I am for all types of medications and technology, and I will do anything you will tell me to do."

"Very well," she didn't seem impressed by my dedication to her. "So what other questions do you have?"

I looked at Mike to confirm he was as beaten as I was, and then I tried to smile at Doctor Mallory, "No, that's all."

"Good."

I had forgotten to ask her about Mike cutting the cord, and what pain medication options was I going to have, and how long was I going to stay in the hospital, and probably other five or ten things. Even the cord blood banking topic, the choice we had made about it, and the fact that we had just the previous day received the blood and tissue collection kit at home, had completely escaped from my mind.

"So now a nurse will give you a TDAP vaccine," her voice was still stronger than my own thoughts. "TDAP is for tetanus, diphtheria and pertussis, which is a whooping cough and the main reason why we do it, as it can be very dangerous for small babies. Your husband needs to get it, too, at his doctor's office or at a pharmacy."

Mike, as hypnotized as I was by the doctor's military authority, could just nod and pretend to smile at her.

"Very well. Then a second nurse will draw your blood for the glucose test. Did you drink the bottle with the orange solution?"

I nodded energetically to placate her.

"Good. This is the one-hour-test, as you drink the fifty-gram-sugar bottle and we check the sugar in your blood one hour later. We will get the results tomorrow, and if it doesn't look good we will do a three-hour-test, to measure the levels of blood sugar in a longer period of time."

When she left the room, Mike and I were like two kids who had just been caught with their hands in the cookie jar by their very severe mother.

"She fucking destroyed me," I grabbed my face in my hands.

"The book was suggested by the hospital: it was on the brochure!" he tried to apologize to me, while we were waiting for the nurse.

"I will throw this birthing plan away, so that we don't even think about it anymore," I announced.

Mike's smile, the best placebo for any medical condition, flashed on his face for a tiny second, as he shook his head, "Come on, it's certainly still good to have, we have already spent some time to think about these things, let's not waste it."

"That's fair, but I'll update all the medical questions to "ASK THE DOCTOR", all capital, just to be sure. Now let's hope the glucose test is fine, so that I won't feel guilty when I'll eat a ton of chocolate as soon as we get home, to recover from mom's reprimand."

Snow days are always a welcome break from the New York routine: offices are closed, people work from home if they have to, but they mostly enjoy the snow outside with their children, or the coziness inside with their significant others.

Both Mike and I woke up the morning after the doctor's visit with emails from our HR departments, confirming the previous day's weather forecasts and officializing the snow day. I stayed in bed longer than usual on that Friday morning, watching the snow cumulate inch above inch outside the window.

By eight o'clock, Mike was fully operational at the living room table, computer and notebooks wide spread, earplugs ready for the first call of the day. I was more lazily finishing my breakfast and setting up my own working station in our bedroom.

My mobile phone's prolonged vibrations interrupted the flow of my thoughts, "Unknown". I wouldn't normally answer if the number didn't show up, but I was in a good mood, even to handle harassing advertisers or political parties.

"Hello?"

"Hello, am I speaking to Amber?"

I didn't recognize the voice on the other side, so I frowned, "Yes, that's me."

"Hello Amber, this is Doctor Mallory speaking."

Oh.

Receiving a doctor's call at eight in the morning was never a good sign.

"Hello Doctor, how are you?"

"I'm... well, I received the results of your glucose test, the one-hour-test you did yesterday."

Oh.

I left my chair and I walked to the living room, where Mike just had to lift his head up and look at my face to understand that something was wrong.

"There are many ways in which the glucose test can go," Doctor Mallory explained. "For some people we find values just above the limit, and we ask them to come back to the practice to run a three-hour-test, to check how the level of blood sugar changes over a longer period of time. For other people, the results are so bad that we don't even need the three-hour test. And this unfortunately is your case, as the limit is 120 and your test came at 230. You failed so hard that I don't need the second test: I can diagnose you right away with gestational diabetes."

Oh.

The word "diabetes" hit me in the middle of my chest, as Mike could tell by the small tears that were starting to accumulate at the inner corners of my eyes.

Diabetes?

Mike moved towards me to hear what the doctor was saying, and I put her on speaker, "I already made you a referral to see an endocrinologist and a nutritionist: a nurse will contact you to give you their names and phone numbers, and please call me back if they are not able to see you next week. It is key that you see both of them as soon as possible, as most likely the endocrinologist will ask you to check your blood sugar a few times per day, and inject insulin daily if the levels are too high. The nutritionist will help you with your diet, which is the first lever we can play with, before going the insulin route."

Blood checks?

Insulin injections?

It all sounded unreal, and all I could do was nodding and agreeing to all her demands.

When she hung up, Mike hugged me, without saying a word.

"Everything will be fine," he murmured in my ear.

How could you know, Mike?

I didn't know much about diabetes, but I had always thought that was connected to sugar and diet, so how could I get diabetes? I had always followed a very healthy diet made of vegetables, fruits, and good proteins, doing my best to eliminate added sugars from any meal. Doctor Mallory hadn't explained much of what the gestational form of diabetes really was, so it was hard for me to picture myself with it and guess what the endocrinologist's appointment was going to look like. Nobody I knew had diabetes, and none of the women who had been harassing me for weeks with their pregnancy stories had cared to mention it.

The telephone rang again, and this time it was one of Doctor Mallory's practice nurses, with the names and numbers to call. I left Mike in the living room and I went back hiding in our bedroom, eyes fixated in the void, my mind a bundle of shapeless thoughts. With a sigh I made the calls, securing the endocrinologist on the following Monday and the nutritionist on Friday. Somehow relieved that at least I was going to see an expert soon enough, I decided to look for gestational diabetes on Google. I read everything I could find regarding my condition: it came with no concrete symptoms; its causes seemed to be related to hormones; it carried some risks for both the baby and myself to develop actual diabetes later in life; there were no available treatments beside diet, exercise, and insulin. At least it didn't sound worse than before. I tried to build a picture in my head: pricking my finger, injecting insulin, going to the doctor, again and again. Being sick. That was not me.

What a retaliation from life, what a sudden push to be constantly thinking about the pregnancy, the baby, and their effects on my body. I had become The Pregnant Woman. If that was the beginning of the relationship with the baby, we were not off to a good start.

THE WEEK WITH SEVEN SUGARY DAYS

Everything was dark. I was in a tunnel, but there was no light at the end of it, or at the beginning, or anywhere. I was standing in a cold black nothing. I moved sideways to touch the tunnel's wall, and I started to trot towards what I hoped was "forward", keeping the tips of my fingers glued to the surface. In the complete darkness, things started to brush my skin, small abominations crawling up my legs, along my arms. Or was I imagining it? I was pacing faster and faster towards an even deeper nowhere.

When I opened my eyes I saw my bedroom in the dim light of an early Sunday morning. I grabbed my phone to check the time and I sighed. While the mobile was turning on, I gazed at Mike's soft profile in the screen's light, the curve of his nose almost invisible under the sheets. He turned the other way, subconsciously escaping from the luminous disturbance.

"Awake?" I found myself texting Rachel. I hadn't told her about my diagnosis, yet, since we were going to have brunch together in a few hours, but now I needed to.

"Sort of," she typed back after a few minutes. More than understandable, at 6:03 am on a weekend.

"What's wrong?" she then added.

I didn't want to bore her, and I hesitated several times while typing my response.

"Come on, you can tell me. Anything," she threw out after my many rewrites and deletions. So I told her everything, and she let me finish, she let me type and type again, message after message, tear after tear.

"I'm coming," she simply stated at the end. "What's a decent time? As much as I love Mike, I would rather not see him half naked in bed."

"Come at ten."

"You will be fine," she told me as soon as I jumped into her arms, on my doorstep. "You have none of the risk factors, so you will fully recover as if nothing ever happened."

A wave of gratefulness submerged me: thank you for talking about me, Rachel, for not making it all about the baby.

"I brought you a sugar-free muffin from the bakery in front of my place."

"The one with all the tasteless vegan gluten-free crap?"

She smiled, "That one."

I smiled, too.

The rest of the weekend slid on my skin. I tried to grasp moments of it, to get distracted from the imminent doctor's appointment on Monday morning, but nothing seemed to stick:

a movie, a dinner, a walk under the frozen rain with Mike, everything came and went. Chloe called again on Sunday night, and this time I hit the red button, without even pretending to have just missed her.

I woke up early on Monday morning, before the alarm went off, and I stared at the ceiling. Mike brushed his hand against my shoulder in his sleep, as if he could sense my distress.

I walked to the endocrinologist appointment as through a dream, defying a cold winter wind and climbing over old snow conglomerates at street corners, dirty memories of the previous Friday's storm. I didn't know what to expect from the doctor's appointment, since I had never seen an endocrinologist, and I didn't even know if it was going to be a man or a woman: I hadn't asked, and the nurses had just said "the doctor". I was relieved when a young woman came into the room. Somehow I had always felt more comfortable with female physicians, even though I knew that to any doctor anybody was just a body, a collection of flesh and blood, cells and electric connections, that from time to time needed a fix.

"Why are you here today, Amber?"

Doctor Palmer broke the ice with the usual questions, more to make me feel at ease than to gain information. She was affiliated to the same hospital as Doctor Mallory, and she probably had already seen all my medical history and latest test results.

"Gestational diabetes is more common than we think," she articulated. "It is caused by all the pregnancy hormones you have in your body, which might prevent your pancreas from producing the right amount of insulin as a reaction to sugar intake."

My eyes wide open, I was staring at her; she gave me a smile to break my evident status of hypnosis.

She opened the plastic bag she had brought with her, which I had barely noticed, and she took out an impressive amount of little unidentified objects. She placed all the objects on the table, in what seemed like a precise order, and she resumed her speech.

"We need to make sure that your blood sugar is under control, to avoid immediate problems for your baby and longer term issues for both of you. The only way of doing so, is to check your blood sugar every day, in the morning before you eat and one hour after every meal."

She opened a small plastic cylinder to extract a flat rectangular cartridge, "This is where you will have to put your blood. I will show you how to prick your finger."

She introduced the flat rectangular cartridge in a small machine, "Once you place the cartridge, the machine turns on. Once there's blood in the cartridge, the machine will show you your blood sugar level. You need to record all measures and send them to me every few days."

She grabbed a small chunky pen, she removed its cap and she inserted a needle before clicking on a button and replacing the cap, "This is the pricking device. Set it up to the deepest reach, since we don't know how thick is your skin. Clean your finger with the small alcohol pad, wait for it to be dry, place the pen on your skin, and then click the button."

I felt the small needle on my finger, as she was holding it with her gloved hands. She started to carefully squeeze my fingertip, "You want to change finger at each measure, since you are going to take many measures per day. Also, try to prick on the side, not right on the tip, where it's less sensitive. You want to keep your finger straight and gently squeeze it, until you have a fairly big drop of blood on your skin. Now, you can approach the machine, until the cartridge very softly touches the blood drop. Make sure the cartridge fills up with blood."

We waited in silence for a few seconds, while the machine processed my blood.

The number 84 then flashed on the screen.

"Did you have breakfast already?" Doctor Palmer asked, frowning.

As I shook my head, a smile came back on her face, "Good, 84 is a good value for fasting. We want you to be lower than 95 when fasting, the first measure of the day, and lower than 120 one hour after meals. If the fasting value is too high, there's not much we can do, and we would need to move to medications. Unfortunately the only FDA-approved drug during pregnancy is injectable insulin. There is a long-acting type and a regular type, both have advantages and contraindications, but we will talk about it if we need to go that way. If the post-meal values are too high, I need you to exercise for ten minutes, with a brisk walk or climbing some flights of stairs, and then recheck the blood sugar. If at this point it's good, then we're good too, otherwise we might again need to use insulin, and start injecting ten minutes before every meal."

Four blood checks plus four insulin injections would make eight needles in my body each and every day, until the end of my pregnancy and potentially even longer, if the insulin production couldn't go back to normal on its own. I didn't know what to think. The overwhelming sensation of being sick was somewhat balanced by the complete calm that came from not being able to do anything about it; the astonishment of never having faced any chronic disease before in my life was muffled by the hope that this could go away in just a few months.

"You also have to check the ketones in your urine," Doctor Palmer was still talking, her voice barely a wind gust against the side of my head. "Every morning you need to collect your first urine of the day in a plastic cup, test it with one of these strips, and record the reading with your blood sugar measures."

She was showing me some thin white strips.

"We would ideally want the ketones to be absent from your urines, to confirm the sugar is being correctly processed by your body. Some traces of them are fine, too."

I walked slowly to the subway, eating the cereal bar I had brought in with me for breakfast. I set the alarm up on my phone for sixty minutes later, and I sat still on the train until I reached my downtown stop. The pharmacy around the corner from my office had already received the prescription and they were eager to hand me my many boxes of things. They all had soothing names, "Comfort this", "One touch that", "Easy whatever". When the alarm went off, a strange panic attacked me: I had barely reached my desk, I wasn't ready with all the machines and cartridges and pieces, and I didn't know how much time I had before it was too late. I hadn't asked enough questions to the doctor. How stupid. I pricked my finger with a lot more pain than what I had experienced at the physician's office, and my hands were so sweaty that the blood drop got all smudged on my fingertip. I managed to get some blood in the cartridge, but not enough to fill it: the machine attacked me with an "Error 5, replace the cartridge and provide another sample" message. I pricked another finger, but this time the hole had ended too far on the side, and not enough blood was coming out. "Error 5". I squeezed my finger so hard, to try to get some blood out of it, that the fingertip suddenly turned blue: I had just given myself a nice looking bruise. I pricked a third finger, and I finally managed to get a good drop out of it, but by now I was so stressed up that my other hand was shaking while I approached the cartridge to the blood, and I ended up blurring the drop myself. "Error 5".

Fuck.

I took a breath, I walked around my desk to calm down, followed by colleagues' wondering eyes, and I finally got back on my chair. I pricked a fourth finger, I gave it a second for the blood to start to peek out of the hole, and I squeezed as softly as I could, to build a round fluffy drop of blood. Focusing on my hand to keep it steady, I grabbed the machine, equipped with a brand new cartridge, and I was somehow able to completely fill the cartridge with my blood. A countdown showed up on the screen: 5, 4, 3, 2, 1, … 103. At least the value was below the threshold, at least a reward.

Huffing and puffing like a marathon runner at the end of the competition, I placed all pieces back in their boxes. The most disappointing thing was not to have anybody to curse for what was happening, apart maybe from my placenta and the hormones it was producing. The baby had obviously been the trigger of the whole pancreas malfunction, but he was clearly not responsible for that, right?

I had to find a way to make the process less of a hassle, if I didn't want to lose my mind on it.

Open the pouch.

Remove the machine.

Remove the cartridge container.

Remove the pricking pen.

Remove one needle.

Remove one alcohol pad.

Open the alcohol pad and wipe a finger, left pinky for fasting, left ring finger for breakfast, left middle for lunch, right pinky for dinner.

Insert the needle in the pen.

Prepare the pen for pricking.

Insert the cartridge in the machine.

Prick the given finger, squeeze to make a spherical drop.

Approach the cartridge and fill it with the blood drop.

If the value is above threshold, come back after ten minutes of activity and retest.

If the value is below threshold, record it on the chart.

Throw away the disposable items.

Place the non-disposable items back in the pouch.

Close the pouch.

If it's an early morning check, grab a plastic cup from the pile.

Place some toilet paper on the border of the sink.

Pee in the plastic cup.

Put the full cup on the toilet paper.

Wash your hands.

Pick one ketone testing strip from the cylindrical box.

Dip it in the urine for a few seconds.

Compare the testing strip color with the sample on the cylindrical box, and record it on the chart.

Throw away the disposable items.

Having a process, by the third or fourth day of that non-stop finger-pricking and blood-testing, made me slide into an appeasing routine, even if my fingertips were still numb from the inexperienced pricking, small bumps where I had given myself numerous bruises. If it was part of my everyday life it couldn't be that bad, after all.

As soon as the thought crossed my mind, my mother's face came up: she had had to do just the same, creating a new everyday routine to accommodate her baby, me. Maybe she hadn't done it in the most perfect way, maybe she hadn't been able to adapt the process to the ever evolving sample she had had in her hands, but she had done the best she had been able to. Surely she had suffered from the same need to be impeccable, the same urge to do everything and anything for her baby.

I sighed.

On Friday I sent a message to the endocrinologist with my blood sugar measures of the week: the levels were quite stable, below or around the thresholds, as she commented, and a targeted diet was going to help to keep them in check. Good thing I had my appointment with the nutritionist on that same afternoon, a time and date chosen so that Mike could come with me. He had insisted to accompany me and he had offered to follow whatever constraints I would be tied up with, to make it a couple's endeavor. The nutritionist, a young woman my age, thought that was a great idea.

I had never been to a nutritionist, so I didn't know what to expect from it: a day-by-day meal-by-meal diet? Suggestions for a balanced intake? Regular appointments?

Maureen, who was going by her first name, asked me the highest number of questions anyone had ever bombarded me with, always keeping her smile up and her kind eyes on Mike and myself. What was my usual diet? How often did we cook at home? How much did I usually eat? At what times? Now that I was pregnant, was I feeling more or less hungry? Was I craving any food? Any non-food items? She explained how some women could crave dirt during pregnancy. Fascinating. Was I eating fruits? Vegetables? Proteins? In what quantities? What did I have for breakfast? And yesterday's dinner? And yesterday's lunch? How was my blood sugar after those meals?

It never seemed to end.

When the questions were finally concluded, Maureen went through all my answers on her computer and, with a very focused look on her face, she started to jot down some notes. She then printed a few papers and she showed them to Mike and me.

"It is very important to limit your carbs intake - not only sugars, but all carbs. Remember that also fibers are carbs."

She briefly looked at us, to confirm that we were following her. I nodded, to keep her going.

"On these papers you can find the number of carbs, in grams, contained in many major foods, organized in their families: starch, like pasta and rice; dairies; fruits and sugary vegetables, as many green and leafy vegetables have virtually no carbs; sweets. Given your body weight, the fact that you're pregnant, and your food habits, I would recommend you to eat two servings of carbs per meal, counting three meals per day, and one serving per snack, counting up to two snacks per day. A serving of carbs is fifteen grams, so you can make all your calculations just looking at these papers, and you can keep having a very balanced and healthy diet, pretty much like you are doing right now. Maybe just limiting the ice cream," she finished with a smile.

It all sounded easy and doable, until Maureen showed me how much cooked rice corresponded to one serving of carbs: a third of a cup, two spoonfuls. How much pasta? Well, pasta was not even mentioned on the table. How much fruit? Half an apple. Or even half a banana, if I felt fancy. How much yogurt? Half a cup. Of plain unsweetened yogurt, because a small pot of, let's say, vanilla yogurt, could have even more than twenty grams of carbs.

I couldn't speak when Mike and I walked outside the nutritionist's office: what was I going to eat for the remaining two and a half months of my pregnancy? How would the baby keep growing? And what if the diabetes didn't go away after delivery? I couldn't believe I was destined to a life of grilled chicken and unseasoned broccoli.

When we came back home, Mike checked how many carbs some of my favorite food contained, "Chocolate Chip Delights, one serving: two cookies, thirty grams of carbs."

The equivalent of a full meal.

"These are small damned cookies!" he couldn't believe it himself.

He quickly opened the freezer, "Vanilla Bean Haagen-Dazs," he read out loud for me. "One serving: half a cup, twenty-five grams of carbs. All sugar!"

I was about to scream. There were not many sweet things I liked, but I loved my weekend morning cookies and I sometimes needed a well-sized ice cream, definitely not half a cup.

"Your Kind bars have only sixteen grams of carbs, so you can keep eating them for breakfast in weekdays!"

Where was all that enthusiasm coming from? I had none of it.

"And my plain Greek yogurt has just nine grams of carbs per cup," he kept going, unaware of my mounting rage. "So I could make you wonderful yogurt recipes during the weekends: Greek plain, with almonds (just a couple of grams of carbs for ten almonds), unsweetened coconut flakes, and perhaps some extra-dark chocolate drops. And you can eat all the cheese that you want!"

The cheese and the dark chocolate, as good as they were, couldn't fix anything.

"I want my fucking cookies!"

THE WEEK WITH SEVEN BEST PICTURE
OSCAR NOMINEES

Gray sky above gray industrial landscapes, the highway 95 South flew by outside the bus window, despite some Saturday morning traffic towards Philadelphia. I still had the dusty taste of my sugar-free breakfast lingering in my mouth, ashier than the view.

"The hotel is right downtown," Mike confirmed, the Google Maps app open on his phone. "Just a few steps away from the theater."

"That's tomorrow night, right?" I checked. Mike had planned our three-day President's Day weekend in Philadelphia down to the detail: he had made reservations to restaurants for lunches and dinners and he had organized evening entertainment; he had identified the best time of the day to visit the Independence Hall and he had booked a guided tour to the

Barnes Foundation, one of the most impressive private art collections in the world.

A smile bloomed on his face, "Yes that is tomorrow night! And tonight we can catch a film after dinner: there's a cinema on the way back from the restaurant to the hotel. That is, if you're not too tired."

My legs were sore from the two-hour ride, as I could notice while walking down the few steps that led to the bus door. I stretched while we were waiting for our Uber, careful not to overstress my back muscles.

"I'm great, and I'm always up for a movie!" I tried to smile back. No doubt we could find something I hadn't already watched for work, in the vast February offering.

We quickly checked in the hotel, and once we had left our bags in the room we were ready to explore the city. We reached a charming alley just in time for Mike's lunch reservation; he had picked a healthy organic place that Rachel would have loved, and which had perfect carb-free soup options. I walked out still hungry but at least unconcerned about my blood sugars. The first glucose challenge came later that afternoon when, after a tour of the downtown area that left me completely famished, Mike stopped in front of the cutest English pub in the city, for an afternoon tea.

"I know biscuits and pastries are not ideal for your diabetes, but you do love afternoon tea, and I wanted you to have something nice."

He frowned, before brightening up again and resuming his speech.

"I know this is not the most marvelous of Baby Moons, I know it is my fault if we didn't go to the Caribbean because I couldn't take any vacation days right now, but I wanted us to have a romantic weekend anyway. I wanted us to savor this time for ourselves—"

I hoped he would stop there.

"—because next romantic vacation will require a certain level of additional planning, with babysitter arrangements and the likes."

He couldn't control his grinning.

I hardly repressed a sigh and a thousand thoughts, focusing instead on the homemade shortbreads, jams, and scones that were waiting for me passed the wooden entrance door.

"Let's go," I then pushed him, convinced I could pretend those sweet delights contained no actual sugars.

"I'm dead," I typed in a text for Rachel, responding to her request for updates on the weekend. I was lying in bed late at night, trying to fall asleep cradled by Mike's soft breathing noises.

"Too much sex?"

I sighed.

"Not even. Imagine having a fifteen pound ball strapped to your abdomen, all day every day."

She replied with a sad face emoji.

"And then imagine having to walk around with it at a fast pace, to burn the stupid sugar you ingested. And obviously the exercise was not enough to lower my blood glucose, so I had to come back straight to the hotel after dinner to run up and down the stairs for fifteen minutes. Do you know how many floors I had to climb to fill up fifteen minutes at an accelerated pace? Seventeen. Seventeen fucking floors up and then down. My legs screaming, my chest exploding, my belly the heaviest thing in the world. I even had to try and recompose before reentering the room, so that Mike didn't call the ambulance thinking I was having a stroke. So that at least one of us can actually enjoy the weekend."

"I am totally there with you, darling," Rachel responded with an explosion of hearts. "And I know how hard it is. But don't let this jerk diabetes ruin your vacation: you're spending a nice weekend doing romantic things with your lovely husband, what more could there be?"

A sudden pain in my groin responded to her rhetorical question.

During the usual Sunday morning video chat with Mike's parents, they insisted to have a picture of me and my belly. Mike immediately accepted with his usual enthusiasm, ignoring the "WTF" I was mouthing to him from outside the phone's camera framing.

He started to laugh as soon as we hung up with his parents, "I loved your WTF face!"

Buddy, that was not a joke.

"I don't want a picture of fat Amber to ever exist in this universe," my pout spoke for me.

Mike took me in his arms and he kissed me, "You are not fat! You are still yourself, even slimmer than you used to be, just with a big belly. Our growing son!"

For once I was not tricked by his charms, as that was exactly my point: I was not myself. I couldn't pretend anymore that everything was normal, with the ever expanding pains, and the gestational diabetes, and the tiredness, and the constant hunger derived by the almost complete elimination of carbs from my diet. It was impossible to look at me and still see me, and not being kicked in the face by my current shape. Round. So very round. Sure, I was not fat, especially with the endocrinologist-friendly regime, but the person in the mirror was not me. What did Mike see when he looked at me?

As it usually happened, we found a compromise. Mike took a picture from quite afar, where my belly would show but not too overwhelmingly, and he sent it to the chat group we shared with his family.

I went back to the photo a few times during what remained of the long weekend, and on Monday afternoon on our way back to New York City. I kept enlarging it on my phone's screen, to check how huge I looked in it, in an unnerving game of self-deprecation. During one of these playing sessions, Chloe's name popped up on my screen: incoming call.

"What the…" I whispered.

"Are you ok?" Mike's spontaneous reflex investigated.

"Chloe is calling again."

"You ought to just answer," he caressed my cheek. "I don't believe she will desist."

I kissed him on the forehead, and I let the call go to voicemail without a second thought.

Chloe would have squeaked in pure joy if she had seen the photo. She would have thought I had become like her when she was expecting her child: The Pregnant Woman, the word "pregnant" being the only thing that seemed to define her. She had told me how she had loved to catch people's eyes hypnotized by her belly, the most evident sign of her new beauty. I had never fished for people's attention or relied on my beauty, as I had never been a beauty queen. I was not curvy and charismatic like Rachel, or petite and feminine like Chloe; I was quite tall and skinny, with reasonably sized boobs that would attract men's eyes only when appropriately exposed. Now my breasts were enormous, for sure. Was that the new beauty Chloe was referring to? All I could see was a belly walking around, the content already more important to most people than the container. Then I would become a mother, and I would never go back to be just Amber.

I deleted the picture.

As soon as I reached the office on Tuesday morning, I went looking for my boss. I hadn't told her about my gestational diabetes, yet, and I didn't want her to think I was hiding something from her.

"My sister had it with all her three pregnancies," Lauren immediately empathized and she hugged me. "I know how annoying and scary it can be. You have to take care of yourself: I've seen how hard you've been working lately and I want you to be selfish for once, and put yourself before anything else."

She squeezed my hand and tears started to accumulate at the corners of my eyes. I hoped they were not visible from the outside.

"We desperately need you here, don't get me wrong," she grinned. "But we need you to have the energy to be the real Amber, strong and opinionated, ready to call on jerks on Twitter and ask tough questions during interviews. I want you to feel good, and I'm ready to have a smaller quantity of that goodness now, and then wait for a few months to have you back."

Lauren hugged me again. I tried to thank her but I almost choke on my tears.

"You will get through it, I know, and you and your baby will be healthy. My sister's diabetes had no impact on her or her children, so you shouldn't worry."

I sighed through a smile.

"You will have your perfect baby and you won't think about diabetes ever again. My sister didn't. Her husband is African American, too, and they have three handsome boys with dark skin and blue eyes. The only concern with the kids growing up has been where to play in the neighborhood basketball games: they go whites against blacks."

"What?" my disbelief was stronger than my emotion.

Lauren shrugged, "I know, that sounds horrible, right? But they are still young, they are neutral to race. They don't see it as a discriminating issue, they just state it as a fact. They don't have jerseys to identify the two teams in the playground, but they have a fairly proportionate amount of African Americans and Caucasians, so they just go with skin color. The problem for my nephews is that they're both, so at first they didn't know where to go."

"Did they find their place?"

Her calm smile comforted me, "Of course they did."

Counting carbs at every meal, giving up cookies and even more regular things like rice, soon took its toll on me. The lack of sugar was transforming me into a panting, whining little person, who would get home at night and collapse on the sofa, and yell at the blood glucose machine any time the post-meal value was greater than 120.

Only two weeks had passed since the first appointment with Doctor Palmer, but when she came into the exam room I was in desperate need for some positive development.

"Thank you for sending me your readings for this week," she nodded as she shook my hand. She gazed at the printed paper she had in her other hand, the table with my numbers from the past few days, and she nodded again, as if she was reminding herself about a decision she had already made.

I tried to smile.

"How do they look?"

"Well, the post-meal values are good," she now looked at me. "But the fasting values are too high. You can see it here: they've been rising over the past five days, and yesterday and today they've been above 95."

Oh.

"Unfortunately the only drug approved by the FDA is injectable insulin," she kept staring at me with a faint smile. "So I'm going to prescribe it to you."

Insulin?

Please no, not the insulin. Not the daily injections, not the needles.

I sighed. I hadn't seen that coming.

"Since the post-meal values are still good, I only need to prescribe you bedtime injections, at least for now," Doctor Palmer's voice sounded softened by some fog. "But keep in mind this is a very typical progression of gestational diabetes: your insulin resistance will keep increasing in the next weeks, and it will plateau at some point between week thirty-four and thirty-eight. The condition is generally fully reversible: you don't have Type 2 diabetes risk factors, so there shouldn't be any consequence for you after delivery. Or for your baby, as long as we keep the blood sugar level under control. Let's hope the post-meal values remain within range, and let's keep doing the walking and the exercising. Let me show you how to use the pen."

She left the room with a kind smile on her face, a soft show of empathy that barely registered on my clogged brain. The condition was generally reversible. What if it wasn't? Was I going to have to deal with diet and injections all my life? What if the baby ended up developing diabetes, too? What if I was giving this incurable life-long disease to the baby? Children's diabetes carried many risks, and it could demand a high toll. For life. What was I condemning the baby to suffer?

Doctor Palmer opened the door, leaving my questions hanging. She showed me how to screw a needle on the insulin pen, select the dosage, pinch the fatty part of my inner thigh, and inject the medicine. I had never been prone to panic, but that simple gesture of pushing the pen on the skin overwhelmed me. Was that the price I had to pay? That didn't sound fair.

My phone chirped while I was waiting for the insulin's prescription to be filled out at the pharmacy, "All good with the endocrinologist?" Mike was inquiring.

"Fasting sugar is too high, so I need insulin. Picking up at Columbus Circle's CVS."

The three dots blinked for a few seconds, while Mike was processing my words.

"I'm done in the office, I can be there in fifteen minutes."

"No problem, I'm waiting for them to fill the prescription," I added with a soft smiling emoji.

Mike had a special sixth sense, always able to detect my needs even when I was not expressing them. And now, I really wanted to see him.

He ran in that late February windy afternoon, and he caught me right before they called my name at the cashier for the pick-up.

"I'm here," he kissed me when I smiled at him.

While walking towards the subway, I gave him the full download from the endocrinologist's appointment, going into all the annoying details of preparing and injecting the insulin in my leg. Every night.

"I am here for you," he said in the end. "We will do whatever we need to make sure you are healthy, and the baby too. I know there's not much that I can do, but I'm here."

He held my hand tight down the subway stairs, in the train, up the stairs again and all the way to our living room, where he finally hugged me and he looked at me straight in the eyes, "I wish I could carry the baby myself, and deal with all this."

I kissed him and I placed his hands on what remained of my belly button, to Mike's surprise.

"You know you are still the most important thing in the world, and you will always be?"

I nodded.

NINE

The baby decided to roll with a perfect timing, making Mike squeak with surprise.

I hugged him.

Later that night I wished Mike could truly carry the baby, as I was struggling with the whole insulin injection process. The pen's leaflet and instructions spread on the bathroom's floor, I was trying to put all the pieces together: the small needle had to go on top of the pen, the dose had to be precisely set up. When my left thumb and index tried to pinch my thigh, I sighed at how much skinnier I had gotten, as there was not much to pinch. The pen firmly in my right hand, I noticed that the needle was peeking outside the injection cap, meaning that I had to push the needle inside my flesh before I could click the button and release the dose. My eyes stuck on the needle, I couldn't move. Seconds poured, one by one. There was no way out: I had to do it.

The needle hurt more than I thought.

I went to sleep.

I woke up with my mind full of horror images from an already forgotten dream, pins in my tight where the needle had hit.

"Did you sleep well?" Mike asked me while sipping his morning coffee on that Saturday, his nose buried in the New York Times open on the kitchen bar.

"Sure. Did you?"

"Like a baby," he grinned. "Do we have plans for the weekend?"

"We have dinner with Rachel tonight, and you know it's Oscars night tomorrow."

He raised his head from the latest news on Syria, to throw an interrogative gaze at me.

"Of course I'm not going! But I need to follow the red carpet and live-tweet the awards."

"Do you need to go to the office?"

"Nah, everybody is in LA."

Right. Everybody was in Los Angeles that weekend, sharing the excitement for the Academy Awards, interviewing actors and directors, enjoying the Vanity Fair after party. I hadn't missed one ceremony in many years. I should have been there.

Mike brushed my hand, "We have a full weekend to take advantage of: what do you want to do? Do you want to go shopping for that new pair of boots you said you needed? Do you want to catch a film?"

Shopping? Maybe without the tiredness, the diffused pains, and the never satisfied need to pee, even if there was no pee to be offered to the gods of the sewers. A movie? Sunday night's Academy Awards were going to give me enough movies for the whole weekend.

The Academy Awards.

"Anything you like, dear," I put up an accommodating grin.

The statuette was the only thought on my mind during those two days, until I turned on the TV for the red carpet on the Awards' day. It was sunny and lukewarm in California, and I could almost feel the cool breeze on my face. Too bad the freshness came from the tears running down my cheeks. Relieved that Mike was out with his colleague Ryan, to let me focus on my typing and tapping, I let the tears roam free and soak my shirt. They kept going: during red carpet interviews,

Jimmy Kimmel's opening monologue, the first awards, even commercials. Something heavier and heavier compressed my chest as the evening went by and the speeches with it. I kept tweeting and typing my article through a thick fog of tears, loud sobs following the rhythm of my fingers on the computer's keyboard. I hanged in there until Tom Hanks recapped the seven Best Picture nominees and he finally announced the winner. I was incapable to allow myself even the smallest smile for having correctly guessed in my latest prediction article. I went to bed as soon as the article was published on the Vanity Fair's website, not before sending a thankful text to my editor who had so quickly reviewed and approved it.

I was still awake when Mike came home, he softly slid under the blanket and he hugged me.

I pretended I was asleep.

ANNALISA CONTI

EIGHT

THE WEEK WITH EIGHT COUPLES WITH MANY QUESTIONS

I opened my eyes to month number eight. Where had all the previous months gone, one after the other? It seemed so impossible that I now had only two months to go.

A clock was ticking inside my head: the countdown had started, and it would advance minute after minute until the day my waters would broke or my contractions would start, or whatever else would signal that labor was coming.

I felt like a prehistoric animal on the day of the big meteorite. I could see it tearing the sky open with fire, dust exploding in the air after it touched down on Earth. I could hear earthquakes afar, volcanoes channeling the anger of a wounded planet, tsunami ravaging the coasts. All I could do was hope the dust would eventually settle and I would survive. Many species would go extinct, many would mutate or have to evolve, and only the strongest beings on the planet would keep conducting their normal lives: insects. I had never before wished I were a cockroach.

Mike didn't seem to be affected by the big milestone, his unflappable smile printed on his face.

"I will always be yours", he would respond to my ironical frowning, but I knew it wasn't true. As disappointing as it was, given all the promises we had made to each other, it was by now as inevitable as the arrival of the baby. It was nobody's fault.

"Are you ok?" Mike squeezed my hand while we were walking towards our destination in the Upper West Side. He had caught me as I was trying to shake doomsday thoughts out of my head.

I put up a smile, "Sure. I'm curious to see what this birthing class will teach us."

We were going to a One Night Intensive Birthing and Newborn Care Class, hosted by one of the nurses in Doctor Mallory's practice, and we had no idea of what to expect from it. We had purposefully avoided the Two Night Extensive Birthing and Newborn Care Class, where the nurse also showed a video, because I didn't want to see any delivery video. I wanted some things to remain a mystery. Both for me, as I didn't want to know too much too soon, and for Mike, as I didn't think he needed to learn the mystic details of the female body during labor.

The class was hosted by a very experienced maternity nurse, who professionally handled eight couples with many questions, some of them quite unusual and others far more relevant. They went from the rational "How do you know if your breastfed baby is getting enough milk?" to the boozy "How many glasses of alcohol can I drink per day if I'm breastfeeding?", which I was tempted to ask myself, but I was defeated by another woman. That turned out to be a good thing, since the nurse opened her eyes wide in disbelief, and she gently pointed out it was going to be only one glass of alcohol. Per week.

Full size diagrams and pictures explained how the baby would move down inside my pelvis in the last couple of weeks before delivery, while the nurse's expert gestures showed where and how the cervix would become thinner and then dilated. I kept monitoring Mike's face expressions: his eyes open wide, he was completely fascinated by how nature had somehow figured this all out. He looked at me with pure emotion, squeezing my hand and making my heart painfully lose a beat every time we crossed eyes. I loved Mike more than anything. I would have never wanted a child without Mike; not just without a man by my side, but specifically without him. I could see the other guys' faces in the room, and some of them were staring in the void while their wives furiously scribbled on their papers, some were yawning, some had their eyes fogged by deep fear. Mike was calm, he took notes. With him by my side, I could face it all. Contractions, pain, effort, exhaustion. And whatever would come next: taking care of a newborn, not ever having held one in my arms; feeding the baby through sleepless nights; braving the never ending tiredness, hopelessness, and without knowing if we were doing it right. Nonetheless, it was daunting.

After the class was over, in the elevator down I held Mike in my arms, stronger than ever, more grateful than ever. He smiled at me and he kissed me: he knew what I was thinking.

"Do you know that you may have to push for two hours?" I texted Rachel for comfort.

"How scary was it?" she asked.

"It was more tiring than scary: the idea of having to make it through all those hours of labor, and then push. It sounds exhausting."

"But you have a child in the end!" she commented with a baby emoji.

"What are you doing?" she added after a few seconds.

"I'm walking up the stairs."

"In your building?"

"Yep," I responded.

"Sugar was bad after dinner.. ?" she investigated.

"145," I tapped back, with a crying emoji.

"What did you eat?" she was surprised.

"The freaking usual boring thing," I was surprised too. "Salad and chicken and some yogurt with almonds. And half an apple: that screwed me."

"Crap, 145 with half an apple, that sucks."

I had to grasp the handrail as I kept pacing faster and faster up and down the stairs.

"I know. I so need a cookie," I typed back, in between heavy pants.

"I'll bring you my sugar-free gluten-free muffins on Friday night."

I responded with the vomiting emoji.

"Is it the athletic effort making you barf or is it a bad joke on my lovely muffins?"

I responded with a heart: I only had a couple of minutes left, out of the fifteen I could spend exercising to reduce blood sugar, and I wanted to get the most out of them.

NINE

I read Rachel's last text while wheezing to reach the apartment door, "Fingers crossed!"

I went straight to bed after the glucose testing machine flashed its triumphant 119.

Only a few minutes seemed to have passed when a deep pain pierced my crotch, and I opened my eyes to a hospital room, where this time I was covered in blood.

When the alarm went off I escaped the most profound darkness of my subconscious, leaving my latest nightmare behind. The beauty of a Friday morning possessed me for several minutes, until I remembered the weekly appointment with the endocrinologist. Doctor Palmer stressed me like a college test: I never knew what new and impossible questions she could ask me. I sighed, I slowly rolled out of bed, supported by Mike's gentle push on the back, and I went in the shower.

"We can keep things as they are for another week," Doctor Palmer commented on the weekly measures. The "for another week" didn't sound promising.

"Message me if the fasting value goes again above 95, so that we can increase the insulin dosage," she kept going. "And I will see you next week."

Her end-of-conversation smiles were always relieving.

I left her office and I shivered my way to the subway, braving the chilly wind coming from Central Park and getting channeled through the Upper West Side buildings. The two long blocks from Broadway to the Central Park West B C subway stop left me breathless, and I jumped on the first empty seat on the train. As I grasped my phone at the bottom of my pocket, a text message made it vibrate.

"How are you? I haven't heard from you in a while and I wanted to check in."

My mother.

I rolled my eyes and I put the phone back in my pocket. I sat staring in the void for a couple of stops, then I pulled the phone back and I re-read the message.

"How are you? I haven't heard from you in a while and I wanted to check in."

She was probably worried. And she didn't even know about gestational diabetes.

Right.

"I should tell her," I whispered, to nobody in particular.

It had always been hard for me to tell my parents when I was sick: as rough as our relationship had been since I was a teenager, I nonetheless had done my best to spare them the heartache, and to spare myself the overprotective rush that would punctually befall. I had never appreciated their dedication, their efforts. I had never accepted their unconditional love, even more powerful considering how spiteful I was to them, especially to my mother. Now that the dreadful effects my diabetes could have on the baby were the first and last thought of my day, now I understood. What it meant to have a sick child, what it meant to feel incapable in front of the disease, useless with the human being one gave life to and one was fully responsible for.

As soon as I exited the elevator at my office floor, I searched for an empty and unbooked meeting room, and I looked for my mother's name in my phone's contacts.

"Amber? Is everything ok?" she yelled as soon as she picked up.

I sighed: suddenly it didn't seem like a good idea anymore.

"What did she say?" Rachel wanted to know more about the rare conversation with my mother, later that night at dinner. Mike grinned from the other side of the table, as he already knew the story.

"She was worried about the diabetes, but I told her everything is under control. It's just some finger pricking, just an annoyance."

Mike and Rachel exchanged looks.

"I mean, I feel good, the baby is fine. No worries!" I added. "She doesn't have to know all the details, it's not that I see her every day, right?"

They nodded.

"Right. And I don't think she cares about the details: it's all medical stuff. Everything will be fine, in any case. Everything is fine."

They exchanged looks again.

"Will you call her more often?" Rachel attempted. "You haven't really been in touch with her."

I took my face in my hands, "Maybe."

My phone rang before I could think about something to add: the sugar alarm. With unhidden exasperation I fished for the diabetes pouch in my purse and I went to the restroom.

With only some salmon and a kale salad in my stomach, I was expecting the reading to be safely below threshold, and the 135 that came bursting on the machine's screen was a kick in the face. As I was pacing back to the table, Mike looked at me. My face must have revealed him everything that was going through my mind, since he fell silent as I approached the table. Rachel was silent too.

"Is it bad?" she squeezed my hand.

I nodded.

"Why don't you ladies go for a walk outside, while I pay?" Mike gestured at us with a smile.

Rachel and I put our coats on and she grabbed my arm, softly pushing me out of the restaurant. It was drizzling.

The light rain transformed into a tsunami, an enormous wave that fell on my head and that pushed me underwater. I went rolling down, far away from the surface. It took me a second to understand where up and down were, and once I had an idea I started to swim towards that direction. Before I could see the surface at arm's length, my chest burning and my heart pounding, another wave crashed on me and it pushed me away, again. Was it truly impossible to breathe?

I woke up scrambling to let a big gulp of air in my lungs, before I could understand it was just a dream. Another nightmare.

I sat up in bed and I shook my head to swipe away the last memories of the night. I looked at Mike, still asleep, his mouth slightly open, and a smirk bloomed on my face. I left the bedroom and I slowly paced towards the bathroom for my morning routine, made of peeing in a cup to measure ketones, and pricking my finger to record the fasting blood sugar level. Already exhausted, I collapsed on the sofa, only to realize I had left my phone in the bedroom. Not to awake Mike, I grabbed my computer from the coffee table, to check my emails and read the news. An email from Chloe flashed in my Inbox. I slapped my forehead and I sighed.

"Dear Amber,

I apologize for disturbing you on your work email, but I have tried to contact you many times in the past few weeks, and we were never able to connect. I understand you are very busy with work and with the fact that you are now expecting a child, so I don't blame you. Nevertheless, I would appreciate if you gave me a call back, since I have a very important matter I would like to discuss with you live. In person would be best, but I understand this would be extremely complicated right now, so a phone conversation will do the job.

Thank you very much and best regards,
Chloe"

THE WEEK WITH EIGHT WORDS TO CHANGE YOUR MIND

I eventually fell out of excuses not to get in touch with Chloe, and on Sunday morning I gave up. Soft sobs came to my ear as soon as she picked up.

Shit.

A low whining noise followed, then some words started to emerge from the primordial soup of her tears, "Hello, Amber," then she legitimately started to cry.

I took a deep breath and I pretended everything was fine.

"Hello, Chloe, how are you?"

More sobbing.

"Are you ok, Chloe? Is everything ok?"

Nose blowing.

"I'm not ok, Amber, I'm not ok."

"I am so sorry to hear that. What's wrong?" that was the wrong question, because I didn't really want to know what crap her head was filled with on that specific day, but I had to go there.

"Well, I tried to call you many times during the past weeks—"

"I know," I was able to intercept her. "I am sorry we never got to talk."

"That's fine," she sniffled. "I am happy you called me now."

She paused. That was unusual.

"You know," she then resumed after a deep sigh. "I have been feeling strange for some time now: not sick, but weak, tired even to hold my sweet baby Jasper in my arms. So I went to the doctor."

She paused again, and she resumed the sobbing.

"And do you want to know what the doctor told me?"

That you should get some rest?

"Please, tell me," I responded, instead.

"That I have breast cancer!"

Oh.

"I'm dying, Amber!"

Oh.

Somehow my brain hung up at that point, and I lost track of what she said next, what I responded. The only thing I could remember afterwards was the question mark carved on Mike's eyes, the expression on his face evolving minute after minute, mirroring mine.

That was what she had wanted to tell me for a month.

I had gotten used to nightmares of the worst kinds, but this was not one of them. As soon as I hung up with Chloe I got run over by a motorcade of undecipherable emotions, which congested into a horrible traffic jam in the middle of my chest. I couldn't respond to Mike's requests for clarification; the only thing I could do right then was to sit on the sofa and stare into the void.

My hands tapped on the phone until they found the right number to call.

"Are you ok, Amber?" Rachel's voice sounded both worried and resolute. We never spoke on the phone, we usually texted.

"Chloe has breast cancer."

"What?"

"I just called her back, and she told me she's dying," I put it as simple as I saw it.

I could hear Rachel's brain gears furiously spin on the other side of the phone, searching for the perfect thing to say, the witty lawyer response.

"I am so sorry," was everything that came out.

We kept silent for a few long seconds; Mike, who now knew what was wrong, sat next to me and he held my hand.

"The strangest thing," I spit out at last, "is that I normally would have called her back sooner. I don't know why I left her hanging on the cliff's edge for so long. Maybe I thought she would do an Indiana Jones and climb up behind our backs, unscathed. Instead she fell. She's dead now."

"Wait a second," Mike stopped me. "She's certainly not dead, don't you let your guilt overwhelm you."

"That's right," Rachel said on the other side of the phone, having heard Mike's words. "What did she tell you? How does she feel? What's her stage? When—"

"I don't know!" I shouted. "I couldn't even listen to her, I couldn't even tell her anything!"

My eyes tickled as I kept screaming, "Who doesn't call back a friend for a month, when this friend keeps calling? Who can be so selfish and blind? Who doesn't understand when a friend is in trouble? What the fuck is happening to me?"

Mike was now holding me in his arms, and I could hear Rachel whispering something in my ear, but my phone was too far now for me to identify her words.

Mike tapped on the screen to put Rachel on speakers.

"—because nothing happened to you, dear," she was saying. "You're still the same, Amber, you're still yourself. You just have a lot going on now. Don't feel guilty: you have no fault in here."

"I have no fault," I repeated. "Are you sure?"

"One hundred percent sure," she responded without hesitation.

"I don't know, Rachel. This had never happened to me."

"I know," she smiled. "You've always been the generous one, the selfless one. We all need to focus on ourselves, from time to time."

"That's all I'm doing nowadays. And I hate it."

Rachel spent her Sunday at our place and, as much as I could appreciate her efforts to distract me and elevate my pitch black mood, I still went to bed empty.

As soon as I regained consciousness, I understood something was wrong: pain was pushing on my chest, as if somebody I loved was dying and I was there in the room with them. As seconds flew by, the scene became clearer and clearer: I was in a hospital, holding Rachel's hand. She was in bed, gaunt, barely recognizable. She had cancer and she was dying.

This was something I couldn't face.

I fought against my own dream as hard as I could, until the sound of my own screams woke me up.

Mike jumped up and he held me in his arms, powerless, as I cried my heart out with the picture of Rachel's death in my eyes.

"Everything is fine," he whispered.

"Never die," was all I could say.

"Never let Rachel die," I continued, when I had the energy to do so.

He smiled and he kissed me, "I promise you I'm never going to die, my love."

That wasn't enough.

"Make these nightmares go away," I prayed.

He held me closer, "I will do my best."

I woke up in Mike's arms, his eyes fixated into mine.

"Did you sleep?" I asked with a yawn.

He scrolled his head: it didn't matter.

We got ready and he insisted to ride with me on the subway to my office. I didn't say no.

It was still early morning when I reached the building, after kissing Mike good day, and Vanity Fair was sleepy in the Condé Nast offices. I sat at my desk and I turned my computer on, in a habitual gesture that instantly calmed me down. I checked my calendar, I reviewed my notes on the article I had on my to-do list for that cold almost-Spring Monday, and I let my fingers roam on the keyboard. That was Amber. I almost didn't feel my belly. Then the baby decided to kick me in the stomach, and we were back to our tumultuous relationship.

The article I was completing that morning was about the recent proliferation of excellent TV shows starring African American women. It was wonderful to see how Taraji Henson's Golden Globe win had finally acknowledged the public's interest in those stories and characters, but the journey towards equality was not over, yet. The elephant still trumpeting in the room was the fact that Hollywood and TV-land still considered African American watchers a niche, a group of people whose interests were not bankable enough, not respected enough. I found it even offensive to classify some shows as "for black people", it sounded so 1950's. The baby was going to be part of the 2010's generation, and I wondered what name would media find for him and his peers: Post-Millennials? Digitals? Screwed? And he would also be a mixed race person in a world I still couldn't depict in my mind: would he still be considered a minority? Would he become the majority, by the time he would be an adult? Would we finally stop identifying people on the basis of their race, or gender, or income? I wished I had some answers.

One week after the Birthing and Newborn Care Class, Mike and I attended an even more visually impactful session: the Infant CPR Class. What could be less tempting than spending two hours discussing a topic whose title contained both the words "infant" and "cardiopulmonary resuscitation"?

At least this second time we were prepared. Mike had taken adult CPR classes a few years ago, so we had a vague enough idea about what we would be hearing about.

The same nurse who had run the birthing class was back for this additional curriculum, and we were ready, pen in hand, when she started the session. First Aid suggestions on how to treat fever and seizures, clear instructions on how to disinfect an open wound, and how never to let anyone but a plastic surgeon put stitches on your baby's face, were followed by the focus of the class: CPR. Each couple was given a doll that impressively resembled an infant, and the nurse explained us how to perform a cardiac massage and mouth-to-mouth respiration to our babies, in case of loss of consciousness. Mike and I continuously gazed at each other while we practiced the resuscitation techniques on the doll, and I found myself grinning at how weird it was to carry out CPR on a plastic doll. Mike kept looking at me. A strange noise captured my attention, and I turned my head around to identify its source. A woman was sobbing.

"What if our baby was unconscious? What would we do?" she was whispering to her husband, who carefully held her hands.

"We would probably freak out," he smiled. "But that would be ok: we could be the best planners and the calmest people on this planet, but how could we keep it cool if our newborn child was in a life-threatening situation?"

"That's right, and that's one of my points," the nurse approached them. "If anything happens and you freak out, just call 911, and listen to what they tell you. As I always say, though: I hope this can be the most useless class ever!"

I slid next to Mike to buzz in his ear, "The woman is nuts!"

He looked at me with a mix of incredulity and scorn, and I noticed his eyes were misty.

What the hell?

"I was joking!" I added, only to receive a frown.

I was not crazy, I knew the baby's life completely depended on us. I was just joking.

"We are going to be the only thing that separates the baby from death," I told Mike that night in the cab, on our way home. "Have you ever thought about parenting in these terms?"

He kissed me on the forehead, more resigned than affectionate.

"Hopefully death will never be that close to him: I don't want you to transform into a witch and start howling spells in his bedroom!"

I looked back at him and I mouthed a long wail, like a wolf in a bright moon night.

"Your phone is blinking," he told me in between laughs.

I looked down towards my lap, where I had put my phone, and a message from Rachel was illuminating the screen, "How was the CPR class?"

"Socially interesting: a weirdo cried," I tapped back, making sure Mike was not looking at my screen as I did.

"A woman? Why?"

"I guess she got upset imagining her baby dying, or something," I shrugged.

"I'm sure she knew that was only a doll, but not everybody is as rational as you are!" she wrote back, with a nerd face emoji.

"Fair point. And with the pregnancy hormones maybe she got over emotional. She probably used to be normal before," I reasoned, genuinely interested in the issue. "But Mike was also kind of moved, isn't it strange?"

"What?" Rachel typed back right away. "What is strange: the fact that Mike was emotional, or the fact that you weren't?"

"I don't know," I responded to Rachel's message later that night.

"You're back! How's the after-dinner sugar?"

"Bad, very bad. 145, and I skipped the apple this time. I already did my first fifteen minutes, but it was still 130. I decided to sort of cheat and I'm doing fifteen more minutes to lower it. I don't think I will survive, though…"

I was slowly climbing the stairs in my building, going up to the fifth floor, from our apartment on the second floor, to then walk down again.

"Try not to die, if you can, ok?" Rachel seemed concerned.

My breaths were longer and slower, my heart was a stone in my chest.

"I'm ok. For now," I texted back, adding a skull emoji, just for fun.

"Optimism is the key," Rachel responded with a thumbs-up emoji. "So what don't you know?"

"I don't know what surprised me: seeing Mike almost with tears in his eyes, or not having any myself."

She waited for me to add more.

"I didn't feel anything: it was just a doll, a puppet looking like an ugly baby. I guess that's it."

"You didn't imagine your baby in that situation and you didn't think "What the hell would I do?""

No.

"What would you do?" Rachel probed.

"I don't know. I would probably freak out like anybody else."

When I opened my eyes, I was dropping off the baby at daycare. I was in a play room, where other children were already crawling, clumsily walking, or crying on their bellies. I placed the baby seated on a mat, and he kept his balance with some effort. A bigger boy came by to say hello and, before I could stop him, he pushed the baby, who fell backwards hitting his head. The baby started to scream like I had never heard anybody scream, so I picked him up and I shushed him in my arms. He suddenly stopped crying. He looked at me straight in the eyes for a second, then he rolled his eyes and he passed out, his body now a dead weight in my arms. The teacher looked at me with a pinch of terror in her eyes. I tried to caress and tickle the baby, but nothing seemed to work. He was still breathing, but his heartbeat was getting slower and slower. He regained consciousness for a moment, he shrieked, and he fell unconscious again. Panic was holding on to my throat, preventing words from coming out. I gazed at the teacher, who was already dialing 911.

"Don't worry," she said. "They will be here in a minute: the hospital is just around the corner."

I sat up in bed as soon as I woke up, and my sudden movements tore Mike off his dreams.

"Are you ok?" he asked, still half asleep.

"Yes. Somebody pushed the baby at school."

He smiled and he let me slide in his arms, "Nobody will ever push him: he will be the Harlem Hooligan and he will dominate the nursery. We will make "On Her Majesty's Secret Gangsta Service" onesies for him, and the message will be clear for everyone!"

I couldn't believe he had just made a movie-related joke.

Doctor Mallory was never much of a joker. Always serious and sporting a professional smile on her face, she measured my belly a few hours later during our monthly appointment.

She nodded while noting the increase in my abdominal diameter, "Your belly is growing just fine, and you might just have slightly more liquid than normal. There is nothing to worry about, though, because this sometimes happens to expecting mothers with gestational diabetes: the amniotic fluid is ingested and urinated by your baby, and babies sometimes tend to urinate more when their mothers have diabetes, to try and eliminate the surplus sugar. As long as your blood sugar is under control, though, we have nothing to worry about."

She didn't care about my missing weight gain, and the pain of my almost-zero-carb diet; the severe exercise requirements; the extreme frustration due to the ban of cookies from my life; the fact that the little heir was stealing all my nutrients, leaving me constantly hungry, perennially tired, never energetic.

"Your blood sugar levels are under control, right?" Doctor Mallory confirmed while I was pulling my pants up.

"The post-meal values are mostly ok, and I'm taking bedtime insulin to manage the fasting glucose."

"Right. Since you are on insulin, the guidelines demand that I put you on twice-weekly fetal monitoring. We need to make sure that the baby's heart beats at good speeds, both while accelerating, decelerating, and at standard rates, to confirm he's not affected by either hyperglycemia or hypoglycemia. Gestational diabetes can go either way for babies: they can get hit by the highs and the lows in the sugar cycle, and we don't want either. You will find a referral at checkout. Go Mondays and Thursdays, or Tuesdays and Fridays, as you prefer. Remember it can take up to sixty minutes each time, since we need to record the heartbeat of a full rest-activity-rest baby cycle."

She remembered she hadn't smiled for a few sentences, and she paused just for a second to fulfil her to-do.

"Any questions?"

I shook my head in disbelief: this freaking gestational diabetes was becoming a real burden. To the weekly checkups with the endocrinologist we were now adding this fetal monitoring twice a week. What else?

"Good. I also made you a referral for the Third Trimester scan, which you should try to book next week. In the scan we will measure the baby weight to confirm that everything is going according to plan. As babies of mothers affected by gestational diabetes tend to become bigger, and sometimes too big, we will probably think about the next steps in case the baby does not show up before your due date: at that point we might not want him to stay in there any longer."

Great, a C-section or an induced delivery would be the cherry on top of my daily cake - a cake that had to be sugar free and carbs free, obviously.

"And I will see you in three weeks," the doctor finished with a smile, leaving the exam room on her soft heels.

"Everything will be fine," Mike didn't lose a second. "I'll come with you for the first monitoring, and I'm sure it will be exciting to listen to his heartbeat twice per week!"

"One more thing to do," I could just repeat. "One more complication."

He stood up from his chair to take me in his arms.

"I know," he murmured. "You've been so great about making everything part of your routine, keeping your spirits high, so try to see this just as another piece of the puzzle. A more annoying and time consuming piece, but still just another fragment of a bigger picture."

I sighed. Two more months.

I was at my desk in the office, working on an article on what to expect during next season of Game of Thrones, when my mobile vibrated: my mother. My first instinct was to let it go, but then I remembered I had promised myself I would be a slightly less horrible daughter, so I picked up.

"Hello?"

"Hello, Amber," my father's voice roared. I had been probably fourteen the last time we had spoken on the phone.

"Oh. Hello, how are you?" I mumbled.

"You mother told me about the complications in your pregnancy. Do you feel good?"

I hesitated.

"Yes, I feel good, thank you," I responded after two seconds of frozen silence.

"The baby feels good, too?"

"Yes, everything is good with the baby, too," I was tempted to add, "Thank you, Sir," but I didn't.

"Very well. What is it that you have exactly? Your mother couldn't quite clarify for me."

"Oh. Well, I have gestational diabetes. It means my blood sugars are a bit too high, due to pregnancy hormones. But everything is under control: I just have to check my glucose a few times per day."

"Do you need to take medicines?" he fished for details.

"Nope. Just walk a bit, to stay active and burn those sugars, and keep things checked," I thought that was enough for my parents to know.

"Very well."

We both stayed silent for a few seconds, each waiting for the other one to say something.

"You know, Amber," he let go of a heavy sigh, "I have always valued discipline and respect for authority above all. I now realize I have been too severe with you, and I apologize."

My eyes opened wide, and I held my breath.

"I wanted you to follow the rules," he kept going on his railroad. "I wanted you to fit in the system, but not to imprison you, rather to make you take the most out of it, to strive in it and to use it to become whoever you wanted to become. I now see how I never listened to what you wanted, I never tried to understand who you were and who you were hoping to become. I am a bad father in the end."

My teenage self was screaming, "Yes, you are!" but I muted her, and I sighed.

"You are not a bad father," I soothed him. "You just did what you felt was right. We were not very compatible when I was a teenager, but then I was hardly compatible with anybody."

He snorted: agreement or smile?

"We all do our best with our children, that's all that matters in the end."

He now truly smiled, "Will you give me a second chance with my grandson?"

Was he going to be an all-allowing grandfather, one who didn't follow any of the baby's parents' guidelines, like my mother was already set to become?

I sighed and I tried to put up a smile, "Sure, dad, sure."

When Friday came, the weekly stress attacks accompanied me to the endocrinologist's practice. Sitting in her waiting room, I looked outside the window and I saw the first signs of spring on the trees outside her Upper West Side office. The due date was getting closer. I shook the thought out of my head when a nurse called me in.

"Thank you for sending me your weekly measures," Doctor Palmer greeted me when she joined me in the exam room. "How do you feel?"

The question caught me by surprise, as she didn't normally ask it.

"Well, I'm ok, I guess. I'm tired. And always hungry. And the belly is getting really heavy. But I believe it's normal."

She put on her soft smile, "It is all normal, I fear."

She paused.

"I see from your notes that you are exercising after every meal."

"I am. The values are always too high, even if I don't eat much."

"I understand," she nodded. "And sometimes the sugar doesn't go down below 120, even after exercise. How long do you walk or climb stairs for?"

"Sometimes I need twenty to thirty minutes," I responded with a grimace.

"That's what I thought," she smiled again, before she took a deep breath and she collected her energy to initiate a new speech. "I think your post-meal sugars are on the verge of getting out of control. As I can infer from your readings, your body is taking more and more time to process the sugars you intake during meals, probably due to increased hormonal levels in your blood. It is all normal: if you remember, we had discussed how gestational diabetes usually plateaus at some point between weeks thirty-four and thirty-eight."

I nodded, still unsure of what would come next.

"You are now in your thirty-first week, if I'm not mistaken, so your insulin intolerance is about to reach its peak. I however think it's better if we try to slow things down and hopefully regain control of the situation. I am going to prescribe you pre-meal insulin injections."

No!

My respiration suddenly accelerated. My nose tickled with incoming tears.

She looked at me straight in the eyes with a soft expression on her face, "I know this might seem like a lot, but trust me: you will get used to it very quickly. You are already doing bedtime injections, so you already have the technique. You will just need to plan a little bit in advance of your meals, as it is recommended to inject insulin ten minutes before a meal. Everything else remains the same: you measure your blood sugar one hour after each meal, you exercise if you need, and you keep sending me your readings and messaging me on the hospital's system if you have any questions. And if your measures slip out of control again, we can increase the insulin dosage to bring them back on our side."

She smiled and she patted my hand, "Everything will be alright. Do you happen to have your insulin pen with you now?"

I shook my head, still unable to speak.

"That would be better if you could start pre-meal insulin for lunch today," she explained.

I nodded.

"I am here if you need anything," she emphatically waved me goodbye.

I didn't move. I kept staring into the void of the exam room until a nurse opened the door wide.

"I am sorry, I didn't know you were still here!" she apologized.

I slowly turned my head to look at her, and she looked back at me with a question in her eyes. I mumbled something and I left the room.

It was chilly outside.

I had to go home to grab my insulin pen and then rush to work.

"I will be late for the staff meeting," I texted my boss. "So so sorry."

"Is everything ok?" she responded right away. "In any case, don't worry at all."

I took a mental note to tell Lauren about all the latest developments of my unlucky pregnancy. Especially since I now had to go to twice-weekly fetal monitoring sessions, she needed to know why I would not be in the office as much as I should have.

I reached the office right in time for the second half of the staff meeting, and I floated through it and the rest of my morning without paying much attention to anything.

When lunchtime came, with the heaviest heart I took the elevator down to pick up some food from one of the warm salad bars around the Freedom Tower. Once I regained the Vanity Fair's floor, I left my lunch on my desk, and I paced towards the restroom with my insulin pen.

The syringe pinched harder this time.

I set the alarm clock and I waited for ten minutes before eating my lunch, now cold and far from attractive.

What a lovely day.

The calendar invite popped up on my phone on a lazy Saturday morning, between a cappuccino and a New York Times article read on the sofa.

"Prepare hospital bag".

Like a verdict I had cast upon myself, inevitable. "Prepare hospital bag". My due date was two months away, and my very forward-looking plan called for the hospital bag to be prepared now. Now.

I slowly stood up from the couch, under Mike's perplexed gaze. I took my suitcase out from the closet and I placed it on the bed; the list open on my phone, I turned my head off. Shit was getting way too real.

The first section in my list was called Hospital Specific, and one lonely item dominated it: the ViaCord kit for umbilical cord blood and tissue conservation. We had to notify the nurses and give them the cord kit upon our arrival at the hospital on the big day. How would we remember, especially if things were to get rough quite early? The only thing I could do was trusting Mike.

The second section, Clothes, contained anything, from pajamas to go-home outfit, for the perfect mom-to-be. Where did I find that list? Probably a craft of consolidation of many sources, from What To Expect When You Are Expecting, to friends and colleagues.

Then the Toiletries came, a full batch of products from head to toe. I hadn't included my insulin in the list, since I had compiled it before the whole diabetes tantrum had been thrown at me. With a sigh, I stacked some needles and alcohol pads in the beauty case that was rapidly being filled with travel-sized products, and I left a note for myself to remember to pick up an insulin pen before leaving the house, when the time would come. I didn't even know if I was going to need it: shouldn't the gestational diabetes disappear after delivery? Not always, as Doctor Palmer admitted during one of our glucose checkups, not always. I didn't want to picture myself injecting insulin and checking my blood for all the years to come, so I shrugged and I went to the following set of items.

I barely repressed a laugh when I read the title of the next section: For Mike.

"What are you doing?" he peeked in from the door as he heard me giggling.

"I'm preparing the bag for the hospital."

I opened one of his drawers and I fished for a pair of underpants, "Underwear for you," I grinned. "Just in case you can't keep it together!"

He laughed at me and he looked for an older pair, "Take the ugly ones, in case I ought to crap my trousers!"

"No please," I shouted in a vaguely dramatic tone. "I will be doing all kinds of crazy horrible things, so try to keep our family's honor as high as you can."

He skeptically raised his eyebrows, then he sat on the bed to keep me company while I finished to fill in the suitcase.

I packed some go-home clothes for the baby, picking them from the pile of outfits we had received from Meredith, Mike's sister, during Christmas. I highlighted some items on my phone, to hopefully remember to grab them at the last second: my phone, my ID and my insurance card.

It was ready.

I surely wasn't, but we had done as much as we could. Now we had two more months to go, a few more pounds to take, several fetal monitoring sessions to pass, many more fingers to prick for glucose testing and thighs to sting with insulin injections.

Such a fun plan for the next sixty days.

THE WEEK WITH EIGHT DAYS' WORTH OF NIGHTMARES

"Now even the hospital bag is ready, so anything can happen!" I was proudly showing off during Sunday brunch.

Rachel smiled at me in approval, while Mike was distracted by his phone.

"Mike, that was so nice of you to join us today," I faked my best British accent. "But if you are indeed busy with work you ought to have remained at home."

He looked up from the screen with a pale embarrassment; he stared at Rachel and me for a couple of seconds, then he put his phone back in his pocket.

"Just one email," he explained, serious.

"I'm just teasing you," I had to clarify. He had become so sensitive: prey of his own maternal hormones?

Rachel looked at both of us and she patted our hands, "At less than two months now, does it start to feel real?"

Mike looked at me to exhort me to answer.

"It's hard to imagine ourselves with a baby," I gave it a try. "What will we do and how will we react when there will be a child in our apartment? A crying screaming little thing?"

Mike nodded, "The abstraction effort that is required way overtakes my capabilities."

"Not even making the hospital bag helped you visualize future events?" Rachel always wanted to get to the bottom of things.

I hesitated, "I just followed some instructions that I had put together months ago, and I didn't think much about it while I was doing it. Does it make sense?"

Rachel pulled off an automatic smile, "Sure, my dear, sure."

I was trying to add something more, to sound more empathetic towards Rachel and Mike, when my phone's alarm sounded: ten minutes had already passed since I had injected insulin in my left thigh, for the first time struggling to find a non-bruised spot that I could reach without too many contortions around my lumbering belly. I twisted my neck to check if any waiter was in sight and ask about our meals, then I sighed as I gave in, and I stuffed my mouth with a sample from the rich bread basket. I still had my phone in my hand, so I set up next alarm in sixty minutes, for the glucose check.

Mike captured the annoyed look on my face and Rachel tried to distract me, "How does it work: you need to start eating exactly ten minutes after the injection, so that the extra insulin can be put to work in your bloodstream?"

I nodded, my mouth still full.

She nibbled at a piece of focaccia, in a show of solidarity.

"Your food is on its way," a waiter assured us, as if he could read our minds.

I gazed outside the window. Even restaurants were hardly a pleasure anymore.

This time I was in a Robert Rodriguez movie. It was most likely Desperado, as a young Antonio Banderas jumped through the window of our brunch restaurant, pieces of glass flying all around his mariachi costume and his flowy hair. Fire and bullets came out of his guns, killing the cook, who now suddenly resembled Steve Buscemi, and our waitress, strangely looking just like Salma Hayek. Everybody in the restaurant was screaming, incredulous horror; Rachel was hiding under the table and Mike was shouting at me to get cover, throwing his hand out for me to grasp it and follow him. I didn't move. Bullets flew in all directions, so close to me that I could perceive their heat on my skin, but I didn't move. Antonio Banderas pointed his gun to my forehead, spitting out some words in Spanish that I couldn't understand.

"Hasta la vista, baby," was the last thing I heard before I opened my eyes in the darkness of my bedroom.

After the thrill of the dreamlike adventure and the close encounter with charming Antonio Banderas, standing up was an ordeal that morning: rolling out of bed was becoming more and more of a physical challenge, a discipline worthy of Olympic status. The effort left me breathless, and even Mike's gentle pushing support didn't have much of an effect. I rolled myself to the restroom to shower and then back to the bedroom to get ready, to the subway station and then on the train, where I bluntly stared at a man until he left me his seat. I walked up the stairs, out in the street, across half of the office's corridors to reach my desk, where my butt crashed on my chair. I could feel each bone, each muscle, and they all ached. With a grimace I remembered I had to get up again and give myself my pre-meal dose of insulin, before waiting for ten minutes to attack my nowadays meager cereal bar.

The sixty minute glucose check wake-up call came after what seemed like two seconds, as I had only written a handful of words for my new article: What The Latest Game Of Thrones Leak Means For Fans And Regular Watchers. I was horrified to find out that the few words I had aligned on the screen totally sucked.

I shook my head to clear my thoughts and decide what to do with my day.

Lightning struck me after a few minutes, and I dragged my heavy ass to Lauren's office.

"Hello?" I confirmed her presence while peeking into her office.

"Amber!" she immediately greeted me. "How are you?"

Long answer or short answer?

I decided for a fair share, "I'm ok."

"How's baby boy?" Lauren grinned at me.

"Well, that's exactly what I wanted to talk to you about," I jumped onto my chance. "Before you start to worry: everything is fine, we're both healthy. But since I am now taking insulin, I need to go to the hospital twice a week for fetal monitoring."

I interpreted her interrogative look as an encouragement to keep going, "Guidelines recommend checking the baby's heartbeat regularly to identify potential negative effects of gestational diabetes on him. They just need to attach a sensor to my belly to record his level of activity and rest and their cycles."

Lauren nodded.

"So I just wanted you to know where I am in case you come looking for me and I'm not here, on Tuesday and Friday afternoons."

"Don't even say it, Amber," she waved her hands in front of me, dismissing my company loyalty. "Do whatever you need: I'm here to support you all the way through. The only important thing is that you and this wonderful baby boy are healthy and carefree."

I would go for that, too.

"And this is his hair - can you see it here, all spiky?"

The nurse moved her mouse's arrow on the screen to point at some long, straight shadows departing from the top of the baby's head. Mike and I looked at each other: he already had hair! Was such a small detail enough to turn the unknown creature squatting in my belly into a real person?

If in the second trimester scan we could see the baby almost in his entirety, literally from head to toes, now we could just get the feeling of his full body, and we could peek into some of the details. The comfortable loft he was living in was slowly becoming a cramped studio. So typically New York City.

The hair was the simplest and yet somehow the most impressive element of the sonogram, but the nurse walked us through brain folds, fully working kidneys, busy with processing the constant flow of amniotic fluid through the pipes, and a maze of legs and arms and fingers. The nurse spent a good portion of the exam evaluating the baby's stomach and the large blood vessels, and measuring the diameter of the abdomen, the best proxy of the baby's weight.

"According to the calculations, and keep in mind there is a ten percent margin of error, your baby weighs already four pounds and eleven ounces."

"Is it big?" I tried, since I had no idea of what a big baby was.

"It is fairly big for thirty-two weeks," the nurse answered with a smile.

"What percentile is he in?" Mike nitpicked.

The nurse looked for a number on her screen, and then she solemnly announced that our offspring was at the seventy-ninth percentile.

"Doctor Mallory had told us he might get big, since I have gestational diabetes."

"As long as the baby is below the ninetieth percentile we are good, but the doctor will tell you what she thinks about it," she tried to reassure us.

Seventy-nine percent sounded pretty high to me, especially considering my narrow hips and not very muscular built: how would I get an eight-pounder out? Hadn't I read that babies can double their weight during the last two months? I sighed and I hoped the baby would be smarter than that, if he still wanted to see the light at the end of the tunnel.

As soon as we left the room, I took pictures of the photos taken during the scan, and I sent them to my parents.

My mother responded in the blink of an eye, "He already looks like you! Can't wait to see you this weekend."

Crap. I had totally forgotten they were spending the weekend in New York. Maybe this time it wouldn't be that bad.

I had scheduled the first fetal monitoring right after the sonogram, so Mike and I were accompanied to a large room at the end of the corridor. It was populated by many small alcoves, shielded by curtains. A nurse helped me lay on a bed and she strapped two sensors on my belly, their long cables connected to the humming machine next to the bed.

Detecting the puzzled looks on our faces, Juliana, the nurse, soothed us with a smile, "This is your first monitoring session, right?"

Mike and I nodded simultaneously.

Juliana played with buttons and wheels, until the sound of the baby's heartbeat came out of the machine. An ecstatic smile twisted Mike's face in a split second; I kept my eyes on the nurse. She grabbed the paper that the machine had already started to slowly spit out, "What we need to do here is collecting information on a full baby cycle, rest-activity-rest, to measure the accelerations and decelerations in his heartbeat, and make sure he has just the right amount of sugar in his own bloodstream."

Three trend lines were forming on the paper, and Juliana's fingers moved in between them to describe what we were seeing, "The first one on top is the baby's heart. We want it to be between 120 and 160 in its baseline, and it can go above or below during those accelerations and decelerations. The second line is your pulse, and we want it to be slow and steady. The third line plots baby's movements: see, now he's moving," as I could easily confirm from the bumps going from left to right in my round belly. "And his heart rate is on the high side of the range. This is good, but we will need him to rest, so that we can identify his baseline and then compare it to the peaks and valleys of his activity. The last line, here at the bottom, records your uterine activity and it tells us if you're having any contractions."

She paused for a second, to check if we were following, and I swiftly thanked her for the explanations. Mike seemed lost in the baby's sounds. Juliana disappeared behind the curtain and into the corridor, ready to go check on other patients and promising she would be back every few minutes to evaluate the trends.

The earlier sonogram must have boosted the baby's excitement, because he kept rolling around at full force for almost one hour. Every time Juliana would come back she would focus on the printed records, her hands moving left and right on the paper to count the minutes that had passed and trying, unsuccessfully, to get to a baseline. She had me lying flat on my back, then sit up, than lying on my left side, then again on my back, trying to get the baby to stop his happy tantrum.

"I'm hungry," I burst out, immediately clearing my throat to regain control. "And he might be, as well: he always goes crazy when he's hungry."

She allowed me to eat some almonds, one of the snacks I always carried in my bag, as my no-sugar diet quite often left me with zero energy. The effect was almost immediate: once fed, I could imagine the baby sitting on a folding chair on the beach, his arms crossed behind his head, sassy sunglasses, Hawaiian swimsuit and all, finally relaxing. Juliana was sincerely amazed, her eyes wide open to follow the printed heartbeat line.

Things went smoothly from there: the heir in flip flops kept quiet long enough for Juliana to get her baseline and the deceleration she needed; he then decided to take a walk on the shore, giving us some sweet accelerations.

More than ninety minutes had passed, when I could finally get rid of the sensors' itching straps around my belly, and rush to the restroom. By the time we got home, we had lost a whole afternoon of work, that both Mike and I had to make up for later that night. At least everything looked good, and whatever was wrong with me and my internal insulin management didn't seem to be affecting the baby. Hopefully next time the belly tenant would be more willing to cooperate in the process.

I woke up with B-movie images in my mind: somebody running after me with a huge metallic syringe from the 1930's, screaming what sounded like terrifying words in German. I shook my head to let the remains of my last nightmare fade away in the dim light of dawn. As soon as I remembered it was Friday, I connected those images to my weekly challenge: the appointment with Doctor Palmer. I sighed and I hoped she wouldn't prescribe me additional injections, for whatever reason.

When I reached her practice's building and I found out all elevators were out of service, I interpreted it as a bad omen, and I used the long minutes it took me to climb up the three flights of stairs to prepare for the worst.

Unexpectedly, the doctor dismissed me fairly quickly, "Your values have been good this week, and I think we started with the correct dosage of pre-meal insulin. Keep messaging me with your readings, and let me know if fasting or post-meal sugars go above threshold."

She wished me a good weekend while waving goodbye and leaving the exam room. Not bad after all.

I texted Rachel as soon as I left the doctor's office, "No tragedy this week!"

She responded with a fireworks emoji, full celebration.

Mike reacted in the exact same way, but he couldn't stop himself from adding some forward looking remarks, "Are you going to tell your parents about the injections or are you going to plan some subterfuges not to have them find out?"

Party killer.

"Relax, they don't even sleep at our place."

"Fair point," he tapped back with a smiling emoji. "What's the plan for the weekend?"

"We are meeting them for brunch, both Saturday and Sunday, and they will come home with us on Saturday afternoon. But Rachel will be there too, so she will capture my father's attention as usually. They are going to a show on Saturday night with Barbara and David, the usual thank you for having them over for the weekend. They go back to Shithole, Connecticut, on Sunday afternoon."

"I can't believe this is the last time I see you before the baby is born," my mother was gripping my hand on Saturday, as she had strategically picked the place next to me at the table, leaving my father and Rachel in front of us and Mike at the head of the table.

I gave a hint of a smile: I couldn't believe it either.

"It's your last month, so I want you to take as much rest as you can. Barb and Dave are being so kind to us: they told us we can come any time when the baby is born, without notice. They will just want to see lots of pictures! They are great friends."

She sighed, exchanging adoring gazes with my father.

"I can't wait to be a grandma!"

She stared at me for a few very long seconds, waiting for me to say something. Anything. There was only one thing I wanted to say.

"I have to pee."

THE WEEK WITH EIGHT GALLONS OF PEE

The first time it happened it startled me. I woke up on Monday in what looked like the middle of the night, my eyes wide open, my brain fully operational. What was going on? I checked the time: a few minutes after four in the morning. A stinging pain going through the lower right side of my abdomen. Was I having contractions?

Nope. I had to pee.

I sighed and I blamed the baby for always pushing against some vital spots. I slowly rolled on my left side, I slid my legs out of the sheets and towards the ground, and I finally stood up from the bed, trying my best not to wake up Mike in the process. Guided by the street light coming in from the window, I reached the restroom. Something in my brain clicked right when I closed the door and I turned the light on: the first pee of the day had to be tested for ketones. Everything looked more complicated at four in the morning, but I managed to grab a plastic cup and pee in it without too much liquid getting on my hands or anywhere else. Once the strip assumed a pinkish hue, the sign of just a few traces of ketones in my urine, I threw everything away and I went back to sleep.

Right.

I was by then fully awake, and I spent the following two hours occasionally falling back to a drowsy state, getting strange blurry visions of monsters pursuing me, and waking up again after just a few minutes. In the end I decided to get ready and go to work.

The day was the hardest since the start of my pregnancy: exhaustion possessed me; a perception of my uterus being impossibly stretched and my other internal organs being kicked around; discomfort, and pins all along my spine; the suffocating demands of continuous injections and blood checks.

While I was pitying myself, my face in my hands, Lauren stopped by my desk.

She caressed my hair, "Are you ok?" she whispered.

I raised my head and I met her eyes. I couldn't find anything to say, so I nodded.

She smiled, "Do you want a cup of tea?"

I nodded again, and I followed her in the pantry.

Later that afternoon, I was pacing as fast as I could in the corridor, to help my glucose reach a safe 120, from the merciless 135 I had achieved thanks to a small portion of rice. I had just climbed two flights up and I was panting my lungs out, when I turned a corner and I bumped, literally, into the magazine's editor in chief. He opened his arms and a large grin popped up on his face.

"Look at you!" he burst out. "You are beautiful."

The honest light in his eyes made me smile for the first time that day.

"After lunch exercise?" he explored.

I hesitated for a second.

"Yes, it helps after a meal."

He nodded, knowingly.

"How do you feel?"

I hesitated again, before putting up a strong self-confident smile, "Heavy!"

He laughed and he squeezed my shoulder, "You're one of those women who wear pregnancy like a dress: the moment you'll take it off, you will get your body back."

I thanked him for having somehow said the exact thing I wanted to hear, and for letting me forget about my physical exhaustion for about five seconds.

That night, collapsed on the sofa, I worked hard to convince myself that I had just had a bad day.

"Sorry for being such a pain today," I apologized to Mike.

He gazed up from the children education book he was reading with exhilarated enthusiasm.

I sighed.

An enormous smile occupied his face as he took me in his arms, carefully caressing my belly.

"I'm always here," he tried to soothe me.

"You will be in Chicago the rest of the week so, technically, you are not always here."

Mike laughed and he smooched me on a cheek, "It's just for two nights: I will return on Friday and then, as I promised, I will be by your side until our baby boy is at least two months old. I know you will enjoy the time on your own, with Rachel sleeping here, the two of you binge watching that bizarre TV show you tried to fob me off with last week… You'll love it!"

I forced a smile, "You're always right," I noticed with a mildly derisory tone.

Needless to say, he was right: I couldn't wait to see Rachel on Wednesday night, and I was eager to have her all for me until Friday night.

I was waiting for her on the sofa, typing the last sentences of an article on a very promising new HBO science-fiction TV show, when Mike texted me, "Just landed! Love you."

I sighed with relief, as my day had started with a too realistic nightmare of his plane crashing and everybody on board horribly dying. There seemed to be no end to the convoluted creations of my sleeping brain.

I texted a series of hearts and kisses to Mike, and I resumed work until the doorbell rang.

"Seamless," Rachel yelled from the other side of the intercom, holding a plastic bag in front of her face. I laughed and I buzzed her in.

"What did you bring?" I asked as I was opening the door to let her in.

"Oh, hello to you too!" she scolded me.

"Right, right. Hello my dear friend Rachel," I mocked her while hugging her and kissing her on the cheeks. "I hope you had a wonderful day at work. Thank you for ordering our dinner on Seamless and bringing it over to your tired whiny friend."

"There you go," she grinned back.

"So what did you get?" I went for it again, while she was removing her shoes in the entrance and dropping the plastic bag on the kitchen counter.

"Pad thai, with barely any noodles and a lot of chicken and eggs for you!"

"I love you," I hugged her again. "Now please let's eat."

"I love you too," she looked at me straight in the eyes. "I love you too, so much, Amber."

"How are you?" she asked me much later that night, after a few hours spent having dinner, chatting, and watching Bring It On for the twentieth time.

I took my time to climb in bed and roll to a decent position, before answering her, "I'm fine."

"Amber, how are you, really?"

"Really? I'm fine."

She looked at me, her eyes two slits.

"Really. You're fine. Everything is awesome," she challenged me, for some reason.

"Don't go all Counselor Chambers on me: I'm telling you, everything is fine. I'm fat and drained, I have bruises all over my thighs and my fingers, I can't eat anything, most days I literally want to kill myself, but everything is absolutely fine."

I smirked and I looked away.

She kept looking at me with her eyebrows frowned, before she took a breath and she gave it a last try, "I'm here for you, always, for anything. Just talk to me."

She was worrying about me way too much.

"I'm fine," I repeated for the last time, squeezing her hand. "But you're the best sister I've never had."

Eventually I got used to the middle-of-the-night pee-alarms, and I accepted them as part of the necessary routine for the last few weeks of my pregnancy. Day after day, I developed impressive skills: rolling out of bed without making a sound; peeing in a cup with my eyes barely open and no spilling on my hands.

The second part of my daily routine was the visual inspection: every morning I looked at myself in the mirror, only my underwear on, to monitor how and how much and where I was gaining weight. Had my ass expanded, yet? Were my thighs getting fatter, beyond the swelling induced by insulin injections? Were my breasts still getting bigger? Did I still recognize myself in the mirror?

Rachel smiled at me while getting ready for work on Friday morning.

"Jealous of these babies?" I joked, hinting at my breasts.

"Man, those are beautiful, indeed," she pretended to admire them. "Can I touch them?"

I started to laugh, and once again I thanked her for being there, as I did when we reached my Upper West Side stop on the subway and I got off. I left her on the train waving at me, both of us looking forward to seeing each other again that night for dinner, before Mike would come back from Chicago. I stepped up the stairs slowly, focusing on my breathing; I had to preserve some energy for the ten minute walk that would bring me to the endocrinologist's practice, my unmissable Friday routine.

"So how was the doctor?" Rachel asked me while sipping her glass of wine at dinner.

We hadn't eaten in a restaurant just the two of us for some time, and I was excited about our date.

"Uneventful," I smiled.

"Which means great," she agreed. "And the rest of your day?"

"The usual Friday text from my mother—"

"That's good, too."

I shook my head and I nodded at the same time, "I guess."

"How about you?" I asked her right away. I had enough about myself and my sad pregnancy stories. "Do you have anything that could make me feel less old and less fat?"

"You know, I always have something," she came closer to me with a conspiratorial grin. "There is one quite new girl in the office, one of the associates we hired last summer, who is starting to show... her personality."

She was interrupted by the waiter, who removed the empty appetizer plates and replaced them with our entrees, but she resumed her narration as soon as she could, "Apparently, on a late night in the otherwise empty office, this girl helped both the male partner and the female senior associate release the pressure they had accumulated on the case."

"You mean, she had some form of sex with one, and then the other? Or..."

"Come on, she was professional: both at the same time."

I raised my eyebrows with some admiration, "What a dedication to her job."

"You bet. Being a lawyer is so hard in this city."

"I know. You're one of the very few who could make it without sleeping around," I winked at her.

"Exactly," she raised her glass and she cheered.

I cheered to her, with my glass of unsweetened lemonade, and I thanked her for being her good ol' Rachel, to which she responded with a little bow of her head.

My phone vibrated, breaking our enchantment: blood check time. I snorted and I took my glucose testing pouch out of my purse. I eyed the restroom and, when I saw the line in front of it, I decided to prick my finger there at the table, partially hidden by the fashionably dimmed lights in the dining room.

Rachel followed my gestures with laser eyes, and she inspected my face expressions when the small machine spit out the answer: 130. She read the frustration in my eyes and she asked for the check.

"Let's go for a walk," she suggested. "I'm sure it will improve right away."

I didn't feel like walking, even less so when the wind and drizzle brushed us as soon as we got out. Rain washed my face. Rachel took me by the arm and she shared her umbrella with me.

"Let me do this for you," she insisted.

As soon as I hopped on my Uberpool ride back home, I received a text from Mike, "Landed!" it just said. I smiled: two days had been short, but I had missed him.

His face fully occupied my thoughts for a few minutes, until a hand opened the car door and a couple sat next to me on the back seat. Uberpool was quite cheap, and convenient if the other clients were at least polite; being Friday night, I was ready for anything. The woman of the couple quickly glanced at my enormous belly before addressing me a smile and turning her head to resume the conversation with her partner. They made a nice-looking couple: holding hands, whispering in each other's ears and smiling with their eyes. They seemed very close, and they seemed to be aware of the preciousness of what they had.

"Just like Mike and I", I thought.

I loved the intimacy of our dates, and how we would always hold hands from opposite sides of the table, our fingers finding their way among forks and glasses.

I fished for my mobile in my bag, captured by an idea.

"Let's talk when you get home," I texted Mike. "I want to institute Friday Date Nights: we get a sitter and we spend some time the two of us. Or with adult friends, if there's a special occasion. Every Friday, no exceptions."

The message notification popped up on my phone a few seconds later, "Waiting for my cab. It's a perfect idea!"

I smiled and I sent him a heart-shaped emoji. My nose started to itch, and a small tear formed at the corner of my left eye. I focused on the street lights passing by outside the car window.

"I love how you planned an unconventional baby shower, where men are allowed to participate!"

Mike was getting dressed for our party, a Saturday afternoon with a few friends, sugar-free snacks and nonalcoholic drinks. He and Rachel had insisted we organized a baby shower, and I had agreed only provided that they avoided anything too exaggeratedly baby-themed. I loathed those ladies-only celebrations, the movie cliché with squeaking women offering dubious taste gifts and building diaper cakes. Rachel had also taken care of the presents: she had collected money from our friends and she had bought an Amazon gift card. Mike and I didn't want to receive any concrete present before the baby came, as it was common in many European countries - but money was always welcome.

Rachel was the first to arrive, well in advance to help with the latest arrangements, and bringing a pack of balloons that she freed in our living room. A cloud of "it's a boy" and "welcome baby" spread towards the ceiling.

"You had to let me do something stupid," Rachel half apologized while hugging me, before resuming her grin. "Shall we put out the food? People will arrive soon."

She and Mike placed cheese on wooden cutting boards, they arranged raw vegetables in colored bowls, and they occupied all our serving plates with a vast collection of sugar-free cupcakes and muffins, all while I was seating on the sofa and peacefully observing the scene. That part of being pregnant was my favorite. For several minutes they kept walking back and forth between the open kitchen bar and the sofa area, getting our coffee tables progressively covered in plates and glasses. We had so many wooden coffee tables in our living room, most of them purchased during our honeymoon in Southern Africa. We had been married for years now, but each piece carried vivid memories of that trip: the places we had visited and the people we had met were still casting a spell upon us. Mike had wanted to travel to Africa to honor his origins and get a glimpse of a continent he hadn't yet visited. He had picked a few countries in

Southern Africa, rather than his own Nigeria, to immerse ourselves in the widest range of experiences. I had followed him in his desire without really knowing what to expect, and we had both come back with our hearts touched by the beauty of the landscapes and the resilience of their inhabitants. Every time I looked at the giraffe-shaped coffee table or at one of the many elephant statues, I could see the colors of a sunset in the Namibian Kalahari desert, smell the perfumes of the Okavango River in Botswana, hear the wind blowing through the branches of a marula tree in Zimbabwe. And it wasn't just the coffee tables and that specific trip: everything in our home told our story. Our furniture had been selected from different stores, ranging anywhere from IKEA to fancy European brands. Most decorations came from our trips around the world: boxes and rugs from an adventure across South America, pictures taken in the UK countryside through the years, small divinity statues from India, colorful frames holding photos of our wedding in Puerto Rico. I wouldn't change anything.

But as I kept gazing around, signs of the baby's presence started to materialize in the living room, remainders of a dream: a bottle of formula among wine glasses, a burp cloth on the sofa armrest, a high chair next to the kitchen bar.

Everything faded away when the doorbell rang, and Mike's work friend Ryan and his wife Cheryl kicked off the party. My boss Lauren and her wife Kate followed a few minutes later, and we all could enjoy some adult-only conversation, before the friends with kids showed up: Leslie and Robert, with their eight- and three-year-old daughters, and Julia and Charles with their one-year-old boy.

Receptions usually degenerate after too much alcohol has been served to thirsty guests, who indulge in the unnecessary additional glass before losing control of their mouths and brains. The issue with this party was the exact opposite: there was no alcohol. Especially for me. Especially when the children started to run and scream and cry and try to color the walls with crayons.

"You have to excuse her," Leslie was apologizing to Lauren for her eldest daughter, who was investigating why Kate was not a man. Lauren was laughing at my evident embarrassment.

At the same time, Robert, who was an MBA classmate of Mike's and whom we had known for many years, was busy with their youngest daughter, who had decided to hide some cherry tomatoes under the living room's carpet, and she was about to smash them.

Rachel and Charles, who had gone to Harvard Law School together and who had been friends for fifteen years, were cheerfully swearing while cleaning spilled orange juice from the floor. Julia was sitting next to me, and we were both deafened by her crying baby.

"He's teething," she explained with a sigh.

I nodded with empathy.

"He's been fucking teething for six months," she then added, with a flicker in her left eye.

Awesome.

"But at least he's sleeping at night now: the sleep training worked, thank God. Do you plan to do it?"

"For sure," I responded with no hesitation. "As soon as possible. I read—"

"Oh no!" Leslie jumped in. "Don't force your baby into an unnatural routine: sleep training can be very dangerous if your baby is small and he can't eat enough. Do you know what FTT is?"

It sounded like a sexually transmitted disease. I shook my head.

"FTT: Failure To Thrive. It's when babies don't get enough food, because you force them to wait too long in between feedings to do the stupid sleep training, so they don't grow, and they get sick. Not worth it."

"I mean, you have to be smart with it, like with anything else," Julia didn't want to let it go. "There are rules to follow and there is a process. I wish I had done it ten months ago!"

"I definitely do not agree," Leslie didn't want to let it go, either. "It's like breastfeeding: they tell you to stop at six months, but I kept going until eighteen, and see how wonderful my babies are now!"

Her eight-year-old was banging her three-year-old's head against the wall. We all looked elsewhere.

"Anyway, you should breastfeed as long as possible," Leslie concluded.

Without a word, Julia removed a bottle of formula from its thermic bag, and she started to feed it to the baby, who immediately calmed down. Leslie followed the scene with a disapproving gaze.

"I bet you even got an epidural, am I right?" Leslie hissed at Julia, whose face opened up in a smile.

"Of course I did, and it was the best decision of my life. Amber," Julia turned her head towards me. "Don't let the fashionability of natural labor trick you: get everything you can."

"Right, at this point we should even be asleep, and just have C-sections," Leslie grunted.

My head was about to explode.

"Excuse me, ladies," I stood up and I paced towards the bathroom, sneaking in the bedroom at the last second. I sat on the bed and I tried to delete the conversation from my memory.

Rachel slid into the room with a grin, and she closed the door behind her back, "I can't imagine why you had to escape that delightful mama drama."

I snorted and I tried to smile back at her.

"At least they didn't get into the details of their own labors: I've already heard their stories so many times that I promise I can't handle one more. Even Julia, who's usually so normal, becomes possessed when there's a baby conversation!"

Rachel sat next to me, "You have to keep telling yourself: they just want to help. They've already been through it and they're trying to pass on their wisdom, or whatever it is they learned through their own experience."

"It doesn't look like help, it feels more like a constant critique, a never stopping flow of instructions," I grumbled.

She smiled at me, "Don't take it personally. It's just their way of sharing what they've been through and showing you their love and affection. You should thank them!"

She stood back up and she threw her hand out to me. I grabbed it with a heavy sigh, and I followed her back into the living room, where Mike welcomed me with a silent grin.

Later that evening, I could swear I saw a pacifier in a corner of the second bedroom. Whether I liked it or not, the baby was already there.

NINE

THE WEEK NINE YEARS IN THE MAKING

"—and then I told him my bed was surely much more comfortable than his, so we should give it a try as soon as possible!"

Rachel and I were having such a great time: dinner at our favorite Mexican restaurant in the West Village, an empty sangria pitcher on the table and a second one strategically placed in front of us. My head was light with alcohol and my laughs were loud. She was totally drunk. As I laughed at her joke, I slammed a hand on my toned belly.

"What did he say?" I asked her right away, filling the glasses and cheering to her fierce pursuit of occasional sex.

"He called an Uber!" she burst out laughing.

I roared with her, so long and so strong that my belly ached. When I touched it, a bump was appearing on it. I looked down to see what was going on, and an excruciating pain exploded in my brain.

I screamed as loud as I could.

"What's wrong?" Rachel jumped up and she ran next to me.

"It hurts!" was all I could say.

I stood up and I kicked the chair far behind me, holding my stomach with both my arms and doubling over in unbearable pain. As I kept shrieking, Rachel and two waiters laid me down on the table and they tried to hold me still.

A beam of agony and blood darted out of my protruded chest, painting Rachel's face in red. Everybody stopped screaming, except me, and the restaurant fell silent.

My abdomen was burning and aching as if somebody had shot me from my interior. I kept screaming my lungs off.

Another gush of blood came out from what was now an open wound in my chest, and this time something followed the blood. A little head peeked out from my abdomen and it turned around to look at me. When its eyes met mine, an evil light possessed them, and the horrid mouth opened wide in a smile.

Before I lost consciousness, I could hear the monster's mouth articulate one word, its black pupils still fixated into mine.

"Mom!"

"Shit!" I mouthed as soon as I woke up. I had watched Alien too many times.

I didn't even need to check my phone to know it was the middle of the night: a perfect darkness permeated the bedroom. I sighed and I resigned myself to look for my lost sleep.

After what had seemed hours of bouncing my huge belly around in bed, peeing in a cup and measuring my ketones, going back to bed and trying to catch some sleep, the alarm went finally off. The phone told me it was Wednesday morning, and in a bolt of clarity of mind I remembered, "I only have six weeks to go".

"What?"

I must have spoken out loud, because Mike's sleepy eyes turned towards me, trying to decipher the words I had mumbled.

"I said: I only have six weeks to go."

His mouth quickly went from a suppressed yawn to a large smile. He crawled towards me in bed and he caressed my cheek, then my belly.

"Six weeks and then we'll get to meet the little lad," he said in between smiles.

"Maybe even less than six weeks," I responded, turning my head away from him to check my phone. "Let's see how next sonogram goes: if he's already too big in two weeks maybe Doctor Mallory will decide to get him out sooner rather than later."

"When did you say you are going to buy the last things from Amazon?" he asked.

"This weekend: as you know the list is ready."

"The same excel file you had prepared for the IKEA shopping, right?"

I could sense the pinch of irony in his voice, but I decided to ignore it, "Right."

Mike gave me a last kiss, before he jumped out of bed, grabbing his phone and heading towards the shower.

I followed him with my usual slow combination of rolling over towards the side of the bed and sliding my feet down to reach the floor. I removed my pajama and I got ready for my morning encounter with the mirror. It always surprised me to notice how normal my legs and hips still looked, as if nothing was going on. But the big round bump was still there, a basketball somebody had stuck in the middle of my torso, forcing my navel to stick out and my skin to stretch to its physical limit. At least I would not be forced to look at that image for much longer: in a few weeks the roundness would be gone. Would I then glimpse the shadow of my old self hidden behind the remaining layers of fat? The changes inflicted to my body had to be just temporary: I hoped I had the strength to take back control, and reverse the trend that had dragged me down the fattening path in the last months. I grinned at the mirror.

Then I had to go to work, and my smile decided to remain securely at home. The good side of waking up early in the morning was that I could usually find a seat on my long subway run from the Upper West Side to Downtown Manhattan. Usually, but obviously not today; signal malfunctions, the MTA explanation for any delay, were pestering the A B C D line that morning. When the train finally approached my station, it was full of furious commuters. I threw myself in the first door, and I held my breath until I reached my office floor.

I walked by Lauren's desk on my way to my spot in the open space, and I peeked in the open door to say hello.

"How do you feel, my dear? Did you recover from the baby shower?" she grinned.

"I don't know," I shook my head in staged disbelief. "It was a hell of a party."

Lauren laughed, but she immediately regained her poise, "You let me know if there's anything I can do for you, ok? Anything."

There was a click in my brain, and words came out on their own.

"Actually, would it be ok if I worked more from home? Coming to the office is a nightmare sometimes."

Wait, it wasn't that bad, or was it?

"That's an easy one!" Lauren didn't hesitate. "You can work from home as much as you want. You can conference in for the staff meetings, and just call for anything else. I don't want to see you here anymore in a couple of weeks! I don't want you to break your waters here in the office: who would clean the mess?"

The way back home was possibly as bad as the way in, as the rush hour crowd pushed me and they shoved me all the way from my building to the subway train doors. Once inside the train, my fellow New Yorkers were so focused on their phones that they didn't even look at me, let alone notice my belly. That wasn't unusual, though: apart from a handful of exceptions when someone, usually a woman, had left me her seat, nobody would even see me. Most of the times I was doing just fine. The thirty-minute ride was manageable, and there were quite a few pivotal stops, like West 4 or Penn Station, where people would change trains and vacate their seats, and my tired ass could find quick relief. But there were times when my legs couldn't hold my weight, and they were becoming more frequent. If I had slept worse than usual during the night, or if I had had a more stressful day, or a longer standing time, or all of the above, then the temptation to ask someone if I could please sit was really high. And yet somehow I never did. I suffered in silence, and I kept waiting, ashamed of myself. As if acknowledging that I was tired would sound like confessing a crime, admitting that I needed help, that I couldn't make it on my own.

"You deserve to sit," Rachel reacted when I texted her about my controversial feeling. "You should just open your coat, put your hands below your belly to sustain it, and wear some badge saying, "Let the pregnant lady sit!". I'm sure people would fight to offer you their place."

She wasn't joking.

"I mean it, Amber: you are manufacturing a human being in your belly, you are using twice the energy than anybody else on that train, and you should be fierce about it, like a pack of Amazons riding their horses in the forest."

"Nice metaphor. Did you just re-read a number of Wonder Woman?"

She responded with the facepalm emoji.

She was right, I knew she was. And yet, I still never asked to seat, I could never bring myself to it. The human mind is complicated.

The little girl came out of the TV screen, crawling on the floor and fixating her zombie eyes into mine, leaving me petrified by fear.

For shit's sake, not The Ring!

I rubbed my face in disbelief in the pitch black of the bedroom, somewhere in the middle of the night. I rolled on my back, to give some rest to my left side, compressed under the weight of my body. With my hands crossed behind my head, I waited for my heartbeat to fall back to a normal pace, before changing position again and preparing to wait for dawn. My brain, fully operative even before the usual pilgrimage to the restroom for the morning ketone check, informed me it was Friday. It was the day of diabetes follow-ups and fetal monitoring. And what else? I tapped on my mobile phone to open the calendar app, and a reminder occupied the second part of the afternoon, after the endocrinologist appointment and the fetal monitoring session: call Chloe.

Crap.

I hadn't thought about her since she had dropped her breast cancer bomb, but somehow I had blocked time on my personal calendar to give her a call. I sighed. What was I going to tell her?

The thought kept me awake until the alarm went off, a few hours later, and in the afternoon it accompanied me to Doctor Palmer and to the hospital, where it echoed the baby's pulse. It sat next to me on the bus that brought me home, silently disapproving of my incapability to find an answer, any answer, to my own question.

Once I got home, I hoped Mike would join me soon, giving me the perfect excuse not to contact Chloe. He texted me to warn me he would be late, instead, and he would join me and Rachel directly at the restaurant, a couple of hours later. Out of options, I went through my contacts and I searched for Chloe's number. Right before it was too late, I remembered I hadn't yet heard from my mother, who had taken the habit to text me or call me every Friday now. With a proud grin on my face, I kept scrolling down my list of contacts, until I found the number to call.

"It's so great to hear from you, my dear! How is our baby boy doing?"

I sighed: my mother's priorities had never been straighter.

"He's doing very fine, thank you. He's strong and healthy, and—"

"That's good," she interrupted me. "Thank you for letting me know, unfortunately I have to go: dad and I are getting ready for dinner. Let me call you back tomorrow, alright sweetie?"

Never a satisfaction from her.

I hung up and I kept the phone in my hand a little while longer, mentally revising how I was going to open my conversation with Chloe.

After one last sigh, the game was on.

"Oh my God, Amber!" she started to sob as soon as she picked up the phone. "I can't believe you're calling me: we just talked a couple of weeks ago. Did you have the baby?"

"No no," I reassured her. "I just wanted to know how you were hanging in there, after the news you gave me last time."

Somehow she managed to cry even louder, "You're such a good friend! I already feel so much better just by talking to you."

"I'm happy you feel better, that's all I wanted to hear," I was totally winging it. "Are you following some treatment? I hope it works and it's not too hard on you."

Chloe stopped sobbing, and her voice became more poised, "Well, yes I'm doing the first chemo cycle, and it's been fine so far. It's very tiring and it leaves me drowsy for two, three days, but then I slowly go back to my normal self, taking care of Jasper and all. And then the following dose comes up."

She sighed, sounding more adult than I had ever seen her.

"In the end Jasper is the one who's suffering the most," she recaptured the train of her thoughts. "He doesn't understand why mommy doesn't play with him, and why she keeps crying, but at least he's happy that daddy is home earlier at night and all day during the weekend."

"How do you feel?"

"I keep wondering why me, what did I do wrong."

I could see her eyes buried behind her grief.

"You didn't do anything wrong," my voice was a soft hug. "It just happens. You just have to stay strong and positive; tell yourself you are going to fight this thing and give Jasper his mom back. You have a family who love you very much, and they will give you all the energy you need. And I'm here, too: tell me if I can help you with anything."

She smiled, "I knew you were still there, somewhere."

"What?"

"You've been hiding from me, Amber. You've been avoiding me, trying to forget about me. I always have to call you to try and talk to you: you've never called me in the past nine years, you know? Nine years. But I never lost faith. I knew you were still there. I know people change, but I was sure you hadn't changed that much. You're a good person. You have been mean to me and you haven't seen Jasper in I don't know how long, but you're still a good person."

A tear rolled down a cheek, but this time it was mine.

"I am sorry."

"Don't be. I'm not a child, I know people change and they find new friends. We should just not forget that we were true friends once, and true friendship isn't supposed to end. I still love you. Just try to remember you still love me, too."

"I do."

I wiped out a second tear as I reported to Rachel my conversation with Chloe. We were at the bar of the restaurant Rachel had picked for dinner, and we were waiting for Mike.

"She's right, you know?" I was telling Rachel.

"I know," she responded. "And I'm happy you know, too."

I nodded, "I promised I will visit her soon after the baby is born: it will make her feel better, a new baby to focus on."

Rachel squeezed my hand and she hugged me.

"See, you're definitely still yourself."

On a cold Saturday, right after a rushed lunch at home, Mike and I went to the hospital for a guided tour of the maternity department. I was already familiar with the huge compound on the East Side of Manhattan, which I had been visiting twice per week for my fetal monitoring sessions, but the delivery department was a brand new adventure for both of us.

Once we reached the seventh floor of the West Pavilion, we were shown to a meeting room by the check in personnel. There, a nurse greeted us and she handed us a paper with some reminders of where to check in once the time would come, and what to bring to the hospital. Mike and I went through the list of clothing and toiletries, and we snickered at each other: with our hospital bag ready in the closet, we felt like pros.

NINE

Once the room was full of expecting couples, with belly diameters and levels of anxiety ranging from slightly smaller than mine to worryingly bigger, the nurse commenced her spiel with a smile.

"Hello everyone, my name is Joanna. Welcome to the hospital tour. I will tell you a few things here, and then we will visit the department, a labor room, and a postpartum room."

She smiled frequently and honestly, like someone who's used to deal with people in emergency situations, who need to be calmed down and reassured.

"You always have to remember to bring two things with you when you check in: your ID and your insurance card—"

"Can we check in now?"

"What?" the nurse looked around to identify the person who had asked the question, and her eyes stopped on a lady with her hand half raised.

"Can we check in now?" the lady repeated.

"No, you can't. You can check in only when you come here in labor. Not now," the nurse kept her smile lit up, then she resumed her speech. "But thank you for your question, and feel free to stop me at any time, of course. So I was saying, always bring your ID and insurance card to check in, even if we already have you in the hospital's system. Once you are checked in, we put you in the triage room to take your vitals and we run a full exam on you, to decide how fast we need to act. If you are just at the beginning of labor, we might leave you in triage for one or two hours, until you get ready, otherwise if you are already in an advanced state of labor, we bring you to the labor room straight away."

"When can we ask for a single room?" the same insisting lady asked.

The nurse kept smiling, "We will see it later in the process, but you can ask for it at the earliest at check in. It's not automatically sure that you will get one, though, as it depends on how busy the department is when you come in."

"Can we reserve it?" Insisting Lady couldn't stop herself.

"Yes, you can," the nurse responded with a sigh. "You can ask for it at check in and we put you on the waiting list."

Insisting Lady nodded with approval.

"Once you are in the labor room, you will remain there until a couple of hours after you give birth, then you will go to the postpartum room, where you will start recovering."

"Can we keep the baby in the room with us?" Insisting Lady didn't even pretend to raise her hand anymore.

A couple of people in the room started to softly chuckle at her persistence.

"Sure you can, if you want."

"Day and night?"

"Usually people prefer to catch some sleep at night, but you can do whatever you want," the nurse looked at her watch, and she kept going at a faster pace. "Remember that there are visiting hours for the postpartum room, from nine in the morning to nine at night, and—"

"How many visitors can I have in the room with me?"

"I was just about to say it," a vein started to pump on the nurse's forehead. "You can have two people in the postpartum room, plus your significant other."

"And in the labor room?"

"Jesus Christ!" the woman who was sitting next to me whispered, and I smiled at her with empathy: Insisting Lady was driving all of us crazy, not just poor Nurse Joanna.

"In the labor room you can only have your significant other and one additional person."

"Nobody else?" Insisting Lady wanted to be sure.

"She wants a full audience for her labor screams," Mike whispered in my ear, making it hard for me not to laugh out loud.

"Poor baby," I exhaled back in his ear, "and poor husband: can you imagine how she must be at home?"

Mike grinned at me, and he mouthed something that looked like "Man, I'm so lucky".

"You bet!" I mouthed back at him.

Somehow Nurse Joanna was able to go through her introductory speech, and we all left the meeting room to follow her in the corridor. We got a quick view of the triage room, before stopping at the main destination of our field visit: the labor room. It was impressive, not so much for the yet amazing view of the East River it offered, but more for the spaciousness of the room itself. A delivery bed, tall and at state-of-the-art medical technology, towered in the middle of the main space, a large room with a closet and a wide restroom; right after birth the baby was carried in a second smaller room, for measurements and first treatments. Mike squeezed my hand while the nurse was describing the equipment that inhabited the bed, and as I looked at him I knew the same thoughts were crossing our minds: we were in good hands, possibly the best in the country. I was not scared of labor and delivery pain and fatigue. Since nobody could forecast precisely what was going to happen, why bother worrying? And now I was feeling even safer. If anything were to happen, I could fully trust the hospital and its personnel to do the best job. And Mike would be there with me all along, my Michael, my rock.

"Are all labor rooms exactly the same?"

How many questions can one ask, Insisting Lady?

"What happens if there is no available labor room when I come in?"

How many details were there to focus on? I hadn't thought about half the things the woman was bringing up, should I get stressed?

Nurse Joanna realized a more efficient approach had to be taken with Insisting Lady, so she put her hand on the woman's arm and she told her in the calmest tone she could possibly handle, "Don't worry, there is always a room. We have emergency rooms and operating rooms for C-sections that we can use for you if no other labor room is available. We can even move you to another floor with that elevator that you see down the corridor. Let me finish the tour, and then you can ask me any other question you might have."

Insisting Lady nodded, halfway between being reassured and not completely satisfied by the nurse's answer.

Nurse Joanna kept pacing towards the bottom of the department's corridor, and she led us into an empty postpartum room. Two beds, separated by a curtain, occupied most of the space. Insisting Lady held her breath and she went to plan B, whispering something in her husband's ear, and encouraging him to raise his hand. He sighed and he silently apologized to the rest of the audience, before asking, "Can I stay here for the night?"

Nurse Joanna put all her remaining patience into building a smile for the guy.

"No, unfortunately you can't," she explained. I believed I saw a microscopic grin on his face.

"You can sleep here only if you guys are able to secure an individual room, otherwise you will have to go home at about nine in the evening."

The husband and Nurse Joanna nodded at each other, in mutual understanding, before she resumed, "This is where you will spend the first two or three days after the baby is born, depending on the type of birth you will have had, natural or C-section. When you are approved for discharge, our services send a wheelchair to your room, to accompany you downstairs to your car or taxi. Daddy usually carries your newborn baby in a car seat, ready to go home."

Nurse Joanna, relieved by having concluded her speech in her allotted time, opened the floor to questions, and Insisting Lady grabbed the nurse by her arm to start her thorough interrogations. Mike and I fled the premises as soon as we could, chuckling and hoping to never have to listen to Insisting Lady's voice ever again in our lives.

Once we got back home, we sealed the day with a big online order for the last baby items, from diapers to organic cleaning products. We had surrendered to every suggestion we had ever received from any doctor or nurse, or read in any baby book. Thanks to the very consistent Amazon baby shower gift card, almost everything was paid for.

Mike chuckled like a kid, "Shit is getting real!"

THE WEEK WITH NINE ITEMS FROM AMAZON

Most of the Amazon order was delivered on Tuesday, as the doorman didn't forget to mention when I got home from work that night.

"You received quite a few packages today," he shook his head in disbelief. He had a good reason, too, since a huge pile of boxes was waiting for me on my doorstep.

I took a picture and I texted it to Rachel, "The Amazon monster will destroy me."

Rachel responded with a Christmas tree emoji.

"Need help?" she added.

Potentially.

"Mike should be home soon," I replied, instead. "And stuff shouldn't be too heavy anyway."

Inspired by Rachel's text, I sent Mike the same picture, with the caption, "It's Christmas!"

He responded after a handful of seconds with a laughing emoji and a heart.

"Any idea when you're coming home?" I asked him.

"I fear late," he added with a sad emoji.

I brought the boxes inside and I opened them, documenting all details in a photographic reportage for Mike.

The biggest package contained an infant bathtub. Considerably bigger than what I had expected, it didn't fit under the sink, or anywhere else in the restroom. I put it in the bathtub with a shrug. The other parcels unleashed a landslide of diapers, diaper wipes, diaper trash cans, organic detergents, pacifiers, bottles, a music toy to hang above the crib, and a mosquito net for the stroller, to prevent officially bugs but mostly strangers from touching the frail newborn.

I quietly cleaned and I organized everything, counting on the soothing effect that external order always had on my internal mental peace. The calm before the storm.

Mike was moved when he came home, to say the least. Now the second room had supplies on the changing table and in the closet, and a jungle of bottle components and pacifiers waited next to the kitchen sink. Mike couldn't keep himself from smiling.

"I guess now we're ready," he told me as he tried to hug me.

"We're still waiting for a couple of items from Amazon," I responded, eyeing the list I had printed in the office, where most of the lines had been ticked. "And we need to pick up the baby bouncer from Stephanie and Marc on Saturday."

His eyes were bright like I had rarely seen them. There seemed to be nothing he had ever more looked forward to.

My smile faded.

"How was the fetal monitoring today? Did baby boy behave?" he asked me as soon as he recovered from the Amazon invasion.

"It was ok."

The light in his eyes turned opaque, so I put up a smile, "He was very calm at the beginning, then he moved, then he got quiet again. Less than thirty minutes and I was good to go."

"It must be so exciting for you to hear the baby's heartbeat so often," he sighed, "I always think about you when you're there, you and the little lad dancing in your belly. I always wish I were there with you, I wish I could come more often."

"Why do you think it's so amazing?"

A sad expression corrupted his features for a moment, before he regained his joyful poise, "You perceive his movements all the time, but listening to his heartbeat is the only way for me to be in touch with him. I imagine him dreaming quiet dreams when the rate is lower, and then getting all enthusiastic about exploring the world when the rate skyrockets. I feel I'm creating a connection with him when I'm there with you and I'm looking at the monitor."

He paused and he scrolled his head, "Building a bond with our baby has always been a priority for me. You already have a privileged relationship with him, because he is hanging out in your belly, experiencing all the noises, the smells and the lights of life through your skin. Every time I touch your belly and he moves, I hope he knows it's me, his dad. Every time I talk to you, I hope he can hear my voice, and he can recognize it once he comes out and I can hold him in my arms."

I struggled to decipher his worries, so I kept rational, "It doesn't matter who has the strongest bond now, because once the baby comes, you and I will be in the same place. What happens in the womb is essential, but I'm not much more than a microwave right now, where a piece of meat is defrosting. The meat will have to be seasoned and prepared before it's ready to be cooked, and we will do it together."

Mike still looked dubious, questions fogging up his forehead. He hugged me nonetheless, holding me against his chest. He caressed my face and my belly, and he waited for the baby to show one of his karate moves, grinning with pride when the movement came.

"I know this baby will make a wonderful steak!" he tried to convince me.

The idea of meat was still on my mind the next day, with images of dancing bacon cheeseburgers floating before my eyes just before lunch. As I was standing up from my desk to embark on the six-minute journey to Shake Shack, I received an updated invitation on my calendar. A press conference had to be postponed, due to movie release delays, and it was now falling during my maternity leave. That was strange, as the movie was still supposed to come out in just a few weeks.

I paused in front of my computer.

Oh.

I frantically scrolled back and forth, I counted and I recounted the days and the weeks on my calendar, but the result was always the same: I was just five weeks away from my due date. My new life was going to start in the blink of an eye. It seemed like someone had just told me "You will move to Buenos Aires in five weeks": I was ready for the move, packed and with a temporary apartment rented in the city; I had my plane tickets and work arrangements there; I had read many books about Buenos Aires, its culture and cuisine and history; but I had never been there, and I had very blurry expectations on how life would be once I would settle down there. Were people friendly? How did food taste like? Was there a lot of criminality in the city? Where there neighborhoods I wouldn't want to go? Was I risking my life?

How did I get here? Somehow I was in the hospital, wearing nothing but a pale gown. I was sweating and screaming, my legs spread open with my feet up in the air, squeezing Mike's hand with mine. Machines were humming, IV lines and catheters were coming out of my body. I was in labor, and it was not going well.

I had been in labor for hours, between painful contractions and ineffective epidural injections. Nurses were yelling at me when to push, and I was doing my best to follow their orders and the rhythm they were imposing to the whole action. My energies were fading away at each push, my brain was getting numb and my will to keep going was losing its grip on me.

After more hours of ordeal, a woman who looked like Doctor Mallory came into the room, she observed the situation for a few seconds, and she decided I needed an emergency C-section. Right now. Somebody put a gown on the Doctor Mallory look-alike, who started to cut my abdomen open like a butcher, with a long vertical incision. For some reason the anesthesia wasn't effective, and thunders of pain shook my body.

I woke up with tears in my eyes, the memory of agony still vivid. Could anything like that happen in real life?

I looked at Mike, quietly breathing next to me.

"If anything happens," I told myself, "Mike will be there."

This didn't completely reassure me, but it gave me something to think about for a couple more hours, until the alarm went finally off and it saved me from the night's terrors.

What the light of a new day couldn't save me from was another Friday: another appointment with the endocrinologist, another fetal monitoring session. I sighed and I tried to roll on my side, my usual routine to get out of bed, only to be stopped by a sudden sciatic nerve pain that inflamed my leg and the lower left side of my back. With tears in my eyes, I implored Mike to help me stand up.

It was all uphill from there. My sugar levels hadn't been good enough this week, and more insulin had to be injected in my thighs, now blue and swollen in all accessible parts. The fetal monitoring took more than one hour, as the baby had no intention to cooperate and make the second part of my afternoon less miserable.

"How are you, dear? Tons of excitement coming your way!" my mother tried to cheer me up via text, failing hard.

"Just go to bed and sleep as much as you can," Rachel texted me. "And be restored for our brunch tomorrow!"

It was a good advice, if only I didn't have a Game of Thrones article to finish.

I tried all day, I even went home straight from the hospital to provide more comfort to my hurting back, but words didn't come to my fingers. The white page stared back at me, merciless.

Ultimately abandoning myself to the exhaustion from the week, I ate some carrots and cheese for dinner, I half-slept through my glucose check and my bedtime insulin injection, and I went into hiding under the sheets.

I didn't hear Mike coming to bed that night.

THE WEEK WITH NINE INCH NAILS

"This is what the last shot in the new trailer for the upcoming season of Game of Thrones could mean: Arya and Sansa, two fan favorites, could not only be finally reunited, but also in Winterfell, in a strong homecoming scene. Will we get to see some wolves in the picture?"

As soon as I finished re-reading my article, I leaned back on my chair and I sighed with relief: I still had my juice. Friday had just been a bad day, and I could still write with intelligence and wit. Being pregnant hadn't taken away all of me, at least not yet, even if I had needed two days to complete the piece. At least I had made it, and I now could allow myself an early night dismissal.

A hand touched my shoulder and it shook me.

A voice whispered in my ear, "Wake up."

I opened my eyes and I looked in front of me, where two smaller eyes were fixated into mine in the shades, the only light coming from the second bedroom. A boy was staring at me. He was small, possibly two or three years of age.

"Mom," he spoke again. "Wake up."

I sat up in my bed, where I was lying alone, and I turned on my bedside light. I explored the boy's features, opaque eyes nestled in a snow-white face, framed by black hair. He looked like a ghost.

"Wake up," he commanded this time.

"I am awake," I mumbled.

"I need to feed," he simply stated.

I sighed, knowing what it meant.

"Did you already kill it?" I asked him.

He nodded, and he pointed his finger towards his room. He then grabbed my arm and he dragged me there. A big dog was agonizing on the boy's play mat, a pool of blood forming on the floor.

As it was custom, I went to the kitchen to retrieve my tools, and I started to collect the blood. First from the floor, with a sponge and a large bowl, then directly from the animal, now dead, with a big syringe positioned on the only wound it had on its body, a deep cut on its throat. The boy didn't blink through the whole process, his eyes two black holes pointed towards me. When I was done, I handed the bowl to the boy, and he grabbed the full and heavy container with no apparent effort. He smelled the blood, his nose almost touching it, and then he started to drink it from the bowl.

He paused after several gulps, the bowl already half empty, to capture again my eyes with his. Blood was drooling on his chin.

"Mommy," he said. "Next time I want a human."

That was the first step of the downward spiral.

He touched my chest with a tiny hand, and my rib cage exploded into flames.

I woke up gasping for air, my heart still burning. I touched the skin under my t-shirt, and I found it alarmingly hot. I mouthed a curse word, before slowly rolling on one side, ignoring the back pain, and crawling to the restroom. In the mirror I saw it clearly: a burning rash on my chest, bright red spots plaguing it.

I assumed it was due to clothes scratching the skin, so later that morning I archived in my closet a couple more tops that were fitting too tightly. I had now only three work blouses and two weekend tops that still fit me, barely enough to go through a week.

By Thursday morning, the rash had covered my belly in red elevated marks which started to itch brutally.

"My poor dear," Mike pitied me. "It's certainly nothing. It will be gone soon enough."

I looked at him, and all I saw was a guy who, like all other guys, didn't care to listen to me. I didn't say anything, and the corners of his mouth slowly turned down, as if I had offended him.

I walked away from him without saying a word, and I kept getting ready for work.

On the subway I furiously checked the internet to find a solution to my burning problem. Was there a cream I could use? The only suggestion was to keep the skin naked, to prevent further friction and irritation. I couldn't tolerate the idea of having to stay home with my abdomen constantly in front of my eyes, not only big and round but also red and ugly, so I dismissed that. Powerless, I kept constantly looking at myself in the mirror to spot new outbursts.

On Thursday morning I noticed the eczema had now reached my thighs. How would I keep performing my multiple daily injections?

By Thursday night, the itch was so intense that night sleep seemed farther than utopia. Any control over my body was lost.

Sinking in the sofa, I texted Rachel, "My life sucks."

"First: no, it doesn't. Second: what's wrong, my dear?"

I described the rash, and she texted back only after many minutes, "I found an Aveeno cream that treats extra-dry and itchy skin, and it can be used also during pregnancy. I'm leaving the office in a few minutes, and I will stop by a pharmacy and bring it to you."

"I don't want to bother," I tried to stop her.

"Don't even say it," she responded immediately, with a beating heart emoji.

Rachel rang my doorbell less than half an hour later.

"Did you freaking fly here?" I was amazed by how she could do impossible things when she had to.

She grinned and she hugged me tight, still in the entrance.

"Put it on right away," she then said, handing me the pharmacy bag with the cream.

"Can you stay?" I tried.

She smiled again, this time with a tender brightness in her eyes, "I can't. I have to go back to the office."

"Wait, you came all the way up here from Wall Street and now you have to go back downtown?"

"I asked the car to wait for me downstairs, no big deal."

I hugged her as firmly as I could.

"You're crazy. And I love you," I grinned.

She looked at me straight in the eyes, before opening my apartment door and leaving, "I love you too, my Sister."

I woke up the following morning, already Friday, with a text from my mother.

"Only four weeks!" she celebrated, with a party of fireworks, dancing ladies, champagne bottles, cakes and pastries. She had recently discovered emojis.

Only four weeks, and then Mike would finally share the burden.

I left the office early in the afternoon to pay a visit to Doctor Palmer. She joined me in the exam room shortly after I was walked in there by a nurse, and the doctor had my insulin and blood sugar tracker printed in her hand. She greeted me with her usual warm smile, before focusing on my papers, circling data with a stroke of her pen and taking notes on the margins. I could hear my heart bumping between my ears: what else could go wrong?

"I see you have been struggling to keep the levels down, especially the fasting sugar, and we had to increase the bedtime insulin several times during the past two weeks. This is not too bad, as the dosage is not too high, yet, and it doesn't worry me."

She pointed her finger to a specific day of the previous week, and she kept analyzing the numbers, "The pre-meal injections seem to fix the levels most of the times, even if in some occasions you still need to exercise to bring the levels below 120. For example in this case, how long did you have to exercise to bring the measure down, from 140 to 115?"

"Almost twenty minutes, I think."

"Let me know if it takes you more than twenty minutes to lose twenty points: this would mean that we need to further increase the insulin dosage."

I sighed and I nodded.

"How are the fetal monitoring sessions going?"

"They're ok," I smiled. At least something was giving positive results. "The baby is always very active, the heartbeat goes up and down, and nurses are happy."

"This is great news," Doctor Palmer grinned back at me. "Let's hope it stays this way."

She paused for a second, her usual way to collect her thoughts before introducing a new topic with a longer speech. What else could go wrong?

"You are due in four weeks," she kicked it off. "This is what we should do for the remaining time: keep sending me your measures, keep coming here every week, and send me a message anytime you need to increase your dosage. After you have your baby, stop checking your blood and injecting insulin; book an appointment with me for six weeks after delivery. At that point we will run the sugar test again, and we will hopefully confirm that everything got back to normal."

How confident was she?

"If you get pregnant again, you will need to do the sugar test in the first trimester," Doctor Palmer then added, as an afterthought. "The risk of having gestational diabetes in your next pregnancies is very high."

Right. There had to be a catch.

"But let's not think about it now: let's focus on this baby first!"

Next on the agenda was the growth monitoring scan. Mike and I met at the hospital's check-in, and we followed the nurse in the exam room with a certain apprehension. What if my troubles with keeping the blood sugar under control, and the consequent constant need of insulin supply, were translating into issues for the baby? What if he was now too big, or too disproportionate? Would Doctor Mallory order an emergency induction, or even decide to cut me open and get the baby out with a C-section? Mike's eyes were locked into mine as I got ready on the exam bed, my top pushed up and my pants folded down to reveal the full roundness of my belly. I grabbed onto Mike's gaze as long as I could, as I would grasp his arm while walking up a staircase, until the first image appeared on the screen. His eyes turned away from me as soon as the nurse placed the sensor on my belly. The familiar heartbeat sound filled the room and the first shadows came up on the screen, transforming Mike into a dumbly smiling version of himself.

It turned out the baby had gained another half-pound, which kept him at the same quite healthy seventy-ninth percentile. Still perfectly proportioned and with plenty of amniotic fluid to move and roll around, it looked like he was still doing fine where he was.

The questions were still hanging in the air, though: what would Doctor Mallory tell us during our next appointment, in exactly one week? Would any additional complications show up, enough to force her to take immediate action? Was the shock of labor even closer than I thought?

I shook my head to clean it up from all omens.

"Are you ok?" Mike squeezed my hand as we were leaving the hospital.

"Sure."

On the taxi to join Rachel for dinner downtown, Mike sent the latest scan pictures to our families, who promptly responded with cheers and excitement at the approaching event. I focused on Manhattan's skyline outside the window, as the car ran on the Hudson River Drive.

"Amber, where are you?" Mike tapped on my knee at some point.

I turned my head to look at him, his eyes radiating green fire each time a lamplight illuminated them.

"What?"

"I said: we're almost there, you can text Rachel that we're just five minutes away."

"Are we late?" I couldn't follow his point.

"Didn't you notice the congestion?" he laughed. "There was an accident on the Hudson River Drive, we're already fifteen minutes late. You texted Rachel half an hour ago…"

"Right."

"Did you listen to anything I said before?"

I slowly shook my head.

He sighed, "My parents are buying their tickets for May twenty—"

"No," I covered his voice with mine. "I don't want to talk about it."

He frowned, "Pardon me?"

"I don't want to talk about it," I repeated slowly, since he hadn't caught it the first time. "I don't even want to think about it, ok?"

"You don't want to think about my parents coming here?"

"No."

He was perplexed.

"Are you upset?" he asked after a few seconds.

"You're always thinking about yourself, or your baby, or your parents, or your work, or your whatever. I'm a bit tired, and I don't care about any of those things."

He inhaled a couple of times, as if he wanted to respond, but he didn't.

As soon as we got to the restaurant, I exited the car and I went inside to look for Rachel.

"There you are!" she couldn't even finish the sentence that I was desperately hugging her.

"I'm starving, let's go," I greeted her.

She twisted her neck left and right, "Where did you leave Mike?"

"He's paying the taxi, I think. He can find us at the table," I responded, and I approached the restaurant hostess to let her know we were all there.

Mike came in a couple of seconds later, immediately relieved when he saw me and Rachel still in the entrance. He hugged Rachel and he exchanged with her some words I couldn't hear, covered by the restaurant's background noise. They both looked at me with synchronized wide smiles, and Mike kissed me on the cheek.

"You tried to escape, but I'm not letting you go," he whispered in my ear.

Escape? What escape? There was no escape anymore.

THE WEEK WITH NINE SERIES OF TEETH

Swimming.

I had never been a swimmer, but I had always liked bathing in the sea, the sense of freedom that came with it, the cheerful sentiment that all worries could remain on the shore, and be washed away by next wave. Now I was swimming in a warm green ocean, accompanied by colorful fish and without any human being in sight. Perfection. I kept floating, diving from time to time to look at the bottom, sand and rocks populated by hermit crabs and clown fish, farther and farther away from the coast.

It all fell suddenly silent: the water was flat, seagulls weren't singing anymore, fish went into hiding. Then I saw it: a fin. Sharp. It was lazily dancing on the water surface until it saw me. It waited for a moment, to sniff my fear, and then it resumed its march, faster. I knew I wouldn't make it, but yet some primordial instincts told me to run, so I turned around towards the shore and I rushed. I was swimming as fast as my lacking technique allowed me, but the fin was coming closer at every second.

I kept going, putting all my energy into it.

Until I sensed its presence next to me. I turned my head to watch my enemy approaching, the romantic stare into the abyss, but it was already too late. Its mouth was wide open, many rows of teeth were ready to attack me. It captured my leg in its jaws, and it pulled me under water. Blood stained the pure crystal of the ocean, as darts of pain coming up from my leg shook my whole body. I had abandoned myself to the predator, ready for my inevitable destiny. I looked up, staring at what remained of sunlight.

I woke up coughing, my throat obstructed as if I were drowning, or somebody were suffocating me with their hands.

"Are you ok?" Mike jumped up in bed as soon as he heard my struggling noises.

"Don't worry," I responded instinctively, to make him go back to sleep. I tried to calm myself and slow down my short breaths, as my chest burned with the itching rash and the baby jumping in my belly pushed on my diaphragm.

I took a deep breath and I rolled back on my left side, neglecting the needles of pain in my back.

"It's only Monday," I told myself before dozing off.

Wednesday didn't start any better, either. My head didn't want to focus on anything at work, my brain pulsated clueless in my skull as I fought to complete an article on Donald Glover's new TV show. The sigh of relief that celebrated the completion of my piece was immediately replaced by a horrified snort: I had written "Danny Glover", instead of "Donald Glover" in many instances; I had misspelled many of Glover's show's cast names and I had misplaced the filming location; I had even reported the airing date as two years from now, rather than a couple of months. I held my head in my hands once I was finished counting my mistakes, and I decided to go for a walk and grab lunch to clarify my thoughts. I was getting slower every day, hobbling to the elevator and in the entrance lobby, mechanically choosing the closest warm salad bar to limit the number of steps, rolling back to my desk. There I had to look for the insulin pen in my purse, drag myself to the restroom and, now with a mirror, look for a spot in one of my thighs that was not too swollen, red, or inflamed, and congratulate it with an injection. The ten-minute timer was now on.

Lunch was an even more tortuous task if I was eating out with a colleague. I had to have my insulin dose right before we left the building, and I usually carried some crackers in my pocket. I had to be awkwardly ready at the ten minute mark with a silly "I'm so sorry, but this pregnancy makes me so famished that I can't wait for another second" as I stuffed my mouth with a Ritz. Which would also make my sugars nicely spike, and therefore prevent me from finishing my food. And leave me starving. What a sequence of embarrassments, which I tolerated only because the alternative would have been to tell everyone that I had gestational diabetes. I didn't want anybody's pity.

"It's not a matter of pity," Rachel was giving me her perspective on Wednesday night. She had come over for dinner, since Mike had some client event.

"But it is: people look at you in a different way when you're sick."

"You're not sick, Amber."

"Yes, I am. I have to inject a medication in my body multiple times per day, every day. I call this being sick."

She frowned and she took my hand, "Your condition is temporary, and everything will be fine again after the baby is born."

"You don't know that," I couldn't let it go. "I could still have diabetes. The baby could still have diabetes. You don't know."

Rachel sighed.

She looked at me straight in the eyes before her train of thoughts left again, "You are always so rational, so please try to be rational this time, too. Most people with gestational diabetes are perfectly fine after giving birth, right? Both your gynecologist and endocrinologist told you so," she waited for me to nod, unconvinced. "So why don't you accept their estimate, why don't you go with the most likely option?"

"Because you never know."

She sighed again, so I took advantage of her hesitation, "I have no risk factors for this diabetes, and yet I got it, so how are you so convinced I won't still have it after delivery?"

She kept looking at me, without saying a word.

"You see? You have to admit that the risk is there."

She now hugged me, "Please try to stay positive. It will be over soon."

Right. Pregnancy would be over in a few weeks, but nothing else would.

NINE

This time I woke up with a rope around my neck. I was standing on a chair, barely managing to keep my balance, my hands tied behind my back. Was it a James Bond movie? Was somebody going to smash by balls until I dropped dead?

There was hardly any light in the room, but I could identify the small silhouette that was standing in front of me: a little boy. He had his hands on his hips, legs wide spread and chin high, and he was looking at me with a satisfied grimace.

"You know this is all your fault, right?" he burst out, his eyes glowing in the dark. "You know what you're paying for, right?"

I had no idea, so I kept silent.

"Speak!" he shouted.

"I didn't do anything," I mumbled, too late to realize that nobody ever survived in a movie after that sentence.

An evil laugh came out of the boy's mouth.

"You didn't do anything? You, poor thing, have no guilt. You were not the one who brought me into this world, right? Who gave me the terrible disease that forced me to get through a series of bionic surgeries, which transformed me into the monster I now am?"

He stepped forward and a light suddenly turned on, revealing metallic limbs and pieces of skull welded on what remained of his body. His eyes were cold LED lights, pale white holes in his face.

He looked at me with utter disgust as he further approached me.

"Now you see what you've done to me?"

"How…" I stumbled.

"How?" he mocked me. "You gave me this disease when I was inside you. It didn't do anything to you, but it did everything to me."

His eyes fixated into mine.

"Mom," he grinned while he kicked the chair under my feet. He left me hanging, waiting for death to come and get me.

I opened my eyes in the darkness of my bedroom, Mike snoring next to me. The phone confirmed what the brutality of the nightmare had already hinted to: it was Friday, and it wasn't even three in the morning.

A daze accompanied me in the following few hours, a flow of missed sleep and pilgrimages to the bathroom plagued by a constant sciatic pain, until the alarm brought me back to reality and it tore Mike away from his peaceful rest.

"Good morning!" he chirped as he slid closer to me, somehow already fully awake. "Are you ready to see our little lad?"

The appointment with Doctor Mallory.

"I'm incredibly looking forward!" he added, now looking at me and expecting me to say something in return.

"Sure."

"Would you want to shower first, to take your time without feeling rushed?"

"Sure."

"Let me find an Uber, now that you're almost ready. Let's go now, the Uber is downstairs. Are you comfortable with the seatbelt? We have plenty of time and we ought to certainly be there on schedule. Let's see what the doctor tells us! Is he moving a lot now, the morning excitement? Do you want some water, so it won't be too hard to provide the urine sample when we get there? Did you—"

"Mike," I stopped him, as soon as I could find the energy to dam the infinite flow of his excitement. "Can you please give me a minute?"

"For sure, my dear. Are you tired? Can I do anything for you? Do you—"

"Mike," I sighed. "Please."

Just shut up.

I didn't need that hysteria right then. I needed to look at the world outside the window, the buildings and bridges running by, and tell myself that I was going to make it. I needed to focus on something calm and rational.

I closed my eyes and I visualized a comforting creation I had completed this week: a sleeping and feeding schedule for the baby. It was a series of instructions and operations to follow, a security blanket which combined lessons from the many books Mike and I had read on the topic. I had told myself I would survive the first months with a mixture of discipline, method, and luck. The only thing I could do now was preparing a plan, and later adapting it to the baby's personality, whatever that might be. With a blond American mother and a Nigerian-Irish father, the baby could fall anywhere in that wide range, but surely he would be born with a racial bias tattooed on his forehead. The color of our skin had never meant anything to us, but the world didn't always agree with us. Sometimes I thought we were being selfish with our decision to bring children to life in a world that wasn't ready for them.

"How are you feeling?" Doctor Mallory entered the exam room with the usual question on her lips, more a greeting than an actual request for information.

"I'm still doing fine," I gave her a proper answer, this time. "Just getting a bit more tired and sleepless every day. And I have this rash on my belly that is really bothering me."

I pulled my top up at her request, and she closely examined my skin.

"It looks like PUPPP to me, which means Pruritic Urticarial Papules and Plaques of Pregnancy. It is a fancy name for a skin rash that some pregnant women get. It's more common among white women who are carrying a male first child, so you perfectly fit the bill."

"Is there anything you can give us?" Mike asked the Doctor. "She can't sleep at night."

"I am sorry, but there's not much you can do, apart from using a lot of moisturizer and wearing soft cotton clothes. The only cure is giving birth to your baby: the rash usually fades away spontaneously a few days after delivery."

Great.

"What I want to do today is take the usual measures, perform a quick internal exam, and then discuss our delivery plan," Doctor Mallory added as she glimpsed at the computer on the desk.

She listened to the baby's heartbeat and then she checked the roundness of my belly with her tape measure, nodding in approval to both results.

She asked me to lay down on the bed and she firmly palpated my cervix, apologizing for the discomfort and commenting that the cervix was still high and closed, confirming her feeling that the baby was not going to come out in the following few days.

She took her time to remove the latex gloves and wash her hands, as if she needed to catch her breath before tackling the big topic she had on her agenda for the day, "I have been in contact with Doctor Palmer on your insulin dosage and blood sugar. Given that the situation is barely under control, I believe our best option is to plan for a delivery a few days in advance, since we don't want the baby to become too big and the risks to increase unnecessarily for either of you. I will put you on my calendar for an induction exactly two weeks from now, on a Friday, when I will be in the hospital all day. This allows us to complete the thirty-ninth week, which is what the guidelines recommend for cases like yours."

Doctor Mallory paused and she looked at us, as an experienced comedian who gauges her audience before running to the next line of her script.

"You will go to the hospital on Thursday night around six. They will be waiting for you, and they will give you a local medication for twelve hours, to soften the cervix. This can kickoff contractions in some women, but generally not much happens, that's why we do it at night. After twelve hours, we will give you IV oxytocin to properly induce labor. It is usually effective, but if nothing happens even then, we will get him out in some other way, so don't worry."

Nobody dared to speak for one long second.

"Any questions?"

I was not afraid of looking stupid, so I dove into it, "If the baby is already big enough and the due date is so close, why doesn't he want to come out spontaneously?"

"We don't really know what initiates contractions; it doesn't depend on size only, or we wouldn't have nine or ten pound babies. That's why sometimes it's better to induce labor: not all the conditions might be met for the process to begin naturally, but some conditions might be already too advanced, or some risks might exist, and the delicate balance might already be off."

She smiled at the end of her response, her final seal of hopeful reassurance.

"We will have a baby in two weeks," Mike told me with spirited eyes as soon as we left the doctor's office building.

"Right."

"Or even less, if he feels like it," he corrected, an ear-to-ear smile on his face. "But in two weeks, at the latest, we will have a baby in our arms. Our baby. Our son. It's crazy!"

I sighed.

"Didn't you know the time was coming?" I asked him, emphasizing the extreme roundness of my belly with a hand gesture.

He laughed, embarrassed, "I know. I guess I'm just too excited right now!"

As if it didn't show.

"At least I won't have to rush to the hospital in pain."

He nodded and he kissed me on the forehead, "Everything will be perfectly fine."

His words kept echoing in my head all day as a bad omen, as I ran on an Uberpool to the office, then from work to the hospital for the biweekly fetal monitoring circus, then to the endocrinologist appointment, and then finally home. I couldn't handle the bus anymore, but car rides on the horrible roads of Manhattan were not much better.

When I finally sat on my sofa, my feet were swollen and my back cramped. The only thing I could do was responding to my mother's "OMG I will be a grandma in two weeks!" text while complaining about it with Rachel.

"My death sentence has been pronounced: I will be as good as dead in two weeks."

"That's not true and you know it: people who love you today will love you even more after they will see the amazing baby!" Rachel did her best to comfort me. "And I will always be here for you."

"I know. You're my only friend."

She responded with a beating heart emoji, "You're my best friend."

THE WEEK WITH NINE QUEENS

Doctor Mallory's plan to induce me one week ahead of schedule had suddenly bumped up the date of my execution. Before I could prepare myself for it, only a few days separated my current social status of "married woman" from the new one of "married woman with children". A shiver ran down my spine as the words formed in my mind.

Drunk with his emotions, Mike was now stuck in his almost-fatherhood facial expression, his authentic self buried under a permanent state of frenzy.

"I am terribly sorry your skin rash is itching and bothering you so much," he told me on Sunday morning, after I complained about yet another sleepless night. "Perhaps you can ask Doctor Mallory to induce you earlier, perhaps already this week. I don't think it will make any difference for baby boy: at this point he's well-formed and ready to go."

"You're that sick of just being with me, already?" I couldn't stop myself from spitting out.

He looked at me with vacuous eyes, incapable of processing my words.

Couldn't he wait for ten more days?

"I was just trying to help you," he mumbled.

"You are not helping," I just let it go at that point.

He kept staring at me with sad eyes.

"Well, it's the last week and a half, anyway. We have been waiting for so long for the baby to arrive and now we're almost there!" he cheered in the end.

My heartbeat accelerated and I could hear my pulse in my ears, as claws of frustration were closing down on my throat.

"I'm going to brunch with Rachel by myself," I announced as soon as I could speak again.

Mike took a breath to reply, but I left him before he could say anything.

I went into hiding in the bathroom, and I sat on the tub's edge for several long minutes. When I finally shook my head and I regained control, my jaw hurt: I had been clamping it so hard that it had stiffened. I massaged my face for a few seconds, before texting Rachel.

"It's going to be just the two of us today!"

"Mike can't make it?"

"Will you miss him?"

Who was more important for her?

"Not if I have you there!" she promptly responded. Good job, Counselor.

"So, did you leave Mike at home?" Rachel asked me once we were seated at the table. Before I could answer, I got distracted by how my huge belly was the target of the whole restaurant's gazes.

"Do you know what they're all thinking?" I gestured towards all the people around us, eating or serving at the tables.

She shook her head.

"How far along is she? When is she going to pop?"

Rachel giggled.

"It's not funny!" I immediately clarified. "It's suffocating: all these people always looking at me, thinking about my body during labor, my freaking uterus, my vagina. Everybody is looking forward to this baby. I'm already invisible to them."

Rachel leaned forward to catch my hand on the table, "They're all looking at you just because your belly is enormous. It's not something you see every day. Nobody is thinking about your vagina, I promise."

"And Mike is the worse," I added.

She frowned.

"He is so fucking blissful," I explained. "He always talks about the baby, he only sees the baby now. Can you imagine what life I will have after the baby is born? Not only society won't even care about me at all, if not for my mother status and duties, but also my husband will completely forget about me."

I wiped a tear from my face.

"It's a scam. It's like that Argentinian crime movie I told you about, Nine Queens, the one where everyone is trying to stick it to everybody else. "

Rachel squeezed my hand, "Mike will never forget about you or value you less than today. I have no doubt."

"You haven't seen him when he is alone with me, how he only speaks about the baby, to the baby even. I already don't exist anymore. Not even my parents are this bad!"

An interrogative look on Rachel's face encouraged me to tell her more.

"Becoming grandparents is the only thing they have in their minds now, their only chance to a second youth, and yet they're quite calm and not as obnoxious as Mike. They totally kept their cool even when I gave them the news of the earlier-than-expected arrival. My mother started to text me on a daily basis, but that's the only change. I guess either they are freaking out but trying to hide it, to preserve my inner peace, or at their age this is the highest level of stress they can put themselves through, so they are auto-regulating themselves not to have a stroke."

I took a breath and I gauged Rachel's reaction, but she kept smiling.

"Are you freaking out?" I then asked her.

She looked surprised for a fraction of a second, "You know I'm used to stress, so I'm not freaking out. But I'm in a waiting mode, too, just like everybody else. We all know these are the last few days, and we just want to make sure everything goes well for you. I want to do everything I can to help you, any way I can."

I wanted to hug her. Her focus on me was what I needed the most.

"I cleared my schedule for the first weekend, to come to see you at the hospital as soon as you feel good enough. And you just tell Mike to call me if you need anything, even on Friday, even on Thursday in the middle of the night, at any point," her voice cracked. "I will be there for you, Amber."

In my mind, Mike was already holding the newborn baby in his arms, admiring his unique beauty and that skin that was going to make him a pariah on both the white and the African-American side.

I had to wipe away another tear and take a breath.

"I know, my Sister."

With the induction scheduled for Thursday of the following week, Wednesday was my last day in the office. It couldn't come at a better time, as my brain had already stopped working. I had spent my last two and a half days on one article, waiting for words to come to my fingers, just to realize I didn't have enough ideas to structure them with. I hadn't been able to decide what I thought about the latest hit Netflix show: was it really mind blowing, or just a rip-off of concepts already seen before? That Wednesday seemed like a mix of the last day of school before summer vacation, and the day before the Apocalypse. I had a long lunch with Lauren, at the end of which we hugged and she passed all her best wishes on to me. Many colleagues stopped by my desk to say goodbye and good luck, with encouraging hugs and handshakes, and some fearful looks. Everyone sneaked in their last unsolicited advice, their last pieces of untested wisdom.

In a last outburst of celebration, I even allowed myself to take an Uber, rather than an Uberpool, to enjoy the ride back home in complete solitude, before silence and quiet would become a memory from the past. New York City flew outside my window as the car rode uptown on the Hudson River Drive, pier after pier, landmark after landmark, the Empire State

Building followed by the Intrepid Museum, Central Park somewhere east, then the Upper West Side before Harlem and Columbia. For the last time I was looking at the city as just myself; next time I would leave my office, in a taxi or on the subway, I would have a child.

My fate was upon me.

More good lucks and goodbyes populated the rest of the week, as I had my last appointment with Doctor Palmer. My blood sugar, much like my brain, had lost any sign of reasonability, measures were always high, and the insulin dosage had to be constantly increased.

"You don't have to worry," the endocrinologist used all her empathy in an attempt to comfort me. "This happens sometimes during the very last few days of pregnancy. Just think that everything will be over in a week, and you will have a beautiful and healthy baby."

"Be strong," she waved as she left the exam room.

"Best wishes," the nurse cheered me while I was walking down the corridor to reach the exit.

"The best of luck," the admin whispered as she swiped my card to collect the copay, as I was getting ready to leave the practice.

"That way to the firing squad," I was waiting for someone to shout at me.

THE DAY OF

How did I get here? Somehow I was in the hospital, wearing nothing but a pale gown. I was sweating and screaming, my legs spread open with my feet up in the air, squeezing Mike's hand with mine. Machines were humming, IV lines and catheters were coming out of my body. I was in labor, and it was not going well.

I had been in labor for hours, between painful contractions and ineffective epidural injections. Nurses were yelling at me when to push, and I was doing my best to follow their orders and the rhythm they were imposing to the whole action. My energies were fading away at each push, my brain was getting numb and my will to keep going was losing its grip on me.

After more hours of ordeal, a woman who looked like Doctor Mallory came into the room, she observed the situation for a few seconds, and she decided I needed an emergency C-section. Right now. Somebody put a gown on the Doctor Mallory look-alike, who started to cut my abdomen open like a butcher, with a long vertical incision. Some other doctors joined her, and they all started to work on my open belly.

When the time came, Mike left my hand hanging outside the bed and he rushed to grab his son from the hands of the nurse. Nobody seemed to notice my torn body, and the blood spilling out of it. Before I passed out, I could hear the baby starting to make noises and everybody cheering around him, not paying any attention to my heart monitor as it suddenly went flat. As I was dying on the labor bed, someone kicked it out of the way, to make space for a baby crib to get installed in the middle of the room. Mike was laughing and chuckling, too absorbed by the marvel of his newborn son to realize he had just lost his wife.

I suddenly woke up from the nightmare and I opened my eyes, recognizing my bedroom and heavily sighing with relief. My phone told me it wasn't even three in the morning, so I did my best to go back to sleep.

No, please, not again.

I was back in the hospital, again in labor, holding tight onto Mike's hand. This time I didn't know how long I had been there or how the process was going, but everyone seemed calmer. When I tried to move my legs and I failed, I understood the epidural was working, at least, and I scanned the room for a contraction tracking monitor, to find out whether I was at the beginning of the process or towards the end. A nurse gently told me to get ready to push, and when the trend line on the monitor spiked and she yelled "Push!" I knew what to do. It all seemed so easy this time. I pushed another couple of times and I heard movie-like cheers on the other side of the delivery bed, where Doctor Mallory celebrated the head of the baby popping out of my body, followed by his shoulders and the rest of his tiny self. That was not too bad, I told myself as I smiled at Mike, who was still holding my hand and caressing my forehead, admired by my strength and dedication to the cause of bringing his son to this world.

"Can we hold the baby?" Mike asked the nurses, hopeful.

The nurses looked at each other and at Doctor Mallory, who remained silent. One nurse swaddled the baby and she rushed him into the separate area of the labor room, where newborns were weighed and cleaned immediately after birth, and treated if something was wrong. Nobody told us anything. I tightened my grasp onto Mike's hand, begging him with my eyes to find out what was going on.

"What's happening?" he choked on his fear.

Nobody responded.

"What's happening?" he now screamed.

"Come here, Mr. Gillingham," Doctor Mallory called on Mike at the end. I could see the two whispering, Mike in anger and disbelief and the doctor with a pitiful expression on her face, but I couldn't hear their words.

After a few minutes of intense whispering and hand gesturing, Mike pushed Doctor Mallory towards me, mouthing something that looked like "No, you tell her".

"Amber," the Doctor started. "Dear Amber, you've done such a great job—"

"Cut the bullshit, bitch, and tell her," Mike stopped her.

Doctor Mallory looked at him, then back at me with a deep sigh, "Something very sad happened to your baby. As you know, we run all the tests, we follow all the guidelines, we try to catch all possible complications before a baby is born, so that parents can decide what they want to do in case the pregnancy should not be viable. Nonetheless, there are still a very small number of medical issues that we are not able to detect. Your baby is unfortunately one of these very rare cases: he is severely disabled, and he won't be able to conduct a normal life, and I fear you and your husband will have to cope with it."

What?

"What?"

"This bitch is saying the baby is deformed," Mike yelled, with a verbal and physical violence I had never seen in him. "He's a monster, do you understand, Amber? A monster! Our lives are screwed: we will have to take care of this monster, who won't be able to do anything in his life - not anything great, just anything at all. Our lives will be such a nightmare!"

I was petrified.

Mike was exploding with rage, and he threw one last hit to Doctor Mallory, "You're done: I will sue you and this hospital. I will destroy you!"

When I woke up again, I was in my room, in my bed, and Mike was next to me, still lost in his own dreams. A soft light was coming in from behind the curtains: it was going to be a beautiful Tuesday morning.

"Are you ok?" Mike asked as soon as the alarm went off and he regained consciousness.

I nodded, and I let him hug my belly. I repressed a sigh.

"Do you have meetings today?"

He grabbed his phone to check his calendar, "I can stay home today and do everything over the phone. I just have a client meeting at 1 pm that I would like to attend in person, but I leave it up to you: how do you feel?"

"I'm great, I was just asking."

Mike shook his head and he left the bed to take his shower.

"Two more days," he kissed me goodbye before he left for the office.

"Two more days," I repeated to no one in particular.

"How are you feeling today?" my phone vibrated with Rachel's text.

I set up my reading-and-Netflix station on the sofa, with my Kindle, tablet, and a bottle of water a few inches away, before I responded to Rachel. It was strange to think that last time I had seen her, on Saturday for lunch, had been the last time pre-baby. Next lunch together, a stroller would be occupying the fourth seat at the table.

It sounded unreal.

"I can't wait to be done with this," I typed. "And at the same time I don't really want it to be over."

She responded with a smiling emoji.

"At least you will feel physically better in two days," she argued. "Lighter. And Mike can do most of the legwork in the first few days. Everything will be good!"

I was not that sure, so I sent her a heart emoji to avoid thinking about anything smart, or even anything at all, to say. The back of my neck tickled: Mike was doubtlessly going to take care of the baby in his first few hours and days, but who was going to take care of me?

I dropped my phone on the sofa next to me, and I picked up the tablet to select something to watch from Netflix.

The Breakfast Club and two episodes of Grey's Anatomy filled my morning, until my stomach kindly notified me that it was empty, despite all the water I had drank, and it needed food. I rolled up from the sofa to grab sliced turkey and brie cheese from the fridge, and a new bottle of water from the pantry. I paid a quick visit to the bathroom, before I followed my thirst and I drank most of the new bottle of water in a few long gulps. Then of course I had to pee again. Already? Pregnant bladders never surprised me in a positive way. I was planning to wait for as long as I could before a new visit to the bathroom, but it seemed I couldn't hold it at all. I rushed to the restroom and I barely made it: the biggest waterfall of pee came out of my body, unstoppable.

Wait.

Unstoppable?

I tried to contract my muscles to see if I could control the flow, but I couldn't.

What did the nurse say during the birthing class? If you couldn't hold it, then it was probably not pee.

Did my waters just break?

I looked into the toilet. What did I know? It looked like pee, but it kept coming out. Was I just becoming fully incontinent all of a sudden?

I was still sitting on the toilet, water incessantly dripping, pondering what my next step should be, when a tearing pain originated in my lower abdomen, cutting my breath. The pain moved down and back as the seconds went by. When it was over, I could breathe again, short hard pants.

Fuck.

Now I had no more doubts. I took my head in my hands and I wept.

A whirlpool of thoughts fogged my brain, from "couldn't you just wait for two more days?" to "where is my phone?".

A second contraction came, lower and stronger than the first one, and I grunted through it for several seconds. The pain woke me up, and I slowly stood up from the toilet to look for my phone. I grabbed it from the sofa, and I got back to my royal seat on the toilet to avoid dripping all over the wooden floor of the living room.

"I think I'm in labor," I texted Mike.

"I'm going to die," I texted Rachel.

Rachel grasped the truth right away, and she texted back after a few seconds, "Did your waters break?"

"Yes."

"Do you have your bag ready?"

"Yes."

"Do you think you can go downstairs and take a taxi?"

A new contraction prevented me from responding right away, as I fought against the first tears.

"I can try," I tapped back after a couple of minutes.

My phone vibrated, and Mike's name popped up on the screen.

"Amber, how are you?" he was whispering.

"I think my waters broke. And I'm having contractions."

"Let's go to the hospital now. I am calling an Uber for you. Can you take the lift down with the hospital bag?"

I started to pant as another contraction was crawling up my abdomen.

"Amber?" his voice betrayed his concern, while he was trying to keep calm to help me.

"I'm ok," I mumbled.

"Your Uber is coming in five minutes, and you ought to reach the hospital in thirty minutes. There's not too much traffic now. I will be there before you, since I'm already in Midtown. I texted the doorman: he is coming there to help you with the bag."

A knock on the door.

"Go," Mike heard it through the phone, as I had him on speaker. "Call me back when you are in the car."

I dragged my feet to the entrance door and I let the doorman in. Felix looked at me with pure terror in his eyes.

"The bag is in the bedroom, in the closet," I told him.

"Bro, we're screwed," I thought.

I dedicated one second to thanking all the gods for having given me the strength to shower and put on some clothes, earlier that morning, otherwise I would have left my apartment in my pajamas.

"My wallet is in my purse, there on the shelf," I gestured to Felix.

What else did I need? The keys were right next to the entrance, and a phone charger was already in the hospital bag. A new contraction, longer and stronger than all previous ones, prevented me to think further, and it pushed me to shout, "Let's go!"

I walked to the elevator gripping Felix's shoulder, sinking my nails in it as the pain rose up on the contraction cycle. The Uber driver was waiting in front of the building, and with Felix's help I slid in the car and I almost laid down on the back seat, while he secured the bag in the trunk.

"I'm in the car," I had enough energy to tell Mike a few seconds later over the phone.

"I'm almost there," he reassured me. "I will be ready for you when you arrive."

"Thank you", I gasped in between the tears from a new contraction.

As soon as the pain was gone and my eyes could focus again, I texted Rachel with an update.

"Let me know what I can do for you," she didn't hesitate, "I can come whenever you want."

Mike opened the door as soon as the car stopped in front of the hospital, and I fell in his arms.

"I'm going to die!" was the only thing I could tell him, my head exploding with agony. All the breathing techniques learned during the birthing class had been wiped away from my brain.

"I'm here," he held me.

He carried me to the maternity department, we quickly checked in and we were moved to the triage room, where a nurse attached fetal monitors to my belly and IVs to my arms.

"When can she receive an epidural?" Mike asked the nurse.

"We need to run the first checks on her, then we'll move her to a labor room, where she can get anything she wants."

She put a hand on my forehead to calm me down in between contractions, "I know it hurts, sweetheart, but we'll be done soon. I had to put two IVs in, one with insulin and one with sugar: since you have gestational diabetes, we need to make sure your blood sugar is stable. Now I will measure your glucose and fine tune the insulin dosage."

I nodded, my jaw contracted in a desperate tentative to fight the incoming contraction pain.

"One, two, three, four…" a shrieking voice came from a bed nearby, in a far corner of the triage room.

"One, two, three, four…" the voice sounded familiar.

Another contraction distracted me, but as soon as I could I focused again on the voice. Where had I already heard it?

"Mike, who's yelling down there?"

He went to spy, his British aplomb pushed as far as it could, and he came back after a few seconds with an incredulous look on his face.

"You will never guess… It's the annoying woman from the hospital visit."

"Wait, what? Insisting Lady?"

He nodded.

"Out of all the fucking people in this city, she had to be here now!"

If there was ever a bad omen, that was it.

"Mike!" I screamed, possessed by another contraction, more painful. "You get me out of here right now! I want a fucking room, and I don't want to hear her voice ever again!"

Scared, Mike ran away to call on the nurse.

With the last grain of salt I had in my brain I texted Rachel, "Please come, I need your good juju."

After minutes which lasted for hours, a room was finally available for me. The epidural relieved me from what had become constant suffering.

Rachel finally arrived.

"You try to relax now," she squeezed my hand and she kissed my forehead.

Mike went to find a bottle of water.

"I'm here," she threw her jacket on Mike's armchair.

I looked at her, my eyes fixated into hers until my vision started to cloud. I thought the epidural was numbing me, but she gave me a faint smile and she wiped tears from my cheeks.

She kissed my hand, "Don't worry."

"I'm so happy you're here," I could finally speak. "I couldn't do it on my own."

She wiped another tear from the side of my nose, "You're not alone: Mike is here."

A sudden dryness in my throat prevented me from replying to her, until Mike came back in the room. Too late.

"I called your parents," Mike reported. "They are on their way from Connecticut. They will go to their friends' house and they will wait there."

I closed my eyes and I squeezed Rachel's hand even stronger.

The epidural was the only thing that kept me afloat. From time to time I pushed the button on the pump to increase the dosing, just a little.

Doctor Mallory's visits tracked the time, as she hourly kept coming back to stick her hand in my cervix and announce the progresses in its dilation.

One centimeter.

Things were getting started.

Two centimeters.
We were on track.

Three centimeters.
Blood sugar levels under control.

Four centimeters.
We were getting closer.

Five centimeters.
"Do you want a fruit gelatin?" Rachel glanced at the food tray a nurse had just brought in.
"I could throw up right now."

Five centimeters.
"How can you still be here after so many hours?" I asked Rachel.
"I had a contingency plan at work in case anything happened," she winked. "Two of my associates are handling my stuff. I am here for as long as you need me."

Five centimeters.
A few more pushes on the epidural pump, to kick back that annoying tingle in my lower abdomen.

Five centimeters.
"I can feel the contractions again now. What's wrong?"
"The epidural can anesthetize you only up, or down, to a certain point: when the baby approaches the exit, the nerves

stimulated by his passage are too far down the birth canal, and drugs can't fully reach them."

"So what do we do now?"

"Let's see how it goes," Doctor Mallory caressed my sweaty forehead. "I will be back soon."

Five centimeters.

Soon was not enough, as minute after minute the pain increased to a level I was by then too tired to suffer.

"Let me find the nurse," Mike sighed at the end, more exhausted than me.

Rachel nodded, while she was feeding me small sips of water.

Doctor Mallory came in after a few minutes, followed by a nurse and a resident. She did another full exploration of my interiors, and then she sat on the bed next to me.

"We've been at this for a few hours now. This is what I think we should do: I want to give it a last chance, and I want to try and use Pitocin. It is a medication that usually enhances contractions and cervix dilation. Given your situation, this should help us get to the last five centimeters, and then we can get ready to push."

Push?

"What do you think?" she smiled at me, her usual professional grin.

"Whatever."

Another IV was added to the line. Who said giving birth was the most natural thing?

Five centimeters.

Higher epidural dose.

Five centimeters.

Squeezing Mike's hand contraction after contraction, throwing imploring looks at Rachel behind a curtain of pain.

Five centimeters.

Rachel the fighter, the Counselor Chambers powerhouse had tears in her eyes.

She stormed out of the room and I could hear her yell to a nurse, "Do something!"

Five centimeters.
What time was it?

Five centimeters.

Doctor Mallory finally came in. She placed a hand on my knee and she tried to communicate empathy with a swift brush. She knew she failed, so she spoke, instead.

"We have two options now. We can keep waiting, as dilation can take a while with Pitocin. I am not concerned with the baby's health, since the fetal monitor has been showing a strong and regular heartbeat, so this is still a viable option."

What about my health?

"Or we can get him out," she finished.

I sensed a movement at the far corner of my eye, where Mike and Rachel had drifted to make room for the doctor.

I had no doubt.

"Get it out!"

Spasms ran relentlessly after each other while the nurses were preparing me for the emergency C-section. Once the anesthesiologist had connected the epidural tube to the spinal anesthesia pump, they transferred me to a stretcher, to drive me across the department towards the operating room.

"And this is for you," a resident handed out to Mike a sterile package with OR clothes for him. "Go get changed in the recovery room, and we will call you when we are ready."

Mike kissed me on the cheek before he followed the instructions.

Rachel hugged me one last time before the stretcher left her behind.

The corridor looked strange from the bed, a white tunnel with cold lights. At least the spinal anesthesia was already showing its effects.

The operating room was full of people who started to manipulate me: nurses pushed me on the operating bed, spreading my arms wide like Jesus Christ on the cross. A vertical sheet was strategically placed between my collarbones and the rest of my body, to prevent me from seeing anything I would have otherwise regretted seeing.

Where was Mike?

The anesthesiologist introduced herself, and she tried to distract me with small talk.

The nurses were bustling about my lower abdomen, cleaning me up and arranging me for surgery.

Where was Mike?

Doctor Mallory and another surgeon came in after scrubbing, taking their assigned places on either sides of me. Grey's Anatomy wasn't that entertaining from the inside.

NINE

I started to wiggle my head around, waiting for the door to open and Mike to finally come in. My breath accelerated.

Where the fuck was Mike?

Two more nurses followed the surgeons: they were going to take care of the baby once it would be out.

Everything looked ready.

I could hear my heartbeat in my throat, blood roaring in my ears.

"Excuse me," I asked no one. "Where is Mike?"

My air pipes slowly clogged.

Nobody responded for some long seconds.

I tried to speak again, but no voice came out.

"The nurse is bringing him in," someone finally acknowledged me.

Tears ran down my nose as Mike passed the door. He allowed himself a quick squeeze of my hand, before a nurse told him he was not supposed to touch me. He smiled at me, his eyes greener than ever, filled with commotion.

Doctor Mallory took a deep breath and she announced she was ready to go. The weight that had been clawing at my throat fell heavily on my chest, compressing all the air out of my lungs. Alarms started to sound.

"Saturation dropping," somebody announced.

"Everything is fine, Amber," the first anesthesiologist sweetly caressed my face, while the second one played with the medicine dosage.

"Amber, what's wrong?" Doctor Mallory asked behind her mask.

I couldn't breathe.

I saw Mike panicking behind my tears.

Before I closed my eyes, I heard all monitors abandoning their regular beeping sounds for a unison, continuous cry.

THE DAY AFTER

Where am I?

Fog.

Where am I?
I don't know.

Labor.

Where am I?
I do know.

I went into labor. I came to the hospital. I was in the operating room.
At least I didn't die.

I keep my eyes shut.

The baby must have been born. I can't feel my belly. I can't tell if the weight is still there or it's gone. It must be gone. I was in the OR, they must have taken it out.

Mike must be holding the baby in his arms. I can see him, ecstatic. I can see my parents, crying. I am here by myself, nobody is thinking about me.

The baby must be absorbing everybody's attentions.

I can see him, too. A little boy with dark skin and big eyes. I can see the swaddling blanket, the little blue hat on his head.

Who will you be, baby boy?
How will the world welcome you?

I can see you at five years of age, playing at school.
I can see you at eighteen, applying for colleges.

How will people look at you at twenty-two, interviewing for jobs, wearing a crisp suit and one of Mike's ties?
What will the world be in twenty-two years?
What will I be in twenty-two years?
What will I be now?

I open my eyes.

NINE

NINE

ACKNOWLEDGMENTS

The first thanks always go to Emmanuel, who so selflessly supports me, and who still believes in me after all these years. I also thank my wonderful beta readers and editors, Libby and Alice.

Most readers wouldn't have this book in their hands if it weren't for Lore, who is my publicist and my agent, my finger on the pulse and my friend. Many readers wouldn't have noticed this book on a shelf or in an online list if it weren't for Daniele's gorgeous cover art and design. I owe both of you guys way more than the credit your work deserves.

The last acknowledgment, because this is really not a thanksgiving, goes to Charles: you didn't really do anything here, but I would have never written this book without you. Duh.

ANNALISA CONTI

ABOUT THE AUTHOR

Annalisa Conti lives and writes in New York City, where she has been spending the last few years of her life. She is a woman who writes about women, real human beings facing drama and challenges, finding happiness and rewards, succeeding and failing. Normal people.

If you like Jane Austen for her honest humor, Gillian Flynn for her descent into human darkness, and Elena Ferrante for her focus on storytelling, you will find Annalisa's tales wildly entertaining.

NINE is her third novel.

Her second novel, AFRICA, was an Amazon Kindle #1 in its category. Reviewers say it is a "fascinating" "astonishing" story of a life-changing journey to the end of the world, "powerful and dramatic, and well integrated into this incredible "decorum"".

Annalisa is also the author of ALL THE PEOPLE, a novel built around a woman's secrets. Reviewers say "you cannot put it down", it is "capturing reader's attention since the very first lines", and it has a "very deep and accurate psychological perspective".

She publishes quarterly episodes in the collection of short stories THE W SERIES, which describe the world of W, a superhero like no other. Reviewers say it is "a classic action story but somehow very different from anything else", with a "writing style packed of action and visual clues as if it was taken right out of a Marvel comic strip".

Find more at:
www.annalisaconti.com
Twitter: @AnnalisaContiUS
www.facebook.com/AnnalisaContiAuthor

Use the #NineBook hashtag on Twitter to share your thoughts on Amber's story and your experiences.

BOOKS BY THIS AUTHOR

Please visit your favorite book and ebook retailers to discover books by Annalisa Conti:

Nine, a novel (2018)
Africa, a novel (2015)
All The People, a novel (2014)

The W Series, a collection of short stories (from 2016)